Gay Witchcraft

ALSO BY CHRISTOPHER PENCZAK

City Magick: Urban Ritual, Spells, and Shamanism

Spirit Allies: Meet Your Team from the Other Side

The Inner Temple of Witchcraft:
Magick, Meditation, and Psychic Development

The Inner Temple of Witchcraft Companion CD Set

The Outer Temple of Witchcraft: Circles, Spells, and Rituals (Forthcoming)

Gay Witchcraft

EMPOWERING THE TRIBE

Christopher Penczak

WEISER BOOKS
San Francisco, CA / Newburyport, MA

First published in 2003 by
Red Wheel/Weiser, LLC
York Beach, ME

With offices at:
500 Third Street, Suite 230
San Francisco, CA 94107
www.redwheelweiser.com

Library of Congress Cataloging-in-Publication Data

Penczak, Christopher.
  Gay witchcraft : empowering the tribe / Christopher Penczak.
    p. cm.
  Includes bibliographical references.
  ISBN 1-57863-281-1 (pbk.)
  1. Witchcraft. 2. Gays—Miscellanea. I. Title.
  BF1571.5.G39P46 2003
  133.4'3'08664—dc21
                                    2003002063

Typeset in 11 point Weiss

Printed in Canada
TCP

8 7 6 5 4 3

Contents

PART I
History and Mythology

PART II
Tools of Our Tribe

PART III
Empowerment—Love, Sexuality, Healing, and Ritual

List of Exercises

List of Charms, Potions, Spells, and Rituals

Acknowledgments

I want to thank some very special people whom I have found on my path: first and foremost is my husband and best friend, Steve, for sharing the magical path with me. I would like to thank my loving and supportive parents, Ronald and Rosalie, as well as the many spiritual community leaders who have been a great example to me, including Laurie Cabot, Jan Brink, Gita, Bryant, Chris Girioux, and Wendy Snow Fogg. Special thanks to: Erik Olson, Alixaendreia, Jessica, Wade, and Morris Weissinger for getting me started on this venture; my covenmates, the Gay Men's Spirit Group, and my models—Casey O'Brien, Kevin Castelli, David E. Boyle, Nathanael Van Aalst, Rob Bouchard, Timothy Bedell, Jen Benos, Aviva Davi, Temptation, Benjamin Carpenter, Paul Carter, and Tim Reagan. Thanks to the many women and men who have shared their stories, traditions, techniques, and support for this project.

Note to the Reader

All of the charms, potions, and other magical formulas in this book are for external use only. Some of the formulas include essential oils and herbs. The reader should take care to use the proper ingredients and methods as advised by the author. Some individuals may have a sensitivity or allergic reaction to certain ingredients and they should consult with a professional before using or substituting such ingredients. The author and publisher are not responsible for any adverse effects or consequences resulting from the reader's use of the formulas or procedures in this book.

Introduction

When I was a child, I never thought I would be writing a book on witch-craft, let alone dedicating my life to it. But life is filled with surprises, and I've grown to welcome them by now. I was raised Catholic. Yes, I'm a survivor of 13 years of Catholic school. Nuns didn't slap my wrists with rulers, but the last four years were in an all-boys high school. While that might sound like fun fantasy, the reality fell harshly short for a closeted boy desperately trying to figure out where his faith belonged.

Catholic school filled my childhood with ceremony and symbolism. Religion class and frequent liturgies were par for the course. I was surprised to learn that the kids in public school didn't have such things. I took them for granted. Mythic symbolism, statues, crosses, incense, and candles became a part of my life. I had a strong respect for the Catholic faith, but I later realized it was not so much the faith, but the ritual—a time for personal connection.

Not until high school did I consciously acknowledge being gay. I couldn't understand it myself, but I knew I felt different about the boys in my class. When religion class turned into morality class—where we discussed such topics as suicide, abortion, and homosexuality—in a single moment, the world came crashing down around me, and I confirmed all my feelings about not fitting into the whole. I intensely believed in something, but it no longer believed in me, or so I was told. The words "love the sinner, hate the sin" rang hollow for me, since I still felt hated, yet had not done anything at all.

That class created a schism between me and traditional Christian faiths. I went through a period of atheism, which in reality was more like a period of anger with Spirit, for some perceived betrayal from the emissaries of the

Church. I later considered myself agnostic, believing in some form of Spirit, but felt that no one could define or interact with it. Spirituality was abstract, not anything personal. I drew closer to science for answers to my questions, and to art for my personal expression.

Fortunately, science and art could not answer the questions I had about life. In the past, I experienced seeing a ghost and I had an out-of-body episode, though I didn't know what these phenomena were at the time. I didn't find any answers, so I kept looking, without much luck. I didn't let go of much of my anger, though. I held on because I didn't have anything to take its place.

Then witchcraft opened a new world for me. An old friend of the family slowly introduced me to Wicca, the modern religion of witchcraft. The foundations were in ritual, the cycles of nature, ancient Goddess reverence, psychic awareness, and personal development. Witchcraft embraced ancient philosophies and practices from all around the world. So many beliefs fit my own. I never believed in the Christian devil, the source of evil. Contrary to popular belief, witches do not worship the devil. They believe it to be a construct of various organizations to control other people, a target of blame, and a scapegoat. Witches believe in self-responsibility, since all you do comes back to you. Many authors of the neo-witchcraft movement cite a greater acceptance of gay, lesbian, bisexual, and transgendered people because of our ancient ties. Several ancient cultures honored such people—my people—for their unique energies and perspective. A few modern groups, or covens, are exclusively gay or lesbian, though parts of the Wiccan community are as homophobic as the mainstream community is.

The more I read and studied about Wicca, the more I thought I had come home, but I was afraid. I was afraid to trust Spirit again.

As I studied the craft, with my friend and her teacher, I had some amazing personal experiences. My first spell—what others call intentions or prayers—produced remarkable results. Through training, I had experiences with psychic magical abilities. The point of such work is not for the sake of accumulating power, but empowerment. Witchcraft gives a personal experience to what modern science, through quantum physics, is telling us; everything is connected. Everything is one. What one person does affects the whole. An experience with psychic healing opened my eyes to a completely new reality. We are connected.

As my studies deepened, I had to swallow a bitter pill. Magick (modern mystics often spell it with a "k" to differentiate their arts from a stage magician's sleights of hand) and, in fact, any form of mysticism, requires an inner harmony and unity. An aspiring witch must work to shed fear, anger, guilt, and hate, while gathering the qualities of love, self-esteem, and acceptance. Though I had found witchcraft, I held on to my anger at the world because I was different. To continue, to learn the mysteries of magick, I had to let go of my safety blanket of anger. Through the practice of the craft, deep self-introspection, and some healing counsel, I did, and my life changed completely. I then knew I was in control of my life, and always had been. The anger was no one's fault but my own—simply my reaction to others. When you honor the sacred within you, when you find the witch's Perfect Love and Perfect Trust, what others do does not matter. Spirit is not a commodity that others can give or deny you. All things are Spirit. Spirituality is simply acknowledging Spirit in your daily, personal life. Witchcraft is one path of spirituality, the one that brought me home and continues to show me new paths to follow.

One such path is teaching. As I never expected to be living life as a witch, I never expected to be teaching witchcraft. The whole process seemed to happen by accident, but I now know there are no accidents. Things happened in exactly the right way to guide me to this path. And as a teacher, I encountered many people with whom I could empathize. Those who felt disenfranchised from mainstream faiths, continually searching for their path, often found their way to Wicca. Quite a few of these folks were gay, lesbian, bisexual, or trans-gendered, coming from feelings and experiences very similar to mine, now feeling the sense of coming home again.

Modern witchcraft offers quite a bit to the gay community. I found a sense of belonging, not necessarily to a larger group, a physical community, but a belonging in my own spirit, and an understanding that people like me have a rich spiritual tradition. All I had to do was reclaim it for myself.

Rather than simply tolerating my kind, these ancient traditions celebrated our existence. Embracing those who are different is a way to learn. As cultures interacted, through trade or warfare, the mythologies and rituals assimilated each other. The Greco-Roman mythologies mingled with those of the Celts. The spiritual traditions of old are keys to creating the new.

Empowerment is the great gift the craft has given me, a gift I continue to use and honor. Each practitioner of witchcraft is not simply a member of the faith, but his or her own priest or priestess. We need no intermediary. One thing I'm extremely grateful for was my mother's personal twists on Catholicism. I received the usual sacraments—Baptism, First Communion, and Confirmation—but she never sent me to First Confession because she didn't believe you had to go to a man to have God forgive you for your sins. You could simply speak to God. It was that simple. When I questioned Catholicism, her opinions on how the Church could be mistaken about confession made me wonder if they had gotten some other things wrong too, like their views on homosexuality. That was a lifeline for me, hoping against hope that someone had pieced together a tradition closer to the truth. I found witchcraft answered those questions for me, and, strangely enough, it became home for my mother as well. We practiced together in our first few covens and still celebrate the holidays and do magick together. The mother and son mythos is strong in the craft, and in my life, too.

Through this book, I hope to share with you the sense of belonging, reclaiming, celebration, and empowerment I feel through my practice. Don't simply read it, but experiment with it. Try the meditations and exercises if you feel called to do them. This work is not the final word on witchcraft for gay practitioners, but a cornerstone for others to build upon—as others have made a way for me—for a solitary practice, for partners, and for the growing community of gay witches, pagans, and seekers.

I don't intend *Gay Witchcraft* to be a historical document or scholarly argument. I'm sure many strict reconstructionist and conservative historians would debate the material, as many historical books on the ancient practice of witchcraft have been debated. Due to many of our historical and cultural biases, all of our resources are suspect, for both arguments. I'm not trying to prove or disprove anything. I believe that if you really want to know the truth, you should ask the source. If you want to know about gay deities, find a way to ask them directly. Regardless of the provable facts, modern witchcraft and its gay practitioners are here, and we are not going anywhere. I present myth and story as folk history, as it was taught and passed to me from many sources. Rather than a thesis, it is a manual of exploration. It represents the experiences I've had, and bits of wisdom that my sisters and brothers have shared with me.

I use "gay" as a common word to denote those pursuing same-sex relationships and identities. Many people dislike the term "gay." They feel it is a limited label, connected to a lifestyle, political agenda, segregated community, or fashion trend. For many, sexual orientation is no more important than your favorite flavor of ice cream. Such people are trying to downplay the differences between us. In truth, we are different from most of the world. We have a different blend of energies and many need to recognize their differences as gifts and blessings. We have different experiences because of it. When I was first introduced to the word "gay," men and women, bisexuals and transgenders used it as a common umbrella term. There is also the shorthand "GLBT," for Gay/Lesbian/Bisexual/Transgender, but it doesn't have the same magick to me as "gay." If you don't identify with the word, replace it with the words you like or no word at all. To me, claiming words such as "gay," "lesbian," and "queer" as something healthy is as important as reclaiming the word "witch."

Some critics say, "Yes, do what you want for a religion, but don't use the word 'witch.' It has too much baggage, too many stereotypes and bad associations. Call it something new." That's even more reason to reclaim it. We must correct the misinformation of the past. We can say the same for the word "gay." Although "gay" originally was used to mean "happy," and then used as a derogatory term, it refers to a group of people who were considered holy by much of the ancient world, like those who were considered witches (the word "witch" has also been used derogatorily). Both words are a part of our culture and identity. Both indicated healers and wise ones. And the modern world will recognize us as such again. We will see the divinity—the holiness—in our unique energies as a gift, as part of the path to recognize everyone's unique blessings.

Some gay pagans in the community shirked the idea of this book, or that gay pagans and witches have any specific considerations or concerns. They didn't want to be separated from the larger witchcraft community. We are not separate, but we are different, with different energies and experiences. Celebrating diversity necessitates recognizing the diversity. In many ways, this book could be considered a basic manual for anyone seeking to learn the ways of the witch, but *Gay Witchcraft* brings together aspects of both identities in a new alchemy that will take us into the next phase of our evolution. It explores topics not found in the typical witchcraft book.

Though I strive to see a community that welcomes all genders and sexual identities, the experiences and exercises I share come from my own life as a gay man. My experience of love magick, sex magick, and ritual union are through the eyes of a man, loving another man, and I do not feel qualified to comment on heterosexual or lesbian experiences in these areas. What little is available on sacred sexuality is usually geared toward heterosexual couples and, through the strongly feminist and Dianic witchcraft currents in modern Wicca, some information seems geared toward my lesbian sisters. With this work, I hope to start filling the gap for my gay brothers, sharing practical experiences and providing a road map for exploring their own sacred sexuality. All the principles, and the majority of the text, however, can apply to all aspects of the community—gays, lesbians, bisexuals, and transgendered people. Even straight people who read this book may see the craft in a different light.

After trying the meditations and rituals in *Gay Witchcraft*, you may reclaim the title of witch for yourself, identifying with those who have held the name in ages past. Or you may simply find witchcraft as a stepping-stone for your own path, taking what serves you and building your own tradition. In either case, the journey is worth the time it takes to find the path.

Blessed Be

Part I

History
and
Mythology

1

The Good
Witch
of the West

There's no place like home.

T he Wicked Witch of the West, with her green face and pointed hat,
was my first experience of a witch. I was terrified of her in *The Wizard
of Oz*, but soon recovered with a little help from my mother.
Unfortunately, that image imprinted the concept of the witch as villain and
evil upon my young brain. Glinda, the good witch of the East, was not as
important in the movie, and came with none of the familiar trappings of
witchcraft we've come to know and love, like the black cloak or flying broom.
Such things were reserved for evil witches. Although I love the movie, it doesn't
paint witches in a flattering light, nor does it flatter the culture that perpetu-
ates the myth of the evil witch.

When I met my first, real-live witch, I was part of the mainstream culture,
and I laughed, making bad *Wizard of Oz* jokes about this woman. She was a
wonderful friend of the family, and had recently "come out of the broom closet" to me about her faith. I thought she was kidding. No one actually calls herself a witch. Witches aren't real. They're in movies and fairy tales. Witches are
stories. They're make-believe. At least that's what I thought. But they aren't.
Witches are very real indeed, reclaiming an ancient tradition of wisdom and
ceremony.

Witches recover ancient traditions from the old, pagan world, the wise
women, cunning men, priests, and priestesses of the Stone Age, to the
ancient, civilizations, and even the post-Christian era. What is now called
European shamanism, or more broadly, core shamanism, was the province of

2

the witches of old. They were the healers, poets, storytellers, counselors, ceremonial leaders, spirit workers, and magicians of their time. The power of herbs and charms was theirs to share. They would work their craft for an individual in need or for the good of the community to ensure a harvest by bending the natural forces to their intention. One of the root words of witchcraft, *wicca*, is said to mean "to bend or shape" by modern witches, and refers to flowing with the natural forces, to bend them and shape them with magick and spells. The second definition of *wic* or *wicca*, is "wise one." *Wicca* was used to refer to male practitioners, and *Wicce* to female practitioners. Witches of today reclaim all these roles and traditions.

The modern revival of witchcraft is usually referred to as Wicca. Witchcraft still enjoys a popular resurgence that started in the middle of the 20th century, as the archaic witchcraft laws were repealed in England and those who kept the knowledge made it more accessible. Some use "Wicca" to refer exclusively to the first traditions reaching the public at that time—Gardnerian and Alexandrian—named after the founders of the traditions.

The word *pagan* is a broader category. Originally meaning "of the land" or "country dweller," pagan is now a larger classification of those reclaiming the polytheistic religions of old. As Christianity contains many smaller categories, paganism contains Wicca and other traditions. Now you can go to any bookshop and get a decent manual on paganism and Wicca, such as Scott Cunningham's *Wicca: A Guide for the Solitary Practitioner*.

The words "Wicca" and "witchcraft," along with "Wiccan" and "witch," are oftentimes distinguished by the practitioners, referring to the actual religion with "Wicca" and using "witchcraft" to indicate the skills of the craft, such as casting spells and making magick. Oh yes, witches do cast spells. Spells are not resigned to the world of fairy tales or superstition either. A spell is simply an intention, a wish. You could call it a form of prayer. Traditional prayers are used for healing and fulfilling wishes by petitioning God. Witches do the same thing, except their prayers come in the form of spells, using natural substances such as herbs, potions, food, crystals, and symbols to send out the prayer. Unlike traditional religions, witches pray to both God and Goddess.

Recognizing and honoring both the Goddess and God are key to understanding the beliefs of witchcraft. The divine is in everything. The divine *is* everything. We are all expression of the divine. Witches see the material world as an expression of the divine through the powers of creation rather than as a place of sin and suffering from which we must escape. A witch seeks to harmonize with the creative cycles as expressed in the turning of the seasons and tides of the Moon.

Creation is not some sterile process, but an act of divine love. The creative spirit, which I call the Great Spirit—all that is—manifested in the form of a Goddess, the Great Mother, who in turn birthed her own son, lover, and husband. The Great Spirit was expressing itself as feminine and masculine. The two, in an act of love and union, birthed all of creation, including humans, animals, plants, minerals, space, stars, and planets.

This might sound ragingly heterosexual, focusing on creation as the union of Goddess and God, but the most important point to remember is that we all are divine expressions of the Goddess and God. Witches honor the masculine and feminine within all beings, regardless of physical gender, sexual orientation, or identity. Everyone embodies both the divine feminine and divine masculine within, but we each contain a unique balance of the energies. Evidence suggests several ancient traditions honored those who did not identify themselves as heterosexual, specifically because of their respect for the unique blend of energies we contain. All magick and witchcraft is an act of creation, and gay people in general recognize, honor, and use both masculine and feminine energy as a part of everyday life.

In witchcraft, sexuality is sacred, not something sinful or wicked. Witches reclaim pre-Judeo-Christian traditions, and free themselves from the concept of sin. Sure, everyone makes mistakes, but the divine simply asks that you learn from them. Mistakes are experiences, not a stigma. Purity is not about abstinence or freedom from physical pleasure. Purity is living in your truth and personal integrity. Although much of the Western world has adopted Judeo-Christian values, what are popularly called "family values" in America, the cultures from which Wicca draws were not as uptight about sexuality. Sex was simply a part of a healthy life, meant to be enjoyed when desired. Sex was often ritualized and a part of worship. The sacredness of pagan sexuality was no less moral or spiritual than traditional Judeo-Christian morals; it simply was not understood because the monotheistic religions were not divinely sexual. One God, usually depicted as masculine, a father, created the world. There was no union with the feminine, no play between the God and Goddess energies. Interestingly, in the oldest, more esoteric version of Judaism and Christianity, we find traces of the feminine presence, but they did not make it to the popular modern consciousness.

In the Charge of the Goddess, one of the few holy texts surviving in Wicca, the Goddess states: "All acts of love and pleasure are my rituals." Modern witches cite this line as an acceptance and welcoming of queer people to the craft. The love is the most important aspect of the worship. Witches create a temple space through the ritual of "casting a circle." The watchwords

of the circle are "Perfect Love and Perfect Trust," meaning a divine, unconditional love for all those in the circle, and all life everywhere. A witch trusts in
the divine, the Goddess and the God, and works in an active partnership, a
personal relationship, to manifest the life he or she wants to lead.

A witch is a mystic, intimately exploring the divine through consciousness-
raising techniques found in ritual and meditation. Since so much of the witchcraft traditions were stamped out during persecutions in Europe, modern
witches have been reconstructing the faith, liberally borrowing from a mix of
cultures and heritages. Since pagan faiths can recognize and honor more than
one cultural pantheon, we're likely to find a witch working with gods and
symbols from the Celtic, Greek, Egyptian, Hindu, and Aztec religions. Modern
popular psychology, particularly the work of C. G. Jung, and quantum physics
have been incorporated into the principles of the craft, giving a more scientific definition to the age-old wisdom. All these cultures and disciplines have
more in common than you would realize, and their diversity is the key to
change and growth. Witchcraft is not a stagnant religion, but one that is living and breathing, adapting and changing with the times. Wicca is practiced
differently than it was 50 years ago, encouraging more eclecticism, and it will
be different again in another 50 years, but some truths remain timeless.

Witches recognize the masculine and feminine energies, the God and
Goddess, and the majority of Wiccan traditions recognize the God and Goddess
come in many forms and with many faces. Particular aspects of the natural
world, such as Earth, sky, seas, Sun, Moon, and rainbows, and more abstract
aspects, such as dreams, war, love, poetry, and healing, are embodied by various deities. Each culture named these deities individually, but they embody
the same concepts. Because these religions were polytheistic (worshiping
more than one deity), such cultures, including modern Wicca, are more tolerant of other religions, because they see other gods as expressions of their own.

If the gods are embodied by the natural forces, then paying attention to
the cycles of nature is an important part of aligning yourself with these deities.
Witches do rituals observing the solstices and equinoxes as well as the phases
of the Moon, particularly the full Moon. Witches believe in creating a sacred
space, a temple that can be erected anywhere, particularly in nature, but your
bedroom is sacred, too. Permanent temples, shrines, and altars are nice, but
you have all that you require within you. Tools simply make the job easier.
Because of this, most witches keep a home altar with important tools, all as a
reminder of the spiritual path. An honest and heartfelt relationship with
nature, whatever aspect of nature is around you—from lush forests to house
plants—is as important as fancy tools. The wisdom of plants, animals, and

minerals is usually a part of the teachings, particularly for those seeking to learn the healing arts.

Witches believe in more than one world. They live in the physical, like most people, but are "walkers between the worlds," meaning they can interact with the spiritual world, like a medium or shaman. They "pierce the veil" between worlds. The temple or ritual circle occurs between worlds, creating a sacred, spiritual space. Personal interaction with ancestors and guides, as well as deities and animal spirits, is an integral component of the path. In fact, such visionary meditations are often called "path workings," because they lead you from one place to the next, both in meditation and your personal life.

From this fact, witches believe in an afterlife, though opinions vary on its exact nature. The vast majority of witches believe in past lives and karma, but that is not universal among us. Through psychic contact with the nonphysical worlds, one can divine information about the past, present, and future. As walkers between worlds, witches are not limited to the present tense, but see time as a whole.

The universe is created from energy, the energy and love of the Goddess and God. Light, matter, spirits, and everything else are simply forms of energy. Like nature, this energy is neither good nor bad; its use depends on the intent of the user. Witches understand energy exists in spectrums that science has not yet codified, and with sufficient will, one can harness that energy to create change. You can call these abilities "psychic" or "magical," for magick is simply creating change in harmony with your will. Witches use the energy for casting spells. Spells, specific acts of magick, are done for a variety of effects, including love, prosperity, protection, and healing. I know quite a few people who didn't believe in spells until they tried one and it worked.

Humanity fears the "curse" of the witch. The vengeful and cursing witch is a stereotype from folklore, and like many stereotypes, there is some fact and some fiction. Most witch stereotypes were historically a part of the witch trials and had no actual basis in the ancient practice.

The typical person would not admit to believing in the powers of a witch, but the underlying fear of witchcraft stems from the belief that one can be cursed and that misfortune will follow. Although curses are part of the history, and some people practice them still, for the most part, modern witches shy away from curses because of their understanding of the Law of Three. Everything you do returns to you threefold. All intentions come back to you. That is how a spell works. Witches are responsible for their thoughts and intentions, because they truly know the power behind them. Witches do not harm others because greater harm would return to them. If someone is bothering you, there are easier, safer, and more sensible ways of dealing with the problem. Conversely, if you do blessings and help people, blessings and help will return to you threefold. We are all connected, and everything affects everything else. Because of this metaphysical law, many pagans are involved in healing and charity work. As you help others, you help yourself and the planet. Some call this the Law of Reciprocity.

Witches have no commandments or book of laws. Our scriptures are the changing seasons. No one can completely capture the essence of the cycles of nature in a single book. Our scriptures must be observed and experienced. We have but one law known as the Wiccan Rede. *Rede* simply means "advice," or "credo." It's not even a law, just a good practice. The Wiccan Rede states, "Do what thou will, and let it harm none." You are free to do as you feel guided to do in your craft, provided you do not hurt others, including yourself. This is not only a guide for magick, but for life, akin to the Golden Rule of Christianity, "Do unto others as you would have done unto you."

Witchcraft stresses personal responsibility. No one in the craft will tell you what you can or can't do. You are the ultimate authority on your life. Although you should respect traditions and elders, ultimately, you walk alone, which is somewhat difficult, but empowering. As "witch" refers to both male and female practitioners, each witch is his or her own priest or priestess, capable of leading ritual and celebrating all the rites. No one but you can judge if the path is right for you spiritually, morally, or sexually. A warlock is not a male witch. The word's generally accepted meaning is "traitor" or "oath breaker," and was an epithet used by those of the early Church. Anyone who uses the world "warlock" today is probably ignorant about Wicca as a religion.

Names such as "the Old Religion," "the Craft" or "the Craft of the Wise" are used to denote this modern religion legally protected in America by the First and Fourteenth Amendments. Joining the practice as a solitary is an easy way to start if you have the self-discipline and desire, but sometimes it can be difficult if you are looking for formal training or to work with a group, usually called a "coven" or "circle." If you choose to work with a group and a formal tradition, you can find various community groups—some open and others more private—all across the country, which is another similarity gay communities have with witches. Check local New Age and occult bookstores to get some leads.

Formal initiation is not necessary. Self-study and initiation is becoming increasingly popular in a world lacking enough teachers for all the desiring students. Several traditions and books recommend self-initiation to the craft. You must be dedicated and motivated to read, learn, and practice. You can start with the exercises and lessons in this book, geared toward gay practitioners. If you are already practicing, you may find a different slant to some of the traditional material.

Anyone with the desire and effort can be a witch, but many of us simply are called to the practice, beyond our personal desires and understanding. Follow the light of your soul and you will find what sustains it.

2

The Secret History

As it was. As it is. As it ever shall be.

You won't find the history of witchcraft, and in particular the history of gay mystics of the craft, in a traditional history book, though our story is the shadow of the modern world's development. Witches have always been present, since clans and tribes have gathered together, and we will always be present in some form.

Although much of the secret history of witchcraft has been reclaimed or corroborated in traditional history and the latest scientific information—from archaeology to advanced physics—it is primarily a story learned orally, to give witches a sense of identity, of roots in the greater mysteries of humanity. Like any oral tradition, the teller of the tale has his or her own personal points of interest, additions, and lapses in memory, so the story changes over time.

Like any storyteller, I have my own slant to the tale. No one told me this version, so I had to find it myself. Earlier in my training, I was fortunate enough to study with a quite famous witch named Laurie Cabot, in Salem, Massachusetts. Her classes were life changing, to say the least. The additional blessing of her class was her decidedly gay-friendly attitude to the craft, which not all traditional teachers have. Gay history was obviously not the focus of her work, but her books and lectures would throw out tantalizing bits of information about gay people. She mentioned them so matter-of-factly, as though everyone knew it. At the time, I was starting college and in the closet, and after my Catholic school experiences, I hung on to any gay-positive words. Also helpful was another gentleman in the class who I intuitively felt was gay, but we never really spoke about it. Just knowing he was there—a happy, well-adjusted and more experienced witch—gave me hope.

From that point, I set out to learn all I could about witchcraft and build my own spiritual practices, but I also held on to the hope of meeting other gay witches, learning where we fit into the history of the craft, and where we would go with the future. My version of this shadow history would probably not be agreed upon by all, even witches, since gay history is such a volatile subject for some, and it is not my task to prove this history to the scholarly world, but to simply relate the research that I explored, and tell you a new tale, to inspire a new generation.

Scholars start the history of witchcraft in different spots. Certain traditions look exclusively to the Celtic tribes, or simply the later European ones. Ancient Egypt, along with other ancient societies, is a popular choice as the birthplace of magick and mysticism. I choose to look back even further. To find the heart of the craft, one must look to the Stone Age.

Before the Pen and the Plow

Our Paleolithic ancestors left very little evidence of their culture, and much of our information about them is informed speculation. Evidently, they were very primal and tribal in makeup, existing as hunters and gatherers. Although they seem primitive to our society, they lived in balance with the land, and had quite extensive religious activities. Their practices were ritualistic and shamanic in form, using simple tools and instruments. They saw the

Goddess images

divine in the forces of nature all around them, because they relied on nature for their very existence. The image of the Goddess, usually as Earth Mother, was foremost in these practices. Our oldest images of art, dating as far back as 10,000 B.C.E. are simple Goddess statues, found across Africa and Europe. They created statues carved and sculpted from clay, bone, or rock, with emphasized sexual characteristics—full breasts and often a pregnant womb. Most famous of these images are the Nile River Goddess and the Venus of Willendorf.

Our most ancient creation stories do not segregate the divine from sexuality. Sexuality as expressed in the Goddess, or even in bisexual or transgendered forms, was a natural part of creation, to be honored and respected as part of the mysteries of life.

While the Goddess is seen as eternal in the Earth, the less-celebrated masculine aspect was most likely seen as an animal lord. The hunt was an integral part of life, and depictions of animal-masked dancers and ceremonies are found in cave paintings from the time. Most remarkable of these cave paintings are those in the Addaura cave near Palermo, Sicily, created close to 10,000 B.C.E. and discovered in 1952. The painting depicts a circle of dancing men wearing nothing but bird masks, in a ritual honoring the bird goddess. They encircle two other bird-masked men, both with erect penises. Parallel lines connect the neck to the buttocks and ankles and the penis of one man to the buttocks of another. Thought by most scholars to be a sacrificial rite in which the parallel lines represent bindings, other interpreters see this as a homoerotic initiatory rite, with the lines possibly representing male energy, or even ejaculation. Even if they do consist of cords, controlling blood flow with cords is known as a way to induce visions. Bondage does not necessarily mean sacrifice of life. The sacrifice could be more sexual in origin. Bird spirits and shape-shifting aspects have a connotation of trangenderism or transformation. Interestingly, the original discoverer of Addaura, Iole Vovio-Marconi, came to the conclusion of the homoerotic initiation.

The evidence shows us that ritual had an important role in these societies, with strong Goddess themes, and the potential for same-sex unions. We believe these societies were more matriarchal in focus. As hunters and gathers, men usually took on the more dangerous roles. Women were needed to preserve the tribe, while a man could father many more children over a longer period. Because they were more likely to survive into later life, women most likely held some form of power or leadership, since they accumulated the wisdom needed for survival. The importance of the Goddess reflected the importance of woman.

Certain tribe members, particularly certain women, possessed greater intuitive abilities, opening to what we would now call psychic abilities. They could commune with the spirits of the natural world and with the ancestors for healing and counseling the tribe. They would guide the hunters to game and the gatherers to food. They petitioned the gods of nature to bring rain when needed, protect the tribe from enemies, and generally bring good fortune. Relationship with these natural forces was the prime motivation of religious ceremony. Spirituality wasn't simply a cultural luxury, but essential to survival.

Shamanism was the primary form of religious and magical work, though the word "shaman" comes from Siberia and a later date, not necessarily referring to the Stone Age Europeans and Africans. Shamanism is the practice of inducing an altered state of consciousness in order to enter a different reality. This different reality has many names—the "otherworlds," "spirit world," or what C. G. Jung called the "collective unconscious," or "archetypal realm." The shaman would bring back knowledge and power for healing and creating change. Drums, rattles, and certain plants were used to induce these states. Deities oversaw all of creation, and could be contacted through trance. We find shamanic techniques in all tribal societies that honor the Earth. Witches were the shamans of Europe in function and spirit, and these ancient wise ones were the forebears of modern witches and shamans. Whenever one is honoring the Goddess and the God, working with energy and spirit to help and heal, one is practicing the heart of witchcraft.

The powers of spirit were not restricted to the wise women of the tribe, though they expressed the primary interest and talent. Men who were not inclined to hunt partook in the mysteries. Our first legends of the wounded healers most likely come from the men who were no longer capable of hunting, through either advanced age or injury. They became the first priests. Not having the cultural prejudices of the Judeo-Christian moral code, homosexuality and bisexuality were possibly more prevalent and accepted in the Stone Age cultures. Gay, effeminate, and transgendered males showed characteristics in natural harmony with the Goddess, and were likely called to do the work of the Goddess. Women had, and still have, their mysteries known only to women. The sisterly priestess orders suggest potential same-sex unions as the cave paintings of Addaura suggest male homosexuality in sacred ritual.

The First Urban Cultures

With the advent of agriculture, writing, and building came the new civilization of the ancient world. The Middle East—primarily Egypt and Sumer, and later, the Mediterranean—was the cradle of the new way of life. We can find parallels to this development in Mesoamerica.

The nomads of the early Stone Age gave way to the planters. When the art of agriculture became widely known, humanity renounced its wandering in favor of settling in one area. The spiritual mysteries were no less important to the farmer, who depended on the gods for rain and a good harvest, but the myths began to change. The images of the God became more closely tied with agriculture, embodied by a god that rises with the spring, bears grain, and then is slain in sacrifice for the benefit of his people, only to rise again. The Goddess still featured strongly as the Goddess of the Earth, though her associations with the Moon, sky, and underworld mysteries grew. Agricultural cults worshiping these new forms of deity arose, and their traditions persist to this day. In spite of all our modern conveniences, we are still an agrarian society. We still depend on planted crops and domesticated animals, rather than foraging and the hunt.

As people settled down, they built cities and monuments, and established places of commerce, trade, law, royalty, military power, and worship. One of the goddesses who rose out of the temple-building civilizations and fertility cults of the Middle East was Inanna. As the Queen of Heaven, she embodied Earth and sky, fertility and war, life, death, and love. Her consort is Dumuzi, who seasonally died and was reborn. Through the development of the Sumerian Inanna, we see her later incarnation as Ishtar in the Assyrian-Babylonian culture. Ishtar's lover was Tammuz. She evolved further still; the Phoenicians called her Astarte, and associated her more directly with fertility and love, rather than war. Her mate was Adoni. The Syrians embody her as Atergatis, as a fertility and wisdom goddess. To the Canaanites, she was Athirat, and her consort was Baal, the agricultural god turned warrior. Her final incarnation, most familiar to the 21st-century reader, is Aphrodite, the Greek goddess of love, migrating to the Romans as Venus. Her evolution through the ages took over 1,000 years.

With the gathering of tribes into villages, towns, and cities, those with special gifts gathered together to form the first formal orders of priests and priestesses, often working in intimate conditions, devoted to a particular aspect of the deity, which manifested as Goddess or God. The rites of goddesses in the lineage of Inanna in particular often involved sexuality and eroticism. In these orders, the companions of the Goddess were called *hetaira* and *hierodule*, denoting female and male mystics, respectively. They took care of the temples, ran rituals, performed divination, healing and worked with the general public as needed. *Hetaira* and *hierodule* have been translated as "prostitute," "sacred prostitutes," or "temple whores" by modern scholars, but the words "prostitute" and "whore" should not carry the same bias they do in this culture. In many ways, *hetaira* translates much better to "companion," implying both priestess companion and companion of the Goddess. The word *hetaira* also applies to loving, perhaps same-sex erotic relationships between women in the Goddess cults. It's possible that the prostitute translation comes from the belief that these priestesses and priests would wait in the garden until someone came and gave them a coin for the Goddess before performing this sacred act. Such unions were sacraments to commune with the Goddess, using sexual energies to induce altered states of consciousness, for both the priest or priestess and parishioner. One touched the face of the Goddess when making love to the sacred prostitute. They embodied the Goddess to bestow love and blessings upon the participant. In these rites, the receptive role was taken by both women and men. The priests of the Goddess, the hierodule, were also intermediaries for worshipers, including otherwise heterosexual-acting worshipers. These homoerotically inclined priests were often transgendered, and possibly eunuchs.

The hierodule sects are found in the worship of many different deities. These priests of Astarte and Athirat are known as *kelabim*, her faithful dogs, *gerim*, or *qudeshim*. The kelabim of Aphroditos, worshiping on the Island of Cyprus, were associated with Moon worship, in which men would dress as women and women would dress as men. They saw the energy of the Moon as both male and female.

Inanna and Ishtar's priests were called *assinnu*, *sinnishanu*, and *kurgarru*. The assinnu were not simply men dressing as women and taking a priestess role. They were believed to have special powers, being both a representative of the Goddess and of the androgynous divine beings called *Asushunamir*. They held positions of power, were revered as magicians and talisman makers, and to simply touch an assinnu on the head granted one the ability to conquer all enemies. They devoted their arts, minds, lives, and bodies to worship of the Goddess. In the mythic descent of Inanna to the underworld, the kurgarra, or Asushunamir, originally were created as one of two divine androgynous beings to rescue her. Later, a caste of priests took the name. They, too, performed the functions of the assinnu, and were seen as physically and magically different from other men. Their musical ability and dramatic skills were used in the divine plays and reenactments of the Goddess mysteries.

The *galli* are the chosen homoerotic priests of Cybele and Atargatis. The word *galli* comes from the Gallos River, a tributary of the Sangarios River in Phrygia, but was later associated with the word "rooster" in the Roman

Empire. The galli may even have ruled Pessinus until 164 B.C.E. and held positions of respect until that point, when they were eventually overcome by invaders. The demise of the Goddess civilizations started with the association of warring tribes ruled by men whose warlike practices would eventually supplant almost all of these Goddess-reverent societies.

The Hindu goddess Bahucharamata still has priests who, like the galli, are called to the transgendered life. Bahacharamata's priests are known as *hijras*. The Hindu gods Krishna and Ardhanarishvara also had similar gender-variant priests.

Cults to the Goddess reached far and wide, across great distances and times. None were greater than the cults of Isis, originating in Egypt and spreading across the Western world. Isis was actively worshiped for over 3,500 years. She, too, is a goddess of many roles: a Queen of Heaven, goddess of fertility, and, by her consort, the resurrected god Osiris, a Queen of the Underworld. Osiris's story echoes the myths of the slain and resurrected gods of the Canaanites, Sumerians, and Babylonians. Eventually Isis's cults were overshadowed by her husband's but, as in the Innana line of goddesses, Isis's sects most likely contained transgendered and homoerotic priests. Some shaved their heads and bodies, while others wore long wigs and let their fingernails grow out. Their role in the traditional rites was to aid in the rising of the Nile every year, through ecstatic dance. Exposing their genitalia was a sign of forgoing the traditional role of father, and freely giving their fertility to the Earth to help the Nile rise. Isis is further associated with homoeroticism through the relationship of her brother, Set, with her son, Horus, and during her difficulties in the death and resurrection of her husband, Osiris, she was known to shape-shift into the form of a man in order to move unencumbered through the world. Gay men are said to have met at the Temple of Isis in Rome.

One of the most unusual and important gay political events occurred in Egypt, during the 18th dynasty. The pharaoh Akhenaton instituted monotheism, doing away with the multitude of Egyptian gods in favor of one Sun god, Aten. The pharaoh was considered god on Earth, and his laws were religious as well as political. The common people, and the priesthood especially, did not favor this decision. His wife, Nefertiti, separated from him over this religious policy. Akhenaton apparently had a homoerotic relationship with his son-in-law Smenkhare, and later named Smenkhare as his co-regent when Nefertiti left, bestowing Smenkhare with names and titles usually reserved for the queen.

The Goddess fertility cults gave way to the classical pantheons of the ancient world. The image of the God was transformed once again as the social pendulum swung further away from matriarchy toward a patriarchal view. The God's symbols became the sky and Sun, and later, war. He was no longer as dependent on the Goddess. The Goddess and God were viewed in a much broader way, with each individual god or goddess ruling over a single aspect of life. Deities of the underworld, love, communication, Moon, Sun, Earth, grain, oceans, rivers, storms, metallurgy, weaving, and the home were all individualized. Since these worlds were polytheistic, cultures exchanged different deities through their travels and trade, giving them different names and changing the myths to include them into their own creation stories. Sky and war gods became the consorts to the Goddess as invaders came into a culture, and eventually the deities married, forming uneasy alliances.

The most well known of the classical mythic pantheons is the Greco-Roman. The ancient Greeks were so precise in their minds and mythology that they attributed a very specific function to each deity. Because of such specifics, their myths are unlike many other cultures, such as the Celtic, where the mythologies are more complicated and intertwined.

The precision and wisdom of the Greeks highly influenced the development of the modern Western world, giving us foundations in mathematics, geometry, architecture, art, poetry, philosophy, medicine, astronomy, sports, and literature. The works of ancient teachers and poets like Plato, Socrates, and Homer are still studied in the halls of higher education. Modern doctors take the Hippocratic Oath, named after the Greek father of medicine. We still find the caduceus—the ancient symbol of the serpent entwined around a staff—in most major medical institutions. It was originally a symbol of the Greek god Hermes.

Since we have embraced much of the logical, left-brained wisdom of the past, we unfortunately have resigned the ancient Greek spiritual mysteries and mythic tales to a less honorable position in our society. Many people see the importance of the esoteric as a fault of an overly superstitious time of humanity's history. Religious texts are now considered fables, not tales of the divine. Homosexuality was often a theme in such myths, but now, when they are retold, same-sex eroticism and relationship is played down in the translation. However, because the ancient Greek culture accepted gay traits among the divine beings, they also accepted their parallels on the human plane as part of the divine order. Divinity is reflected in humanity, and vice versa. In no other culture do we have such well-known records of publicly accepted homosexuality, in fact or in sacred myth. But like the Greeks' esoteric and religious beliefs, many of our contemporaries view their acceptance of homosexuality as another unfortunate characteristic of an otherwise great ancient culture, and such unwanted customs were put to rest with the introduction of our "modern" religions and beliefs. In fact, as the Greco-Roman culture "advanced" and focused less on the mysteries and more on commerce, government, and war, the view and acceptance of homosexuality declined.

The Mediterranean cultures grew out of the Goddess temple sites, and initially had similar rites, practices, and priests. Although the common understanding of Greek homosexuality is of older men with younger men taking a receptive role, many expressions of gay love occurred among equals and among women. The gods Apollo, Hermes, Zeus, and Hercules were known for their bisexuality, taking both male and female lovers. Achilles' mother tried to keep him from the Trojan War by hiding him and disguising him as a woman. He did enter the war, however, and became the lover of the Trojan prince Troilus, and then later, his comrade Patroclus.

The word "lesbian" comes from the Greek island of Lesbos. Lesbos was the home to Sappho, a lesbian poet, musician, and priestess to the goddess Aphrodite. The Greek Amazons were warrior women who were not exclusively lesbian, but historical accounts and archaeological evidence strongly imply they may have been bisexual. Such women were skilled warriors and hunters, lived alone with women, rejected heterosexual marriage, and allied themselves with galli, the homoerotic priests of Cybele. They worshiped the independent goddesses Artemis/Diana, with her companion Britomartis, and Athena, with her companion Pallas. Perhaps these female companions were lovers and consorts to the goddesses. Same-sex unions were recognized and blessed by these goddesses and gods.

The Rise of the Roman Empire

The Romans built the culture of their empire upon the foundations of the Greeks, including taking the Greek deities and renaming them, but generally keeping their functions and myths. Zeus became Jupiter, Aphrodite became Venus, Hermes transformed into Mercury. The planets of traditional astronomy are named after the Roman deities. With the infusion of Greek thought, the Romans initially kept similar views to homosexuality. Even emperors engaged in same-sex relationships, such as Emperor Hadrian and his lover Antinous. In later periods of the Roman Empire, Mars, the god of war, would hold prominence. Mars is one god most lacking homosexual or transgendered qualities in our modern image of him, although earlier images may have depicted him as a healing god.

During the expansion of their empire, the Romans encountered two cultures to the north that would have a tremendous impact on modern witchcraft—the Celtic and the Teutonic. Both were polytheistic; this much they had in common with the Romans. But the Celts and Teutons were more migratory, organized loosely in tribes and often plagued by fighting between the tribes. Although highly sophisticated people, they did not have the cities and temples that the Romans viewed as constituting civilization.

The Celts migrated from the East, possibly sharing a common history with the ancestors of the Hindu societies of India. They came in contact with the Romans and Etruscans and absorbed many of the native European tribes during their migration to Gaul, or modern-day France, and then to the British Isles. The Celtic peoples' primary organizing force was the order of Druids—priests and priestesses, judges, diviners, storytellers, magicians, and healers. *Druid* comes from the word for "oak," or *duir*, and means "to know the oak." The oak is the tree of life and death, and the Druids were well versed in magick and the spirit world. Modern witches feel the Druids laid a foundation for present-day witchcraft. The Druids saw both Goddess and God in life and land. Like our Stone Age ancestors, they had a Goddess focus in their myth and culture. Unfortunately, the Druidic tradition is oral, and their secrets were never truly committed to written word, only to memory, so most of it was lost. The myths we have today are reconstructions and fragments from a later time, but from what does survive, it seems the Celts accepted transgendered themes and same-sex unions.

Lewis Spence, author of *The Magic Arts in Celtic Britain*, states the Druids could shape-shift between sexes. Men could appear as women to suit their purposes. When transforming into animal shapes, these priests and priestesses would become an animal of their opposite human gender. Myths suggest the legendary Celtic hero Cu Chulainn had an intimate relationship with his foster brother, Fer Diadh, though they were later forced to battle one another and Cu Chulainn slew his beloved.

The Gwidonot was a pre-Christian Celtic band of warrior women with attributes similar to the Greek Amazons, and the likelihood of lesbian relationships among the women is strong. Arthur Evans, on page 19 of his book *Witchcraft and the Gay Counterculture*, states, "Celtic men were notorious for their homosexuality." He cites the 1st century historian Diodorus Siculus: "Although they have good-looking women, they pay very little attention to them, but are really crazy about having sex with men. They are accustomed to sleep on the ground on animal skins and roll around with male bed-mates on both sides. Heedless of their own dignity, they abandon without a qualm the bloom of their bodies to others. And the most incredible thing is that they don't think this is shameful. But when they proposition someone, they consider it dishonorable if he doesn't accept the offer!"

After the rise of Christianity, the Druidic orders were not so tightly organized. To survive, they drew strongly upon their bardic training, musical abilities, storytelling, and divination talents. In Ireland, a figure known as a *filidh* performed similar roles and rituals. Like the transgendered priests of the Middle Eastern goddesses, the filidh represented the Goddess. A special relationship existed between the king of the land and his poet, or filidh, though it is unclear if the relationship was openly or symbolically sexual in nature.

The Teutons dwelled in northern Europe, eventually settling into the Germanic and Norse tribes. Their gods represented the harsh land upon which they dwelled, ruled by the powers of fire in the summer and ice in the long, dark winter. Although most often depicted as a masculine, warrior race, the Teutons had their share of gender-variant mystics. The shamanic arts of *Seidr* are a province of Freyja, the falcon-cloaked fertility goddess, but males who learned her secrets became known as *ergi*, her transgendered and/or homosexual priests. Seidr is a form of magick, inducing trance through shivering and shaking, and using music to create change. Her priests may have emulated her dress and ornamentation. The ergi were also now known as Seidrmen. Although the ergi had a special place in this society as transgendered or homosexual holy men, same-sex union was also a part of everyday life.

The Rise of the Christian Empire

The religious persecution of pagans and gays alike did not occur until a new religion from the Middle East—Christianity—began its rise. Originally, the Christians were a minority persecuted by the Romans. Here we have the familiar image of Christians being thrown to the lions in old movies. Eventually a few noteworthy individuals converted to Christianity, forever altering history.

The bias against homosexuality began much earlier, having roots in the Old Testament and the Judaic faith. The Hebrews came to the land of Canaan, and found the Canaanites actively involved in Goddess worship, sacred sexuality, homoerotic/transgendered priests, and ritual "prostitution." Some monarchs of the land, seeking harmony between the two faiths, housed these pagan priests and priestesses within the monotheistic Hebrew temples. Seeking to disassociate themselves from these practices, less tolerant rulers began legislation and campaigns to eradicate the erotic practices from the land, making the popularly quoted laws of Leviticus and Deuteronomy and the familiar tale of the destruction of Sodom and Gomorrah, after which anal sex was named, and subsequently labeled a crime. In actuality, the tale of Sodom and Gomorrah is about inhospitality to strangers, not sex.

Christianity built its foundation on Judaism. The original teachings were based on the words and actions of the prophet viewed as messiah, Jesus of Nazareth. He preached unconditional love, but later his words were mixed with dogma. The original Christian religion was gnostic and much more personal and free flowing, and Jesus himself can be seen as a sacrificed god of sorts, akin to the Egyptian Osiris, Greek Dionysus, and the Middle Eastern Goddess consorts Baal, Tammuz, Adonai, Adonis, and Dumuzi. Later, the newest Christian records, or testaments, were fused with the holy texts of Judaism, the religion Jesus came from, to form the Bible. Conservative Christians often put Gnosticism in the same category as paganism because, by the conservatives' standards, both shared unorthodox views, including sexuality and the belief in personal divine revelation.

In the 4th century, Emperor Constantine, a powerful convert to Christianity, ruled the Roman Empire, and used his power and influence to begin the purge of certain pagan aspects from the empire and surrounding lands. In particular, he persecuted the gay and transgendered priests of various goddesses, including priests of Aphrodite/Astarte at Aphaca, near modern Lebanon, and those of Isis and Hapi in Egypt. Constantine was evidently homophobic, and felt these priests were betraying their gender and, through their Goddess worship, consorting with demons. Any deity or divine force not a part of the Christian trinity was considered a demon or evil spirit. The emperor felt it was his duty to use military might to cleanse the land.

The entire empire adopted Constantine's faith, as the Edict of Milan made Christianity the official religion of the Roman Empire in 313 C.E. Soon, all pagan practices were banned by the government, including dancing while wearing animal masks, and seasonal rites. Those practices that could not be legislated against became part of Church doctrine. Many witches, myself included, almost shied away from the modern craft because the rituals can seem very Catholic, but in reality, they were originally pagan. The horned god Pan and the Celtic horned god Cernunnos were fused into the Christian concept of evil—the devil. By combining his image with the concepts of a battle between light and dark from Zoroastrianism, the early Church fathers attempted to scare people to the Christian faith.

Witchcraft, magick, and mysticism still survived, in hidden groups, in simple folk magick, and with the wise women and men who lived on the outskirts of the communities, while the Roman Empire declined rapidly, and completely dissolved. Witchcraft was divided into "white magick" and "black magick," generally regarded as helping and harming, respectively. White witches were encouraged somewhat, while legislation against black witches increased. Modern witches no longer use the distinctions "white" and "black," since they smack of racism and white European ethnocentricity. Modern Wiccans do not see the world in terms of white and black and shades of gray. We look to the entire spectrum of colors to make our craft.

In 800 C.E., the pope initiated the Holy Roman Empire, by crowning Charlemagne the first emperor of the new driving force of Europe. The Catholic Church was the unifying force of the land at this time of small kingdoms, and created the empire to protect itself from the Lombards and the Eastern Byzantine Empire. Conversion to Christianity again became a priority, and the formerly tolerated hedge witches and wise men soon came under fire.

Heresy, defined as worship, belief, or action conflicting with official Church doctrine, became punishable by death. The Church considers belief in the old religions and magick heresy. Witch hunters changed the very definition of the word "witch" to include the Christian version of the devil. Using hysteria to help root out non-Christian practitioners, the witch hunters accused pagans of all manner of gruesome acts—serving the devil, fornication with the devil or his emissaries, casting curses to harm townsfolk, stealing children, eating babies, desecration of churches, and reciting the Catholic Mass backward. None of these actions was ever a part of ancient pagan religions. To believe in the devil, one has to be a Christian, but pagan roots were never in Christian soil.

Folk magicians, witches, herbalists, midwives, and esoterics were accused of heresy, put through trials none could hope to pass, and sentenced to death. Most were not even witches, in the most technical sense. They were simple folk, victims of rampant hysteria and prejudice, who admitted to being witches simply to avoid a more gruesome death. The ranks of the heretics were not confined to witches. Jews, homosexuals, and transgendered people were all considered heretics. As the hysteria reached a fevered pitch, spreading from the Catholic Church to the Protestants, anyone was fair game in the witch trials of Europe.

Witches refer to this period of persecution as the Burning Times, since many were put to death by burning at the stake. Other common means of execution included pressing with stones, drowning, and hanging, after first torturing the "witches" to get their confessions and save their souls. Author

Arthur Evans, in *Witchcraft and the Gay Counterculture*, suggests the term "faggot," used to refer to queer individuals, originates from these persecutions. A faggot is a bundle of sticks, used for kindling. Faggots are used in cooking and home fires, and were used in the burning of heretics. When the words "faggot" or "flaming faggot" are used to refer to homosexuals, it is in reference to the Burning Times. Academics have strongly argued against this point, but in any case, it makes one think about the etymology of such slurs. "Faggot" and "fairy" possibly have a connection, as the root word, *fagus*, refers to the mythic ruler of the beech trees (a source of kindling), who devolved with the pagan faiths into a tree spirit, or fairy. What was once a derogatory remark is now a title claimed by gay men on a pagan spiritual journey. Evans suggests some historical records equate heresy with homosexuality. In the historical records, it is often unclear if someone is being accused of witchcraft or homosexuality. A popular defense against the charge of heresy was to show a wife and child to prove one wasn't gay.

The witch trials lasted for the duration of the Holy Roman Empire, and those few who survived with the secrets of witchcraft went completely underground, keeping the secrets between family members. Household tools, like knives, brooms, cauldrons, and candles—tools everyone had—became the secret instruments of the witch. Since they were commonplace, no one could accuse you of heresy simply for owning them.

The Goddess's special priests survived in their own way during the Middle Ages, particularly through the eastern European *calusari*, who worshiped the Goddess in the forms of Aradia and Artemis/Diana, whom they called Doamna Zinelor. The calusari preserved the healing and blessing rites, and it was believed their abilities were dependent upon not having intercourse with a woman.

The Knights Templar, a Christian order, were accused of worshiping an androgynous being named Baphomet and engaging in same-sex unions during ritual. We are uncertain if such claims are true, or if they were merely a ruse to upset the growing power and wealth of the Templars. In any case, many of these knights were tortured and burned like those accused of witchcraft.

For the most part, positive references to paganism, Goddess worship, and homosexuality were erased from the history books. Remaining mentions are tainted with the beliefs and prejudicial dogma of the time. Christians purposely destroyed much of the lesbian Sappho's work, and the musical scale from the Isle of Lesbos was not named after its people, as the other Greek modes were named, such as the Dorian mode. The Lesbian mode was renamed Myxolydian. And that is but one example of how the records were subtly changed. A rich, loving, and magical lore was almost completely erased from European history. From a queer point of view, all our historical records are suspect because we'll never know what was changed, intentionally or unintentionally.

European explorers were shocked to find the very heresy they sought to stamp out in Europe thriving abroad, in most nature-reverent societies. Gay priests and priestesses have been found in the Americas, Africa, and Asia. Unfortunately most westerners to first chronicle these roles looked upon them with scorn or disbelief, as they were usually coming from a white, male, heterosexual, and Christian prejudice.

In the Aztec temples, missionaries and conquistadors found native priests serving as hierodule of the goddesses, through dress, act, and sexuality. Though not as a rule, in certain tribes of northern Native Americans, including the Navaho, Mohave, and Hidatsa, shamans had a ritual identity involving transgender characteristics and gay relationships. Such individuals were healers, diviners, guides, and spiritual leaders of the tribe, called by the divine to a "two-spirit" path. "Two-spirit" is a relatively modern term used to describe such people, but the practices are ancient. The Navaho called their transgendered shamans *nadle*, and they greatly respected them. To have a nadle born into your family was considered a great blessing.

Modern witches speculate that their spiritual ancestors fled to America to escape the Burning Times, but the trials followed them here, most notably in the infamous Salem, Massachusetts, witch trials in 1692 to 1693. The end of the Salem hysteria marked the end of the Burning Times, with a few exceptions. It is important to note that no one was actually burned in America, though execution was meted out in numerous other ways, usually hanging. It is more likely that most victims of the hysteria, in Europe and America, had little to do with the true craft. The Western world entered the age of reason, and relegated all myth, mystery, and almost religion, into the realm of superstition as we flirted with the god of science.

The Modern Age

Beneath the veil of reason, the esoteric arts were coming back into play, particularly at the end of the 19th century and into the dawn of the 20th. Spiritual information from the East, Asia, and India was subtly spreading across the world, planting the seeds of belief in psychic ability, the spiritual worlds, astral projection, and karma. Scholars, under the shield of scientific inquiry, began researching the old witch and fertility cults. Lesbian involvement in witchcraft was noted in the *Canon Episcopi*, in its description of the rites of Diana in Milan.

Early in this modern age, men of the upper and middle classes would gather in gentlemen's clubs to study the Western mysteries of the Kabbalah, astrology, numerology, tarot, and Egyptian magick. They had the time and resources to carry out their research.

In the 1890s, George Cecil Ives founded the Order of Chaeronea, a gay spiritual organization in Britain, using the works of his friends, Oscar Wilde and Edward Carpenter, along with the work of Walt Whitman and Ives's own material, *A Book of Chains, Eros' Throne,* and *The Graeco-Roman View of Youth,* inspired by the Greek traditions. Ives's order based its name on the last battle of the Sacred Band of Thebes, dating back to 338 B.C.E. Eros was the god of the Chaeronea order, and while Ives may have focused on homosexual love between the generations, primarily between males, his order appeared to honor same-age and lesbian relationships as well. Self-esteem and respect were key to the teachings of an initiate, but much of the tradition remains unknown from what is, arguably, the first modern homoerotic spiritual order.

Most notable of the better-known groups was the Hermetic Order of the Golden Dawn, founded in England in 1888. The rising star of the Golden Dawn was a bisexual mage by the name of Aleister Crowley. He stayed with the Golden Dawn for a short time before moving on to the OTO, or Ordo Templi Orientis, and eventually founded the Thelemic Mysteries, his own system of spiritual exploration and ritual magick. He was greatly misunderstood by his contemporary society, and ours still struggles with his renouncement of the normal social rules, restrictions, and mores in favor of his intense pursuit of magick. He granted the modern magician a large library of his works, rituals, and correspondences. Many people greatly admire Crowley's work, though some find fault with his character. His style of writing is purposely veiled and ornate in order to dishearten the dilettantes on the path. Even now, people accuse him of Satanism and all manner of "black magick." Crowley had his character flaws, as many do, and led a very public life regarding his spiritual path. Such matters of sexuality and magick spark enough controversy on their own; add to the mix an unapologetic, unconventional magician, and the situation is ripe for sensationalism and alienation of the more traditional sects, even in the occult world.

As for our interest in Crowley, he is most noteworthy to gay practitioners because of his pioneering work in the modern exploration of sex magick. Crowley's exploration of mystical wisdom through same-sex unions was highly influenced by the work of Edward Carpenter, a British writer, activist, and mystic who linked homosexuality to psychic and spiritual gifts. Perhaps our own well-documented experiences of "gaydar," an intuition that enables us to identify others with a similar energy, is one of our natural psychic gifts. Through it we recognize our similar spiritual DNA and make a connection.

With Victor Neuburg, Crowley undertook the ambitious Paris Workings, three and half weeks of sexual and sadomasochistic rituals, involving the gods Jupiter, Hermes, and Pan. (You can find Crowley's "Hymn to Pan" in his book *Magick in Theory and Practice.*) They began in 1913, on the 600th anniversary of the death of Jacques De Molay, the last grand master of the Templars. During this involved process, both recalled and relived a past life when Crowley was a hierodule priest/ess of the Goddess and Neuburg was "her" male lover. The purpose of the ritual was spiritual wisdom and material success to continue their studies and experiments. The two came to the conclusion that through our various incarnations, life after life, we are more apt for a homosexual or transgendered life when in transitional lifetimes, switching between the sexes. They also concluded that homosexual energy is turned toward inner, magical, and shamanic practices while heterosexual energy is directed outward for the creation of children. Perhaps this is why many religious laws state that child-bearing must be a possibility of intercourse, outlawing birth control, mastur-bation, and same-sex unions. The churches feared the energy would turn inward and awaken magical abilities. Perhaps priests and nuns take a vow of celibacy because it is a way to turn sexual energies inward toward spirituality, but not actually manifest this energy as psychic or magical phenomenon.

Late in life, Crowley had a nonsexual relationship with Gerald Gardner. Gardner, heterosexual by all accounts, is considered the modern father of Wicca. Initiated into an English coven in 1939, he brought the teaching of witchcraft to the public after the repeal of the Witchcraft Act in 1951. In 1954, he published *Witchcraft Today*, and then *The Meaning of Witchcraft* in 1959. Cynics claim modern Wicca is a fabrication of Gerald Gardner's and that Aleister Crowley actually wrote Gardner's first Book of Shadows, a book of rituals and spells. The book was reworked to be more Goddess-focused by his high priestess, Doreen Valiente, though both Valiente and Gardner were inspired by Charles Leland and his book *Aradia: Gospel of the Witches*, which is based on material gathered from Italian witches. Crowley passed away in 1947, before any of this material was published.

Gardner's tradition is now called Gardnerian Witchcraft. Alex Sanders, ritual magician and witch, soon released his own material, quite similar to and possibly borrowed from Gardner's Book of Shadows, though Sanders claimed it came from a family tradition taught to him by his grandmother. Now his tradition is known as Alexandrian Witchcraft, and he was known as the "King of Witches," at least in his own circles.

From these two very public roots spread the witchcraft renaissance of the 20th century. Both traditions survive, and in some areas, thrive today. The major criticism of Gardnerian and Alexandrian witchcraft is the formality of the rituals, orders, ranks, and initiations of the covens. Observers and former members feel the rituals can be as dogmatic as the mainstream Christian rituals from which seekers are trying to escape. Emphasis is placed on the union of the high priest and high priestess, as emissaries of the God and Goddess. Coupled with a focus on the fertility cult aspect, both of the land and physical creation of the child from mother and father, these forms of witchcraft leave those with a same-sex orientation feeling a bit out in the cold. Because of these fertility and heterosexual stresses in traditional modern witchcraft, many covens and circles are secretly or even publicly hostile to queer folk. Some of the prejudice can even stem from an original Judeo-Christian upbringing.

From the more formal Gardnerians came the Minoan Brotherhood, a secret organization for gay witches founded by Lord Gwydion (Eddie Buczynski), in New York City in the middle 1970s, and a Minoan Sisterhood was also forming. The focus for the brotherhood was much the same as traditional witchcraft, but exclusively for gay men and with a slant toward the ancient Greek mythology of Minoa. The brotherhood and sisterhood would worship separately during the Moon rituals, but would come together for the seasonal celebrations. The brotherhood of various covens, in the Minoan tradition are still active today.

More family traditions came "out of the broom closet" as the saying goes, revealing themselves, starting new covens, and taking on outside students, in both formal and informal settings. Many were inspired by the traditionalists to formalize and adapt their own family folk magick. Most modern witches doubt claims that entire traditions survived in secret, but many threads of wisdom survived to be woven into a new tapestry.

Reviving interest in Native American religions, striking a similar chord to the witchcraft and pagan movements, became intermingled with the craft in America. These neo-witchcraft and neo-pagan traditions grew slowly, but steadily, catching the interest of those disenchanted with the mainstream monotheistic and patriarchal religions.

Inspired by the new Goddess-focused religions that saw the divine in feminine form, and by recent archaeological discoveries, such as the Neolithic Anatolia sites, which give evidence of a sophisticated matriarchal culture, feminists adopted the tenets of the craft into their movement. Not all were eager to claim these ideals, as not all were eager to claim the words "witch," "Wiccan," or "pagan." Some simply embraced Goddess reverence. The American author Starhawk, most known for her work *The Spiral Dance*, has been and continues to be a great influence on modern Wicca and Goddess spirituality.

One particularly feminist branch of Wicca is the Dianic tradition, which surfaced in the 1970s. Revering the goddess Diana as Moon and Earth, rituals in this tradition are almost exclusively feminine, focusing symbolically and physically on the Goddess energy and not the God. They celebrate the rites of women, such as menstruation and menopause. Some Dianic covens are strictly lesbian, and use same-sex eroticism in their rituals. The work of Zsuzsanna Budapest can be credited with the formation of much of the Dianic movement.

Mirroring the Dianics comes the gathering of male and gay male spirituality. In 1975, Arthur Evans founded one of the first gay spirituality groups, called Faery Circle. In 1978, Evans wrote *Witchcraft and the Gay Counterculture*, a groundbreaking work detailing the history of gay spirituality. In 1979, Harry Hay and his partner, John Burnside, founded the Radical Faery Movement, reclaiming the word "fairy" as a being of mystery and magick, instead of a word of hatred and bigotry. The Radical Faeries is a loose affiliation of gay men weaving the principles of queerness, ecology, anarchy, community, transformation, paganism, and self-love into a wonderful whole. Although not traditionally Wiccan, they borrow from Wicca and Native American traditions, retrieving traditions of the past while forging into the future. The Radical Faeries are nondogmatic and free-form when creating ritual. In many ways, they are the inheritors of the spiritual traditions of the calusari and the hierodule. They have been inspired by and formed alliances with their sisters in the Dianic covens and the feminist movements.

Modern fairy mythology was initially inspired by Mitch Walker's *Visionary Love: A Spirit Book of Gay Mythology*. The new movements of gay spirit continue to influence and inspire others to create and share.

Prior to the Radical Faery Movement, but congruous with its tradition, we find Gavin Arthur and Llee Heflin. Gavin Arthur was influenced by Edward Carpenter, whom he met while in San Francisco. Arthur's own research focused on astrology and sexuality, as outlined in his book *The Circle of Sex*, published in 1966. He explored the balance of sexual energies, creating definitions and scales of greater depth than simply heterosexual, homosexual, and bisexual, and related such combinations to a clock, with correspondences to days, seasons, and other energies.

Building upon the work of Aleister Crowley, Heflin wrote *The Island Dialogues*, a magical, channeled (received from spiritual entities while in a trance state) work involving male homosexual tantra, chakras, and the Kabbalah. The teachings, completed in 1973, go beyond ritual and sex into the deeper spiritual mysteries, shamanic journey, self-healing, and self-love.

Margot Adler revealed much of paganism and witchcraft in America, bravely including material on Dianic and Radical Faery Groups in her book *Drawing Down the Moon: Witches, Druids, Goddess Worshippers, and Other Pagans in America Today*. Michael Thorn formed a gay men's coven called Kathexis Anthropos in the 1980s. Greg Johnson and Sparky T. Rabbit organized the Sons of the Bitch coven and started the Faggot Witch Camp. Italian witch Dr. Leo Martello campaigned for gay rights in traditional witchcraft. In addition to writing about gay history, Tom Cowan wrote *Fire in the Head*, an excellent guide to Celtic Shamanism, and coauthored with Laurie Cabot *Power of the Witch*, a staple for those beginning their witchcraft journey. In the 1990s, Donald Engstrom, artist, writer, and Wiccan, revealed the details of his own magical universe filled with queer-positive deities. In 1995, Valkyrie Cougar PenDragon shared her story as a transgendered high priestess. Authors and pagan community leaders continue to be supportive and increase awareness of the ancient practices of the Goddess and God.

The process of spirituality is an increasingly hot topic in the gay community. Many gays and lesbians feel ostracized by the mainstream religions in which they were raised. Some have tried to reconcile, but many are searching for a tradition that will openly accept them, as they are, with no struggle or reconciliation. We are seeking positive images, role models, and archetypes of the divine, perhaps something to which we have a historical connection. I found all this and more in witchcraft.

The coming-out experience in modern society is akin to a magical or shamanic initiation. Regardless of whether it is easy, hard, early, or late in life, coming out changes you, your life, and your perspective forever. Magical initiations open you to a new world. If you come to the magical path after coming out, you know what an initiation can be like, or, like me, you may choose the magical path at an early age, and come out a few years later. Each opens a new world, and opens new doors.

Simply by being gay, lesbian, bisexual, or transgendered, you have an experience different from the majority of people in the world. As we've seen in the past, queer mystics were healers, teachers, artists, poets, scholars, and aides to the community. They were visionaries. And they still are. We are now the visionaries. Is it no wonder why so many queer people find happiness in the theater, music, writing, and art? These arts are sacred. We want to creatively express our experiences and share them with others, to help others understand our unique view as those who dwell between worlds. As they understand, hopefully they, too, will heal and find joy. Many of us work in arts, health, counseling, and service industries because they are the only ways our society really supports these natural tendencies. We are going forward, yet intuitively, spiritually, remembering our roots.

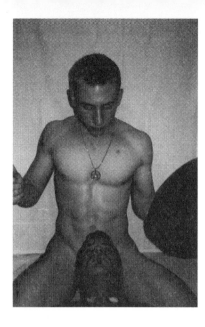

3

Queer Myth

Goddess of the Moon
Lady of the Night
Keeper of the Mysteries
Shine your silver light upon my soul
And unlock the treasures of the ancestors contained within me.

Who are the gods? Who are the goddesses? I am asked these questions frequently, and they are the hardest to answer, because individual witches have personal definitions of witchcraft, so everyone involved in the pagan religions embodies a personal view of the deities and their spiritual worlds.

We are fascinated with the deities of ages past, and the resurgence of Wicca is a testament to the belief that the wisdom of our past contains the seeds of our future, but as modern thinkers, most of us feel somewhat restricted from trying to return to a worldview from the ancient times. The world of the gods and goddesses is not outmoded or archaic in the 21st century. Their very nature cannot be defined. We cannot pigeonhole the forces of nature into what we surmise was our ancestors' belief system. The nature of the gods and goddesses is eternal, yet ever changing and adapting, like life. Most important, our view of them changes, prompting a personal relationship with them.

Pagans recognize the one spirit running through all life, the creative force in whatever manner you recognize it. You can call it "God" or "Goddess," focusing on either gender, but I feel it embodies both genders, as we soon will see in our creation myths. Some recognize the duality embodied by the creative force by naming it "Great Grandmotherfather." New Agers call it "MotherFatherGod," while others call it "Divine Mind" or "Tao." I call it "the Great Spirit," borrowing a nongender-charged term from native traditions. In the end, the name does not matter. The gods of ancient mythology embody the forces of nature, personified and serving as intermediaries among the vast energies of the Great Spirit. If you focus on one aspect, it is easier to see the whole.

My favorite analogy for the Great Spirit is a diamond, which contains many facets, many faces. Each face is an individual deity. Each face is beautiful, as is the whole, but sometimes the whole diamond can be overwhelming. You can give an individual facet more detailed attention. Some religions recognize the diamond and do not see the facets. Some focus on one or more of the facets. Witches can see the value in both views.

The gods and goddesses could be the spirits of nature they embody. The storm and sky gods are the spirit, the energy and consciousness, of the sky. Some native traditions look at the Great Spirit as the Dreamer, dreaming the world into form. The Dreamer creates other dreamers, who dream up portions of the larger picture. One dreamer dreams of rocks; another dreams of trees. Yet another dreamer creates the Moon. Each of the little dreamers is a goddess or god, with a particular providence of influence. Each culture recognized these dreamers as individual beings. Although they had different names and descriptions, surprisingly enough, many attributes and myths are the same. Perhaps the storm god of the Greeks and the storm god of the Norse were the same spiritual being, simply wearing a form, a mask that each culture was comfortable recognizing.

C. G. Jung, who worked with esoteric concepts, called these beings "archetypes." The archetypes are psychic entities that exist in what Jung called the collective unconscious. All of humanity, and possibly other beings, connect to the collective. Mystics refer to it as the astral plane, shamanic realm, or dreamtime, but they all point to the same thing. Individual people, and through them, individual cultures, could tap in to the same archetype image, but dress it in a manner that suited the particular culture or time period. Norsemen in Northern Europe would not see their storm god dressed in a toga, as the Greeks would. Climate and cultural attributes play an important part in the descriptions.

The archetypes of the ancients are eternal in this collective unconscious. Though not generally accepted as divine beings by the majority of society, they emerge in society through our art, movies, music, and television. Joseph Campbell said that the initiation of the hero—the classic heroic archetype found all over the world—is retold, for the modern generations disinterested in Greek mythology, in the story of Luke Skywalker and the *Star Wars* series. Director George Lucas is definitely tapping in to some archetypal themes.

Sometimes individuals live very archetypal lives. These popular icons become a part of the new mythos of the modern world. The renowned genius Einstein fulfills the magician archetype, reminding us of Merlin the magician, or Thoth, the divine scribe of Egypt. Marilyn Monroe reflects aspects of the love goddess Aphrodite and the sometimes tragic end of her affairs. John F. Kennedy lived out the sacrificed king archetype, similar to Tammuz, Osiris, or King Arthur. We even called his time in office the new Camelot. Jim Morrison of the classic rock band, The Doors, created his music to open the doors of perception, evoking the wine, poetry, and madness of the Greek god Dionysus. Occultists even claim a similarity between Princess Diana and the Roman Moon goddess Diana, known as Artemis to the Greeks.

Perhaps the gods of old were similar people who embodied these universal archetypes. As time passed, their names were revered as gods and forgotten as men and women. Such an exchange would explain a lot of the more human behavior of some gods and goddesses.

Ultimately, the true origins of the gods are unknown, but the gods themselves are knowable. By studying myths and history, we as modern individuals can connect to these divine facets of the diamond, and gather a wisdom and personal connection to the forces of the universe. Through the mystics, artists, musicians, and witches will reveal the new tales of wisdom for all to share.

In the Beginning—Creation Myths

The first creation story I learned was that of Genesis. In six days, God created the world. On the seventh, he rested. God created the first humans, starting with Adam, the first man. From Adam's rib he created Eve. Eve's association with the serpent led to defying God and a fall from grace. The divine couple was banished from the perfect paradise, the Garden of Eden. The "witty" argument homophobes use to persecute gays, "God created Adam and Eve, not Adam and Steve" sprang from the Genesis mythology. Like all mythologies, it is subject to change and reinterpretation as society changes. Unfortunately, certain fundamentalist followers of this mythos do not view it as a form of myth or a symbolic representation of spiritual truth. Rather, they see it as a literal description of actual events. Because of this, many people have learned this is the one truth, and no room is left for interpretation. Such beliefs disturb moderate followers, but even these moderates do not present, or even explore, the other version of their mythic history. I certainly was surprised when I did.

As a student of witchcraft, I was asked to learn not only everything I could about my own religion, but about other religions as well. The path of the witch is not always easy, and if there is a path more suited to your personality, beliefs, and life's purpose, witches encourage you to find it, even if that takes you away from the craft. Since modern witchcraft borrows from many cultures and traditions, a wise student learns about all these sources, and the eternal truths found in the heart of most of the world's religions.

The common translations of the Bible are not the only ones. In one Genesis account, the word God is translated from the word Elohim. We now take God to be singular and most likely masculine. Elohim is actually a plural noun, and translates to "creative spirits" or "gods." The Judeo-Christian and Muslim faiths are monotheistic, meaning they believe in one God, while pagans, being polytheistic, honor a multitude of gods. Here we have evidence that the Biblical creation story may have occurred with many godlike spirits, similar to pagan mythology. In one section, Genesis accounts, "Let us make man in our image and likeness. Male and female he created them." Surely this invites the interpretation that God, or the Elohim, had a female aspect in its plurality.

Yahweh, the father god of the Bible, is believed to be the supreme creative spirit, and in the context of the Old Testament, other gods were considered false idols. Yet we have evidence that this father god may have been feminine, or comprised several spirits. It is entirely possible that Yahweh was one of many gods in a Middle Eastern pantheon, a god of the sky and fire. He may have connections to Yareah, a Moon deity of the Canaanites, from whom the Hebrews strove to disassociate themselves. We know little of Yareah, but quite possibly this was an androgynous or bisexual god. Perhaps the followers of Yahweh rewrote the myths in an attempt to make him paramount and eradicate traces of the other deities.

In Hebrew mysticism, Yahweh is an approximation for the unpronounceable name of God, transliterated in English as YHVH. It has no vowels. In ritual magick it is pronounced by spelling it out, Yod, Heh, Vahv, Heh. Throw in a few vowels and you get Yahweh. Each letter is a power in Hebrew, and the four letters symbolize the four elements, earth, air, fire, and water. Two, the first and third, are masculine, while the second and fourth are feminine. Here we have something quite strikingly similar to the Elohim, and not the patriarchal God envisioned by most. The letters when stacked from top to bottom in Hebrew, make the shape of the Adam Kadmon, the Kabbalistic spiritual template of humanity. The Adam Kadmon is both male and female, balanced, the ideal of all humanity.

The Adam Kadmon reminds me of one of the "lost" Genesis stories about Adam's first wife, Lilith. In the beginning, God created the being now known as Adam, but it was androgynous, being both male and female. God divided the being into two, Adam and Lilith. Lilith would not be subservient to Adam, particularly during intercourse. Lilith left the Garden of Eden to strike out on her own in the world. Later she was reviled as a demon, an enemy of the Hebrews, murdering children and mating with demons to create monsters. Like Eve, and a sure cousin to Pandora and her box, Lilith became a scapegoat. Here you see the start of a very similar theme in the history of witchcraft. Some witches consider Lilith to be the first witch.

We need to understand how myths can, and have been, rewritten. One retelling is not necessarily right or wrong, but it is always important to understand where you get your information. With a little digging into the familiar Bible story, you discover it is similar to many pagan creation stories. Even the pagan stories were often changed as the patriarchy gained power with the new warrior culture, making Goddess reverence a scapegoat. The sexual, androgynous, or bisexual aspects of creation are important in many pagan creation stories, for each aspect, in spite of being stripped from our spiritual history, is key to life.

In variations of the Greek creation myth, the universe was born to chaos. From the chaos, the goddess Gaia birthed herself into being as the Great Mother. Gaia most often refers to the Earth Mother. She gave birth to her son and husband, Uranus, the sky father, and the two began creation. This goddess was revered as the fount of life, but eventually was supplanted by patriarchy. Her symbol, the python—another goddess/snake association, like Eve's temptation—was slain by the Sun god Apollo. Her temple at Delphi, renowned for its oracles, was taken over by priests of Apollo. Her gift of prophecy became his gift. Typically, the snake is said to represent winter, which the Sun slays, but in reality, the snake embodied the powers of life and death wielded by the Goddess.

The Sumerian goddess Tiamat, depicted as a dragon—another serpentine image—is akin to Gaia. Her serpentine visage is a sign of sexuality, often considered a phallic symbol, denoting a type of androgyny. In the original myths, Tiamat fertilizes herself to create the first of the Sumerian gods. Some cite her mate, the deity Apsu, as male while other authors view Apsu as female. In later myths, obviously rewritten, the grandson of Anu, Marduk, slays Tiamat, and uses her body to create the world. Marduk is given the greatest power and highest rank among the Sumerian gods, possible evidence that his followers gain power in the culture and rewrote the myths to reflect his, and their, greatness.

The creation stories of Egypt were rewritten many times. One of the oldest involves the deity Khepera, the scarab beetle god, one being prior to the division of male and female, though most often used in association with male pronouns. Khepera rolls the Sun across the sky like a dung beetle rolls a ball of dung across the Earth. The beetle is continually resurrected from the Earth, rising each day with light, just as Khepera resurrects itself from nothing. Khepera created the cosmos through masturbation, or through sex with his shadow.

Another version gives credit to Neith, a gynandromorphous creator deity stated to be the "father of fathers and mother of mothers." Amazons of Libya worshiped her. She is the goddess of the Nile Delta, the source of life in Egypt. She was later associated with wisdom and the goddesses Nut and Hathor. The Greeks associated Neith with Pallas Athena.

In other Egyptian myths, the genders of the familiar Earth and sky deities are reversed, with the goddess Nut being the sky and the god Geb embodying the Earth. Through the hills and mountains, his phallus reached up to his sky-mate to create the next generation of gods, four siblings—Isis, Osiris, Set, and Nephthys. These early Egyptians could see the masculine traits of Earth and feminine traits of the sky, making them a bit different from the cultures around them. And while most cultures saw the Moon as feminine, the Egyptians had both Moon goddesses and gods, such as the gods Thoth and Knoshu.

Two of my favorite Egyptian creation myths, in terms of introducing a sacred form of sexuality, include the elder gods Thoth and Ra. Thoth is attributed as the scribe of the Gods. Associated by the Greeks with the purportedly androgynous Hermes, Thoth sought to bring balance as court magician and advisor to the pantheon of Egyptian gods. Thoth was an early Merlin archetype, yet much more divine in stature, advising gods instead of kings. He may have been greater than the other gods, but he did not seek to rule. Some say his magick was so great, he created the universe with it. One of his aspects was of an ibis, the other, an ape. As an ibis, he gave birth from the void, or chaos, to the cosmic Egg, and hatched the universe and eight major Egyptian gods.

In other myths, Thoth counseled Ra, the supreme Sun god and creative force. Ra, like Marduk, was given the highest rank and prestige by his followers on Earth. His wife, Rait, or Rat, a feminization of his name, is not clearly defined in the myth cycles, suggesting Rait is simply the feminine form of Ra, and perhaps at one time this god was seen as a goddess, or at least one who could transform genders. Obviously, the Sun played an important part in Egyptian life. The Egyptians claimed Ra created the universe solely from an act of masturbation. His semen became the cosmic waters that brought life, starting with the air and rain gods, Shu and Terfnut, who begot Nut and Geb. Ancient Egyptian art and religion were far more sexual than most texts lead us to believe. The first to bring the ancient Egyptian artifacts to light in the West were the sexually repressed Victorians, who were aghast to find so much art-work and statuary showing erect penises. In an effort to maintain "decency," they broke off and defaced the artwork. The ancients who came up with such marvels as the pyramids and the Sphinx knew the importance of sexuality in a culture. Let's hope we will reclaim this wisdom.

From these creation myths, we realize many views of creation exist, from that of the fundamental Christian to the strictly scientific big bang theory, and the variety of pagan beliefs. The common element from a multitude of sources is the androgyny and sexuality inherent in the act of creation. While most of our culture shuns these attributes, traits many queer folk have, the ancients celebrated these qualities and saw them as divine and essential to life. If all life is made in the likeness of the divine, we all have these qualities. A wise one cultivates them into personal strengths.

Queer-Positive Deities

The archetypes associated with homosexuality and gender variance are the gods of magick, creation, healing, inspiration, and the arts. The cliché of every gay man being a dancer, actor, painter, author, or designer is not far from the truth because these arts lead to the discovery of spirit. They are sacred. Those involved in medicine, as doctors, nurses, and counselors of all kinds, are embodying the healer archetype, through the acceptable forms of healing found in the modern society. Images of the butch lesbian resonate with the ancient warrior priestesses, strong in body and spirit. Even the stereotype of the gay construction worker falls under the builder-creator archetype. As you explore the divine images with gay themes, you find the archetypes of artist, shaman, divine child, warrior, ruler, parent, and sacred lover.

The following deities are those gods of homoerotic magick. Since mod-ern witchcraft borrows from many time periods and locations, this listing is not restricted to the typical Celtic, or even European, influences, although they are the most popular. Though the names may be familiar, parts of their story may not.

We may never know which myths are true, figuratively or historically, but such uncertainties should not prevent us from working with new images, myths, and truths to take us into the next century. As you build a relationship with the goddesses and gods, you can ask them directly and get the answers most suited for you.

Adonis/Tammuz (Phoenician/Greco-Roman/Mesopotamian): The name "Adonis" now refers to a strikingly beautiful male, but the original Adonis is a cross-cultural deity, showing up in Phoenician and Greco-Roman mythology. Adonis is often equated with the Mesopotamian Tammuz, with whom he shares many attributes and stories. Most noted for his relationships with goddesses, including Astarte, Aphrodite, and Persephone, Adonis was also the beloved of the god Dionysus. Adonis and Tammuz are fertility gods, representing the vegetation of the land, in a constant state of life, death, and resurrection. Adonis died from a boar's attack, which mutilated his genitals. In the much-celebrated descent-of-the-goddess stories known in many cultures, the Goddess travels into the many layers of the underworld to retrieve the spirit of her consort. Adonis is seen not as a king, but as a lover, somewhat effeminate or homoerotic. His priests in Athens were homoerotically inclined, and, along with priestesses, they celebrated his life and death by planting gardens of Adonis, and then uprooted them only a few days after sprouting. In the Greek magical papyri, Adonis is invoked for lesbian love spells.

Apollo and Hyacinth (Greek): Apollo was initially the Greek god of light and later was associated with the Sun. His twin sister is Artemis. As the god of music, dance, divination, healing, and artistic inspiration, he can grant these gifts to others. Apollo is known for taking many male lovers, most notably, Hyacinthus, or Hyacinth, a mortal youth. When he was tossing the discus with Apollo, it struck Hyacinth with a mortal blow. The western wind god Zephyrus, who desired Hyacinth and was angry and jealous of Apollo, caused the accident with his winds. The Sun god could not save his beloved, but from his wound Apollo created the Hyacinth flowers, a symbol of youth cut too short. Hyacinth later became a divine patron to those pursuing same-sex love.

Aphrodite/Venus (Greco-Roman): Aphrodite embodies the powers of love on every level, especially romantic love. Known as Venus to the Romans, and associated with the morning and evening star, the planet Venus, she was renowned for her gifts of attraction and beauty. She originated—along with the Furies—from Uranus, the sky god, springing forth from the foamy sea where Uranus's genitalia had fallen after being castrated by his son Chronos. She is usually displayed as a beautiful woman rising out of the sea, as in Botticelli's painting, "The Birth of Venus." As she walks on land, she trails flowers behind her, even in the most barren of deserts. Her aid Eros is the original archetype for the Valentine's Day cupid, shooting his arrows and making people fall in love. She had many lovers, most notably Ares the war god and her husband, Hephaestus. She bore Hermaphrodite from her union with Hermes.

Artemis/Diana (Greco-Roman): Artemis is the huntress, the goddess of wild things, the protector of women and children, and the maiden aspect of the Moon. From her bow, she fires silver arrows, the shafts of moonlight to illuminate her path. In many versions of her myths, she is the archetype of the strong, independent woman, goddess of Amazons and unsympathetic to those of traditional masculinity. After her birth, she immediately got up and helped her mother deliver her twin brother, Apollo. Artemis rejects many traditional roles, such as marriage and conventional society, and feels kinship to those beyond traditional roles. Her festivals included same-sex eroticism involving both females and males. As the Romans' Diana, she took on a more maternal, universal goddess archetype, and became the mother of Aradia, her avatar in 14th-century Italy, who taught the Goddess's craft.

Astarte (Phoenician/Canaanite): Astarte is a manifestation of the Great Mother Goddess of the Paleolithic cultures, identified with the earlier goddesses Ishtar and Inanna, and later the Greco-Roman Aphrodite/Venus. Versions of Astarte were worshiped throughout the Middle East, Egypt, and even across Europe, with the spread of the Roman Empire. She is a Queen of Heaven, and patron of love and war. She, too, is involved in the resurrection and fertility myths of Adonis, also known as Adoni, or lord. Though usually remembered in feminine form, like other goddesses, she does have mixed gender incarnations, sometimes depicted as a hermaphrodite, and later the Phoenician records mention King Astarte. Astarte's temples were served by the kelabim and possibly a gender-variant order of Amazonian women.

Asushunamir: In the Sumerian myth of the descent of Inanna to the underworld, the god Enki created the Asushunamir, companion spirits, to rescue Inanna from her dark sister, the underworld queen Ereskigal. Although "Asushunamir" translates as "he whose face is light," these companion spirits are neither male nor female. Ereskigal cursed them for their trickery, stating they would forever more eat and drink from the gutters and hide in shadow. Innana blessed them with the gifts of prophecy, healing, and magick. Technically not gods, but divine spirits, the Asushunamir spirits are often identified with the galatur and kurgarru, the transgendered priests of Inanna.

Many modern gay pagans consider the Asushunamir as representing the creation of the first gay spirits, and refer to them in ritual evocation as the Queer Ones. Some refer to the Queer Ones as aspects of the Old Ones or

Ancient Ones, beings who are divine, yet not recognized as supreme creative gods. They relate to the old myths of the Fey, or Faery Folk. Depending on the source, the Faery are either associated with ancient Celtic or European gods whose power and stature in the world dwindled due to lack of acknowledgment, respect, and worship by humanity, or they are a combination of elemental, nature, and tribal spirits. Cultures all over the world have stories of little ones living in the land, under the hills, and deep in otherworldly forests. Many gay men reclaim the Faery Folk as their spiritual ancestors, since the word "fairy" has been linked to effeminate, gay, and transgendered men. Most likely, the original tribal cultures from which these myths spring didn't have the same taboos against male homosexuality, so, in truth, they are our spiritual ancestors. The Fey Folk have been associated with joy, ritual, sexuality, pleasure, art, music, and theater—all avenues of creative and divine expression found in the gay communities.

In a translation of a myth of Inanna called "From the Great Above to the Great Below," found in the book, *Inanna Queen of Heaven and Earth*, by Diane Wolkstein and Samuel Noah Kramer, the God Enki creates the galatur and Kurgarra to rescue Inanna from the underworld:

From under his fingernail, Father Enki brought forth dirt.
He fashioned the dirt into a kurgarra, a creature neither male nor female.
From under the fingernail of his other hand he brought forth dirt.
He fashioned the dirt into a galatur, a creature neither male nor female.
He gave the food of life to the kurgarra.
He gave the water of life to the galatur.

With the food and water of life, they tricked Ereshkigal and resurrected Inanna.

Athena/Minerva (Greco-Roman): Springing fully formed from the head of Zeus, without aid of a goddess, Athena is presented as the wise warrior woman of the Olympians. She has the ability to transform into a young man. Her affairs often end on a tragic note, and most modern myths present her as celibate, though such descriptions were probably added by the patriarchal rise, to demonstrate a strong warrior woman could not have love. In one such myth, her "brother" Hephaestus makes her armor, for "her love." He means physical love, while she assumes platonic love. I find it hard to believe such a goddess of wisdom and strategy would misunderstand such an offer. Most likely, our modern Athena is a sanitized version of the ancient Minoan snake goddess. Her darker half was shed and cast off as the gorgon Medusa. Modern Athena carries a shield with Medusa's face on it. Athena is the goddess of strategy, weaving, and invention, who is credited with teaching humans how to graft olive branches onto trees, yielding more harvest. The city of Athens is named after her. She is often called Pallas Athena, in honor of her friend (or possible lover) who died as a youth in a spear throwing accident. Minerva is her Roman name.

Baphomet (Europe): Baphomet is not a traditional pagan god, but one most noted for its link to the Knights Templar. Pictured as a hermaphrodite, with breasts and a penis, Baphomet was also a mix between human and goat, a perfect mix between male and female, human, and animal, although something akin to the traditional Middle Age view of the devil. Baphomet is a deity of fertility and wealth. To curb their growing power and influence, King Philip IV of France claimed the Knights Templar were worshiping Baphomet and practicing homosexuality, two acts of heresy in the eyes of the Church.

Baron Samedi (Vodoun): The Voodoo loa (law) named Baron Samedi is a god of the dead and magick, but is also evoked for help in daily life. His place is the cemetery and his symbol, a skull. Samedi is depicted as transgendered, wearing a combination of men's and women's clothing of black and purple, possibly representing his walk between two worlds, the living and the dead, in the same way that his sunglasses, with only one lens, do. He sees in both worlds. The Baron is known for his sexually suggestive movements indicating a desire for anal intercourse.

Bona Dea (Roman/Italian): Bona Dea is the "Good Goddess" about whom little is known. She is a goddess of healing, magick, prosperity, and women. In fact, her cult did not allow the participation of men, and none of her mysteries were to be shared with the outside world. Most of our information on Bona Dea comes to us from the written accounts of male scholars lacking a personal connection to her rites. Her ceremonies possibly included lesbian acts of love as a part of worship.

Bran (Welsh): Bran the Blessed is a Celtic hero/god of the mystical otherworlds. In many Celtic myths, the line between divine and mortal, spirit and flesh, is less visible than in most other mythologies. The legends were passed on orally, and recorded only much later by Christian writers. To preserve the story, yet not blaspheme, the gods and goddesses were transformed into heroes of folktales as the stories are told and retold. Bran is a patron of magick, battle, and resurrection. His main tale is the rescue of his sister, Branwen, who in many ways seems like his feminine half. She was abused by Matholwch, her husband and king of Ireland. Bran's army defeated Matholwch's men and rescued her, but Bran was fatally wounded. His head was eventually severed and continued, after his death, to speak and give magical advice. Eventually it was buried in London. As an interesting note to his history, Robert Graves, the somewhat controversial author of *The White Goddess*, believed Bran was worshiped by an order of homosexual priests, and Amathon, a version of the Green Man, wrests Bran's secret magical name by seducing one of Bran's priests.

Cernunnos/Herne the Hunter (Celtic/Proto-Celtic): Cernunnos is the fabled Horned God, a central figure in modern witchcraft. He represents the god of the waning year and animal lord, the complement to the Green Man. Usually depicted naked, sitting in a lotus position, with stag antlers and a torc (Celtic neck ring resembling a choker) around his neck and one in his hand, surrounded by the animals of the forest. Some renditions portray the Horned God with an erect penis, surrounded by men with erections as well. Very little of Cernunnos's original mythos survives, so old are his cults. Worship of him, primarily in Gaul and other Celtic territories, is believed to predate the arrival of the Celts. We don't even know his proper name; Cernunnos is a Roman variation. He has been equated with Herne the Hunter and even the Greek Pan and Dionysus due to their similar associations with nature and shamanic trance work. Herne is a figure of British folklore, the God of the Wild Hunt, appearing at times of crisis. Cernunnos is sometimes associated with the chalk carving of the god figure at Cerne Abbas in Dorset. The figure is not horned, but associated with fertility, due to his depiction with his exaggerated phallus. Cernunnos is an aspect of the Great Father God, a force of nature, like the Goddess—loving, gentle, and receptive, but also fiercely protective and powerful.

Chin (Mayan): Chin is described as a small child or dwarf, and is a deity of magick, divination, and the destiny of rulers. He introduced homoerotic relationships to the Mayan nobles. The nobles would obtain youths of the lower classes to be the lovers of the nobles' sons. Such unions were considered legal marriages under Mayan law.

Damballah (Vodoun): Damballah is the serpent god of the Voodoo loa and although Damballah is portrayed as a father figure, he has an androgynous nature and can manifest homoerotically or bisexually. Invoked for guidance, peace, and prosperous good fortune, Damballah is the god of rain and rainbows, making a modern connection to the queer rights movement.

Dionysus/Bacchus (Thracian/Greco-Roman): Dionysus is the son of Zeus and a mortal woman named Semele. Myths paint Zeus's immortal wife, Hera, as the villain, tricking Semele to her death while she was still pregnant. Zeus could not save her, but saved his child, and implanted the unborn child in his

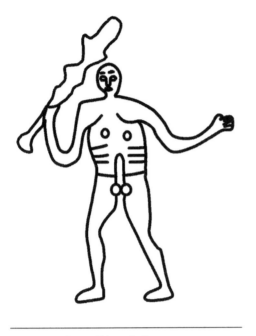

Cerne Abbas chalk carving

thigh, carrying him to term. Thus, in this myth, Dionysus is "twice born" and associated with immortality and Zeus is transgendered and associated with birth. Older myths cite Dionysus's early death and rebirth, as well as a serpent, perhaps Persephone in disguise, as his mother. Hera plagued him after his birth, so to disguise himself, he learned the art of shape shifting into various plants and animals, and dressed in women's clothing to avoid detection. He kept company with woodland creatures, animals, nymphs, and satyrs. Depicted as soft and feminine, yet virile and strong, Dionysus is a balance of extremes. His myths, too, contain both ends of the spectrum. As a god of ecstasy, wine, and love, he traveled the world with his teachings, before ascending to Olympus as one of the twelve main deities. Like Jesus, but predating him, Dionysus spread his message and gathered followers to his cult. Some expressions were peaceful and loving, while others were more extreme and violent. His female followers of the more extreme rituals were called the Maenads, or Bacchante. Noted for his associations with Aphrodite and Persephone, taking a sacrificial Adonis-like role in several stories, Dionysus was less well known for his love affairs with men, including Adonis and Hermaphrodite. Dionysus is both an upper-world god of light, as a newborn child of innocence, and one who has braved the underworld, in search of his mother's spirit, to come back with the power the shamanic realms has to offer. As Bacchus to the Romans, this god was depicted less beautiful, and more masculine, yet he retained his softness and sensitivity. Dionysus is quite the example of balancing gender identities as a path to enlightenment.

Ereshkigal (Sumerian): Sister to Inanna, and Queen of the Underworld, Ereshkigal is the dark goddess of the dead. She is like the crone, and associated with the power of transformation and destruction, with Greek Kore/Persephone,

Hindu Kali, Celtic Morgan, and Norse Hel. In Egypt, Ereshkigal was petitioned for gay male love spells.

Eros (Greek): Eros is most popularly known as the cupid image of
Valentine's Day cards, and as the aid to Aphrodite, shooting arrows to make
mortals and gods alike fall in love. The mythic, truly worshiped god Eros is
much different from our conception of him. Like Dionysus, he contained a
mixture of feminine and masculine energies, being soft, gentle, loving, effeminate, and childlike on one hand, and ancient, wise, aggressive, and masculine
on the other. Eros is the patron and protector of homosexual love. He, along
with Hermes and Hercules, could grant blessings upon male couples—the gifts
of loyalty, eloquence, and strength, respectively. Eros is a major deity in the
Orphic Mystery Schools, associated with the dolphin, flute, lyre, rose, and
rooster. As a patron of success in battle, he was called upon by warrior/lovers
before a fight, because many in the Greek world believed the love men had for
each other would unite and lead them to victory.

Erzulie (Vodoun): Erzulie is the Voodoo loa of love, seduction, and beauty,
who grants the gift of manifesting beauty to those in the creative arts, such as
painters, musicians, poets, and designers. Although similar in some ways to
the Aphrodite archetypes, Erzulie also contains darker elements akin to the
underworld goddesses. Her symbol is the mirror, not only to admire her beauty,
but in Voodoo, the mirror is the symbol of the spirit world, the gateway to
the realm of the loa. She is sometimes known as a loa of tragic love, for she is
Erzulie Ge Rouge, Erzulie of the Red Eyes. She weeps constantly because no
man can love her enough. Some practitioners consider her a patron to gay
men and lesbians. Men "ridden" by Erzulie often display transgender traits.

Freyja and Freyr (Norse): The Norse myths divide the gods into two tribes,
the Aseir and Vanir. The Vanir tribe is considered earthier, embodying the
natural forces. The Aseir represent the more intellectual aspects demonstrated
by sky-god cultures. The two tribes clashed and eventually the Aseir won the
conflict. As a sign of peace, the tribes traded members. Freyja and Freyr lived
in Asgard with the Aseir as part of the agreement. Freyja is the good goddess
of these ancient people who would become the Norse. She is the goddess of
the land, fertility, eroticism, and magick. She specialized in a shamanic magick called Seidr, the practice of inducing shamanic states through shivering
and shaking, and sex magick acts are also attributed to her. She wears the
golden falcon cloak, which carries her into the otherworlds like the bird of
prey. Freyja taught her magick to the god Odin, the all-father of the Aseir. This
great goddess later became a goddess of battle, and her initiations included the
rite of boys becoming men and warriors. Although modern practitioners of the

Norse traditions, the Asatru, are often seen as dominantly heterosexual and sometimes even unwelcoming of gays, it appears possible their ancient spiritual ancestors had homoerotic overtones in actuality, or ritually, like most ancient cultures. Becoming a warrior was a form of blood brothering. Ritual anal intercourse may have been a part of that warrior bonding. Her brother, the god Freyr, also embodies the earth, like a vegetation king, growing, dying, and then resurrecting. Sharing attributes with the traditional Wiccan horned and green gods, Freyr is sometimes depicted with an erect penis, and fertility icons are present as part of his worship. He is also a patron of magick, shamanism, water, eroticism, love, peace, boars, horses, and stags. Freyr seems to keep his associations with peace, an association many queer men identify with instead of focusing on the more patriarchal and warlike gods, while other gods, including his sister, were directed toward war. His priest may have been homoerotic or transgendered, and well versed in his sister's form of shamanic magick. In many ways, Freyja and Freyr are like two sides of the same coin, even in name. To modern pagans, they represent the primal Goddess and God of the land, the Lady and Lord seen all over the world.

Ganesha (Hindu): Ganesha, the breaker of obstacles and binder of evil, is usually depicted as a four-armed, plump, elephant-headed man, riding a rat. Ganesha is a benefactor, a wise, gentle, and loving god, acting as an aide and intermediary for other deities of the Hindu faith. He is the son of the goddess Parvati. One myth claims his father is the god Shiva. Another says he was created by Parvati from clay and dust, to be both her son and servant. Lesser-known myths say he sprung from the union of Parvati with the goddess of the Ganges River, Ganga, or another handmaiden goddess. Shiva beheads him in a fit of anger, as Ganesha protects the inner chambers of Parvati. The goddess replaced his fallen human head with an elephant's head. Shiva later gave control of his armies, his own power, to Ganesha. The inner chambers of the goddess represent the inner, sacred power, and the power of sexuality, as he is said to guard the root chakra, and kundalini. The gates to the kundalini energy are the vagina and anus, and the elephant-headed god has been linked to homoerotic forms of worship involving anal sex. Ganesha is mixed in terms of sexuality, masculine in gender, and as represented with the elephant's trunk, but also is soft, tender, and portrayed with breasts. He opens the gateways that block our path, removes obstacles, and protects travelers. Speaking from personal experience, Ganesha is a powerful ally to have when overcoming challenges placed before you.

Ganymede (Greek): The most famous male lover of the Olympian god-king Zeus, Ganymede was a prince whom Zeus coveted. Taking the shape of an eagle, Zeus snatched Ganymede up to Mount Olympus to be his lover and his cupbearer, pourer of the golden ambrosia, the nectar of the gods. Ambrosia, like other sacred liquids, is associated with semen. The sign of Aquarius is associated with Ganymede.

Gwydion (Celtic): Brother to the Welsh warrior Gilfaethwy, Gwydion is an archetypal magician figure, whose attributes were later absorbed by the Arthurian legends in the figure of Merlin. Gwydion is a trickster, as well as a magician, associated with the Celtic otherworlds and rites similar to shamanism, shape-shifting, and transformation. To woo the lady Goewin from the warrior/magician/king Math, Gilfaethwy asked for Gwydion's aid. Though greatly skilled, they failed, causing a war with the King Pywll. Math punished them by transforming them into animals of the opposite gender and having them mate, producing a deer, pig, and wolf, who were later transformed by Math into human men, the heroes Hyddwn, Hychtwn, and Bleiden. Gilfaethwy took the female role twice, but Math made them both retain their human consciousness within their animal incarnations, as punishment. The results, however, were quite wonderful, creating three heroes. Such myths can construe an archetypal reality that preceded events of ritual transgenderism and homoerotic worship among the Celtic people. Only later, as the myth was retold to Christian audiences, does the same-sex union become punishment for misdeeds. Gwydion later guides the development of the warrior Lleu, much like Merlin did with King Arthur.

Hecate (Greco-Roman): The archetypal goddess of the witches, Hecate is the triple goddess of magick, justice, travel, the night, and the crossroads. She guards the roads of travel, sailors, horses, dogs, and wealth. As Hecate Triformus, she is the one who is three, embodying maiden, mother, and crone, but is most often seen as the crone, the dark goddess of the underworld—the bringer of light or terrible darkness, as a goddess of blessings and curses. Her symbol is the torch, carried into the dark night. As a handmaiden to Aphrodite and Persephone, she is a goddess of love, evoked for gay male love spells going back to the 3rd century C.E. She is also linked with Diana and Proserpina by the Romans, as triple Moon goddesses, and with Artemis, Luna, and Persephone in various triplicies, by the Greeks. Though most typically viewed as a Greek goddess, worshiped by priestesses, her roots trace back to Thrace, and she was honored by gender-variant male priests called *semnotatoi*. The Romans did not change her name when they assimilated her from the Greek pantheon.

Hermaphrodite (Greek): Hermaphrodite is a deity of both genders, having a penis and breasts. One myth states Hermaphrodite is the child of Hermes and Aphrodite, hence the name, and contained the best attributes of them both.

Another myth states a nymph named Salmacis pursued a mortal man who spurned her. She asked that she and the mortal be joined forever, and the gods did just that, fulfilling her exact words, and not her intention. The gods melted the two together into one being with both masculine and feminine attributes.

Hermes/Mercury (Greco-Roman): Although called the messenger god of the Olympians, Hermes has a much greater sphere of influence. True, he is the god of travel, but he is not restricted to any place or role. When speaking to his father, Zeus, he asks to go anywhere he chooses, and takes the role of messenger and psychopomp, traveling between the heavens, Earth, and underworlds. A psychopomp is a guide for souls who takes the dead to the underworld, and new souls to Earth. The psychopomp is the divine archetype of the shaman and magician. As one not bound by traditional roles and obligations, he is free to go and do as he pleases. Hermes took male and female lovers as he desired. With Hercules and Eros, he is part of a homoerotic trinity. His son is the god Pan. Although a male deity, Hermes is androgynous, and carries a lot of boyish charm. Called "Mercury" by the Romans, and associated with Thoth of the Egyptians, Hermes was evoked during the 3rd century in Egypt for gay and lesbian love spells in Hellenistic (Greek) magick. Dill seeds are considered the "semen of Hermes." Hermes is also credited with giving humans the gifts of writing, mathematics, music, geometry, games, gambling, gymnastics, and wrestling. He is even said to be the inventor of masturbation.

Invoked for protection when traveling, Hermes is another Greek patron of the crossroads. He is the god of both intellect and cunning, and as a trickster spirit, he is a patron of thieves. The symbols of Hermes include the winged sandals and cap, the caduceus, and the wand. The caduceus symbolizes the currents of kundalini, rising in a spiral, and later pictured as a double helix, like DNA, or the currents of masculine and feminine energy blending together. Now it is the symbol of modern medicine, as Hermes is a patron of healers. Hermes is a versatile god of many talents, trades, and attributes.

Horus (Egyptian): Horus is the avenging son and a savior figure, a divine child in the Osirian cults. Horus is the falcon-headed god. One of his eyes is the Sun and the other is the Moon. The son of Osiris and Isis, he revenges himself against his father's murderer, his uncle Set. Although Horus

Caduceus

and Set were in constant conflict until Horus's eventual victory, one myth relates the story of oral intercourse between Set and Horus, and Set consequently gives birth to Horus's child. The child is either the Moon god Khonshu or the scribe of the gods, Thoth. Thoth is also associated with the Moon and homosexuality, although in most stories Thoth predates Horus. Homoerotic reproduction is common between divine personages, and their union often signifies birth of a mystical truth rather than a physical child. This particular birth suggests that the child of light and the god of darkness, nephew, and uncle are really two sides of the same deity, much like the cyclical Oak and Holly King of Celtic myth. Unfortunately, many scholars interpret the saga of Horus and Set as the struggle of good versus evil.

Hypnos (Greek): Popular in mythology is the story of the Moon goddess Selene, who loved the boy Endymion. Most versions tell us she was so distracted by her love that she failed to pull her Moon chariot across the sky, causing darkness and the phases of the Moon. The gods punished her by putting poor Endymion to sleep, yet she still visits, continuing the dark phases of the Moon. The underworld god Hypnos, god of sleep, also loved Endymion, and he put Endymion to sleep, so they may share time together through dreams.

Indra (Hindu): Indra is the Hindu sky god, with many similarities to Zeus. Both bisexual and transgendered, Indra loves his wife, Indrani. Indrani and Indra are viewed as the feminine and masculine sides to one being. Indra also loves the Moon god Soma, who elicits comparisons to Ganymede. The word *soma* also refers to the drink of the gods, like the Greek ambrosia, an offering, or potentially a psychotropic substance, real or mythic, which opens the gate to the gods. Soma also forms a union with Agni, the Hindu god of fire.

Isis (Egyptian): The most beloved of goddesses, Isis is the Great Mother goddess of the Egyptians, the mother of gods and pharaohs. As the goddess of the land, agriculture, Moon, heaven, the underworld, healing, and magick, she is essentially the goddess of life. Her worship started in Stone Age Egypt, but was later incorporated in the more patriarchal myths of Ra, Osiris, and Horus. Even so, she plays a pivotal part in such dramas. Her worship spread into Europe, particularly as a result of Rome's contact with Egypt, and only diminished with the rise of Christianity and the violent conversions associated with it. Christianized emperor Constantine forbade her worship and rites, desecrated her temples and killed her priests and priestesses. Actually, she was worshiped almost twice as long as Christ has been, and modern pagans are reviving her worship. Her cults and mysteries may have been similar to or even inspired the Eleusian mysteries of Persephone and Demeter. Although associated with homosexuality through her son Horus and brother Set, Isis, like other goddesses of her time and place, is served in ancient times, and today, by gay and transgendered priests and priestesses. Priests of the ancient world grew out their hair and nails, wore skirts, engaged in ritual sex, fertility rites, and possibly ritual castration, all to the dismay of later Christian observers. As the Great Mother, she welcomes all genders, orientations, races, and classes to her worship, and is considered one of the most popular and well-known goddesses in the modern pagan movement.

Kali Ma (Hindu): Known in Hindu myth as the destroyer, the warrior goddess, and devouring mother is Kali. She is a dark goddess of magick, tantra, thieves, warriors, and death, with many arms carrying weapons, skin like ebony, and wearing a necklace of human heads. She is the destroyer of demons, and the wife/mother of Shiva, the dissolver. In modern practice, Kali is the harsh mother called upon to destroy what does not serve, including our own egos and illusions. She is both beauty and horror personified, forcing us to face our fears. Most people misunderstand the power of Kali. She is not a monster. She is akin to the Celtic war goddesses and crones, like the triple Morgan and the Cailleach. In the Hindu traditions, she is like Mother Nature. Male worshipers sometimes dress as Kali, with fright wigs, masks, and dresses, or ritually cut themselves with swords, as a symbolic castration.

Loki (Norse/Scandinavian/Germanic): Originally, Loki was a fire god, later absorbed by the Teutonic tribes. In Norse myth, he is adopted as Odin's blood brother. As his myth changed over time, he was demonized much like the Egyptian Set was. Loki is the trickster, in the positive and negative associations of the word. Although oriented to fire and light, Loki is as much a mercurial figure as Hermes and Thoth, working in words and clever unpredictability, like a combination of The Fool and The Magician of the tarot. Later his words turned to lies and his pranks turned much more malicious, siding with the enemies of the Asgardian gods, causing the death of Balder, the Sun god, son of Odin and brother to Thor. Loki is credited with starting Ragnarok, the Norse Apocalypse the gods desperately tried to prevent. As a shape-shifter, Loki is associated with transgenderism. To help Thor recover his hammer, stolen by the giants, he dresses Thor as Freyja and disguises himself as "her" handmaiden. Later disguised as the giantess Thokk, he prevented Balder's resurrection by refusing to cry for Balder and defying the goddess Hel's vow to release Balder from the land of the dead if all would shed a tear for him. Loki also assumed Freyja's form and cloak, indicating magical and shamanic associations with the goddess, although it appears Loki never had a cult or priesthood exclusively his own. He transforms to a mare, gets pregnant, and gives birth to Odin's eight-legged magical steed Sleipnir. Because of it, Loki, as a male god, is associated with homosexual union, called "argr" by Odin, an abusive term in old Norse for a sexually receptive male. Related to the word "ergi" that may indicate a sexually receptive male and one versed in Freyja's magick. Loki also fathered the Midgard Serpent, Fenris Wolf, and Hel, the goddess of death.

Macha (Celtic): Macha is an aspect of the Celtic triplicity known as the Morgan. Her name means "battle" and she is associated with both the crow and the horse. Three Machas have appeared in Celtic myth. The first is the wife of Nemed. Another is Cimbeath's wife, who becomes a war chief, herself. The last, and most unusual, is Macha, the wife of Crunnchu. She came to Crunnchu as a fairy lover, making him promise never to reveal her identity. She becomes pregnant with his child. Foolishly, Crunnchu brags to the King in Ulster that his wife can outrun any of the king's horses. The king accepts his challenge, demanding Crunnchu's head should the latter lose the bet. Macha, in her mortal guise, is forced to run the race, and she wins, immediately gives birth to twins, and reveals her divine nature, cursing the men of Ulster for their treatment of her. For nine generations, in times of great crisis, all the men of Ulster experience a feminine transformation, living the pains of childbirth. Such androgynous transformation could signify a strong goddess cult influence in Ulster, originally demonstrating not a punishment, but an understanding of the goddess Macha. Although a goddess of war, she is also a goddess of life and sovereignty, giving birth under harsh conditions. Both Emain Macha, Ulster's capital, and Ard Macha are named after her.

Morrigu/Morrigan/Morgan (Celtic): The Celtic trinity of war goddesses are known by the name Morrigu. One version contains the goddesses Anu, Babd Catha, and Macha. Another version consists of Babd, Macha, and Nemain. All are associated with battle and death, but also with life. On Samhain, the Morrigan mates with the Dagda, with one foot in the river and one on land, symbolizing the veil between the worlds opening as spirits pass through it. In the revival of modern witchcraft, she is one of the most popular Celtic goddesses, associated with the Great Mother of the Earth, sea, and cosmos. In later myths, she was transformed into Morgan Le Fey of the Arthurian legend, sometimes ally and sometimes villain.

Odin/Wotan (Norse/German/Scandinavian): Known as Wotan the Wanderer in Germanic myth, Odin is the all father and king of the Aseir, the warrior gods of the Norse pantheon. Credited with creating, with his brothers, the nine worlds of the Norse cosmology Odin, is a god king and mercurial figure, a traveler, binder, and inspirer. Odin is very shamanic, hanging himself from

the world tree to gain knowledge of the runes and giving his eye for knowledge. He is attended by two ravens—Thought and Memory—the head of
Mimir who granted him knowledge, and the spirits of the warriors of Valhalla
and the Valkyries. ("Valkyrie" means "choosers of the slain," a group compris-
ing of Amazon-like warrior goddesses acting as psychopomps to the souls of
heroes, leading them to Valhalla.) He is the god of nobles, leaders, warriors,
poets, magicians, and mad men, evoking a frenzy or fury for battlers. His son
Thor is the chief god of the common folk. Odin is known to have assumed
feminine dress and identity when it suited his purpose. Freyja initiated him
into Seidr shamanic magick, a form traditionally reserved for women and
transgendered/homosexual men. He is blood brother to Loki, and their bonding has homoerotic overtones, much like the process of warriors bonding in
the rites of Freyja.

Osiris (Egyptian): Osiris is one of the few fertility gods of the ancient
pagan world not specifically associated with homosexual relationships, as
Adonis and Dionysus are. His only association comes from his brother Set
and his son Horus. Originally a god of fertility, he is killed by his brother Set,
and resurrected by his wife, Isis. Angered by his resurrection, Set dismembers
him. Isis finds all the pieces, except his penis. She resurrects him, placing a
symbolic phallus in the correct position. Because of his inability to create new
life, Osiris becomes lord of the dead. Either prior to his second death, or
through the magical workings of Isis after his second resurrection, he con-
ceives a child with Isis, named Horus, who continues his battle against Set,
with the aid of Anubis, Nephthys, and Thoth, and eventually wins, becoming
the new pharaoh, ruling in Osiris's name. The flooding of the Nile River is
said to be the semen of Osiris, the life-giving waters resulting from his acts of
self-pleasure in the realms below. Pharaohs may have imitated Osiris during
their enthronement rituals, masturbating before the image of the gods. These
rituals later led to public masturbation as religious worship in Egypt. Such acts
of religious sexuality can be found also in ancient Phoenicia, Babylon, and
Assyria.

Pan/Faunus (Greco-Roman): The horned god Pan incarnates the power of
the land and animals, the power of wild things, into an archetype of immense
power. Often viewed as the primary representation of the Wiccan godforce,
Pan is the goat-legged god of music, creativity, poetry, nature, animals, sexuality, and even terror. He is the god of life and death, though not often portrayed as a lord or king, but somewhat as a trickster or nature spirit, cavorting
with nymphs and satyrs. Originating the term "pansexual," Pan loves both
men and women. Artwork depicts him playing the panpipes, penis erect and

chasing after men and maidens, particularly shepherds and young men to whom he is teaching music. He has been associated with Dionysus and Ganymede. Unfortunately, his visage was partially adopted by Christians to embody the devil, or Satan, though Pan's pagan historical worship had absolutely nothing to do with Satan.

Quan Yin (Asian): Quan Yin, or Kuan Yin, is the Chinese goddess of compassion. She sits on an island and listens to the prayers of the world, particularly those of women, children, and sailors. In Buddhists terms, she is a bodhisattva, one who forsakes her own union with divinity to remain behind on a spiritual plane, to guide and help the people of the world. She could be thought of as an ascended master or saint. Quite possibly Quan Yin was once depicted as male, from Indian origin, as Avalokiteshvara, and later viewed as a female figure, since union with the divine reconciles the female and male aspects. The Buddha is generally shown as male, so his companion, Quan Yin, was depicted as female in the 8th century. As a bodhisattva, Quan Yin is seen as beyond this world's concept of gender, and can change gender at will, as needed.

Sedna (Native American/Inuit): Several myths paint Sedna has a gynandromorphous creation deity, served by two-spirit shamans. Others depict her as a young woman who lived with her female partner at the bottom of the ocean. She is a mother goddess of life and death, of animals, particularly sea creatures, hunting, heaven, and destiny.

Set (Egyptian): Set, or Seth to some, is the brother to Isis and Osiris, the divine mother and father of dominant Egyptian myth. He is also husband to his sister Nephthys, a dark goddess who lacked Set's association with evil and later defected to her sister Isis's cause. Set is considered the god of evil by the Osirian cults of Egypt, but more rightly he is the god of the harsh forces, the desert, the tests of the world, and the mysteries of death and sacrifice. He is distinguished by his red hair and fair skin—a far cry from the other Egyptian gods—suggesting a previous incarnation and set of associations from another people that were later absorbed into the Egyptian pantheon. His redness is reminiscent of the red sands and dust storms. He is also considered pansexual. Much later he was connected with Typhon, the serpent chaos god and nemesis of Zeus. Typhon is associated with the watery chaos serpent creation goddess Tiamat of Sumeria. In modern mythology, Set slays his brother Osiris twice out of jealousy and twice Isis returns him to life, though finally as a god of the dead. The two begot Horus, who continues the fight. Though Set himself was Horus's nemesis, the two have oral sex, Set swallows Horus's seed, and gives birth to a child.

Thoth

Tezcatlipoca (Aztec): As the Father of Witches, Tezcatlipoca walks the jungles in many forms, including a jaguar, coyote, monkey, or woman. He is the patron of sorcery and divination, often depicted holding his namesake, a black obsidian, or "smoking," mirror. Seen as a dark solar figure at times, he is the mirror image of Quetzalcoatl, with whom he battled often. As a magician and shaman, Tezcatlipoca grants miraculous healings, although he is associated with death and sacrifice. Tezcatlipoca and his priests are associated with transgenderism, homosexuality, and ritual prostitution similar to the cults of the Middle Eastern goddesses.

Thoth (Egyptian): The myths surrounding Thoth are numerous and varied, ranging from his role as a primal creation god to that of guide and aide to the ruling god, or son of Set and Horus's homosexual union. His is pictured variously as a man with an ape or ibis head. Thoth's title, "shepard of the anus," comes from his association with the ibis, which fastidiously cleans its anus with its beak. He is primarily a god of writing, communication, magick, invention, justice, and the Moon.

Tlazoteotl (Aztec): Tlazoteotl is the "Eater of Filth," "Dirt Goddess," or the "Shit Goddess" who takes all the darkness of the world, all the horrors, pain, and suffering and transforms it to purest gold. With these attributes in mind, Tlazoteotl can be viewed as an underworld, dark goddess figure, bringing the wisdom of the shadow to her people. She is a powerful goddess of life and death. Viewed as the archetypal witch, even in the Americas, she is seen partially nude, with either horns or a conical hat, holding a snake and riding a broom. The rabbit is her animal. Along with Xochiquetzal, she is mother and protector of the *huastecs*, transgendered, lesbian priestess. She is also linked with male homosexuality in her form as "Goddess of the Anus." In most recent times, in a pop-culture, graphic story called *The Invisibles* by Grant Morrison (Vertigo/DC), she is associated with a shamanic drag queen named Lord Fanny.

Xochilpilli (Aztec): Known as "the prince of flowers," Xochilpilli is the Aztec patron god of flowers, physical pleasure, fine food, dancing, singing, games, entertaining, and perfumes. Although he is a giver of curses as well as blessings, his festivals are known for their lack of human sacrifice. Xochilpilli is a corn or grain god, partaking in the fertility mysteries of the spring equinox, much like a New World Adonis, with his mother and lover, Xochiquetzal. He is a patron of gay men, gender variance, and male prostitution. As a form of the god Naxcit-Xuchitl, he is said to have introduced homosexuality to his people. As Naxcit-Xuchitl, he ruled the Age of Flowers, or the Cosmic Cycle of the Four-Petaled Flower. Though most records of this time are derogatory, the general, less hostile position marks it as a time ruled by women warriors, where a form of Xochiquetzal was prevalent, and men focused on the arts and possibly same-sex relationships. Perhaps the Four-Petaled Flower age was a New World matriarchal age.

Xochiquetzal (Aztec): An Aztec goddess of the underworld and of spring flowers, Xochiquetzal is somewhat akin to the Greek Persephone in that regard, though others relate her to the biblical Eve. The rain god Tlaloc is her husband, though Tezcatlipoca fell in love with her and took her away. Tlaloc then brought the great flood. Xochiquetzal is the mother of Quetzalcoatl and Xochilpilli. Marigolds, the Moon, red serpents, deer, spiders, butterfly wings, and thorns are her symbols, as she is a goddess of weavers, painters, sculptors, craftsmen, smiths, poets, and those engaging in nonreproductive sex. She is a protector of lesbians, along with Tlazolteotl, and is strongly linked to gay and transgendered men.

Yemaya (Santeria): Yemaya is the orisha of oceans, rivers, and water, a divine mother. The orisha are like the loa of Voodoo, but Santeria practices have a particularly Spanish flair. Yemaya is a great sorceress, a powerful patron of magick, and is known to shape-shift into a man at times. As a warrior woman, Yemaya is linked to transgendered and lesbian women. Water is generally associated with healing, cleansing, and emotion, so Yemaya is appealed to for healing, particularly now, to wash away HIV/AIDS, as she is also seen as a patron to gay, bisexual, and transgendered men.

Zeus/Jupiter (Greco-Roman): Zeus is a sky and storm god, the carrier of lightning and rain, and the leader of the Olympians. The son of Chronos the Titan and grandson of the sky god Uranus, Zeus led his siblings to victory against the Titans. He divided creation among his brothers. He gained the heavens, Poseidon the seas, and Hades the underworld. Zeus is both a beneficent father figure and a stern patriarch, but always the supreme god. Zeus is associated with the planet Jupiter, which is his Roman name, and the granter of fortune, blessings, and prosperity. His wife is the sky goddess Hera, although he is known for his liaisons with both men and women, siring numerous offspring. Zeus is a shape-shifter and often uses the ability to seduce unsuspecting young men and women. In the Orphic mythology, he is transgendered as Zeus Arrhenothelus, being both mother and father. Later myths completely abandon Zeus's transgendered aspects, but he retains some motherly attributes. Zeus gave birth to the goddess of wisdom, Athena, directly from his brow, as he did Dionysus from his thigh. This ability to carry a child to term echoes Zeus's older attributes and we should not forget them.

If you want a wonderfully detailed and well-researched overview of queer gods, goddesses, heroes, and their cultures, I highly recommend *Cassell's Encyclopedia of Queer Myth, Symbol and Spirit* by Randy P. Conner, David Hatfield Sparks, and Mariya Sparks. It is the most comprehensive and convincing work on this hidden mythology. I also suggest you explore other deities from these mythic cultures, and learn about those that do not have any known queer themes, to have a balanced view of the divine myths.

Part II

Tools of
Our Tribe

4

Going Within

Only through silence can we truly hear
the words of the Goddess and God.

As walkers between the worlds, witches learn the art of contacting the spiritual planes, the divine, inner planes of consciousness, from which true wisdom, guidance, and healing springs. Before you can enter such wonderful realms, you must get the key.

The key to unlocking these powers is your own consciousness, and control over your consciousness. With proper control techniques, you can alter your awareness. Mystics, saints, shamans, and gurus around the world have been known to be able to control the workings of their body and mind, to resist pain and injury, heal, and receive psychic information. Walking on burning coals without injury is a dramatic example. Witches learn a similar control, but the methods are sometimes different.

The key to controlling your consciousness, your perception of both the "outside world" and "inside world" is, quite literally, your brain waves. Mystics know there is no difference between outside and inside worlds, or between dream and reality. They are simply different points of view. The Hindus call our "real world" the physical universe, the "Maya," meaning "illusion." Our separateness, lack, and desire are all illusions. The truth is our unity and connection in the divine. Changing your world, your reality, is as simple as changing the TV channel, once you know how to enter an altered state of consciousness and shift your brain waves.

Brain waves are energy. They are measurable and divided into groups. Each category has a specific measurement range, measured in hertz (Hz), or cycles per second. Each category also indicates certain brain functioning. Brain waves could be in several different groups in different areas of the brain, but for our purposes, we are discussing the average, or dominant, group.

Normally, we emit beta waves, ranging from 12 to 16 Hz. In fact, we live most of our time in beta awareness; it is our normal waking and functioning state. Through it we are tuning in to what most people consider the "real," or physical, world. Beta is an important category because it allows us to fulfill our basic human needs and functions, like work. But since work has been such a major component to our society, beta has become the dominant thought state.

The alpha state ranges from 8 to 12 Hz, and is a relaxed but aware state. We may have simply turned our awareness away from the physical world. Daydreaming, accelerated learning, and ceremonial consciousness are based in alpha. If you have ever driven somewhere and didn't remember the ride—you still functioned and were aware, yet in a somewhat light trance state—you were probably in alpha. Closing your eyes for five minutes and simply breathing normally will put you into an alpha state, even if you don't know it. Most people don't even realize when they're in it.

Deeper into our inner consciousness is theta, 4 to 8 cycles per second. Here we focus on an inner reality. The witch will have visions and other-worldly experience, still aware and awake, but tuning in to another, more fluid reality.

Delta is the deepest state, from 0.5 to 4 Hz, indicating a deep trance or sleep state. When we sleep at night, we fluctuate between these altered states. They are all perfectly natural. You have even higher brain wave states indicating a higher awareness or insight to the world.

Gerald Gardner practiced and taught an eightfold path for raising power and attaining the key to these magical states of awareness. His time in the East influenced much of his practice. The eight keys range from inhibitory methods, meaning those that relax and center, and exhibitory methods, those that excite the body into altered states. The names and execution of the paths are different within the various traditions of witchcraft, but these are the basic forms. Not all are appropriate or necessary for every individual practitioner, and often two or more of these techniques will be executed at the same time. The divisions are somewhat arbitrary, since many do not have clear-cut lines between them.

Concentration, including visualization and pure intent, is the first path to cultivating consciousness. There are many visualization exercises for entering altered states of consciousness. Astral or shamanic travel, through projecting your consciousness outward, is the second method. Such trance work is also called "pathworking" and is akin to a daydream created and controlled through your will. The visualization techniques help this process. The third method involves control of the body, usually through breath work and body postures, and thereby stimulating the flow of blood. Some older texts refer to the use of binding cords to control blood flow, but I don't know any modern witches who use such practices. Sound, including ritual, mantra, chant, song, drumming, and prayer, is the fourth path.

"Opening the gates" is the fifth path, referring to the use of various substances to enter a meditative state, including incense, wine, and drugs. One should learn to walk the other paths, using inner technology, before relying on other substances. Most traditions that use intoxicants do not use them for recreational purposes, and insist on prior training. The sixth technique is movement, particularly ecstatic dance. The seventh path is pain. The scourge is a ritual tool akin to the cat-o'-nine-tails, and is used to induce pain and focus the will to enter a spiritual state. Actually, the movement, from gentle lashing to more intense strikes, causes blood to move to the affected area, changing inner physiology to alter brain waves. Because of the association of the scourge with sadomasochism and the Catholic Church, as it was a tool in use with the monks and brothers until the past few hundred years, many witches and covens refrain from using this path. For some, ritual piercing and tattooing has taken its place, to induce a greater awareness in rites of passage. The last path is called the Great Rite, or ritual sex, either symbolically or physically. Sexual energy, alone or with a partner, can definitely induce an altered state of awareness.

My preferred method, personally and for my students, is the art of concentration through meditation. Meditation is using several of those techniques, such as visualization, pathworking, and ritual to go within and open our own inner gates before venturing too far into the other worlds. Aspiring witches so often want to start with the spells, rituals, and astral travel, but you must build a strong foundation before you build any higher. Knowledge of yourself, your own emotions, mind, and spirit, your motives and your fears, is key. Such knowledge will help you travel the inner planes and return with wisdom and healing. Meditation is one of the best tools to receive such personal knowledge. Recent studies tell us there are additional benefits from meditation. Mystics knew these blessings all along. Those who practice meditation regularly, and I suggest at least three times a week, report greater clarity, stress reduction, enhanced immune system, and greater intuitive abilities. You clear the subconscious of harmful thoughts you were not even consciously aware of having. My allergies disappeared after I started a regular meditation practice. It was incentive enough to keep up with the practice, instead of taking a side-effect laden pill every day.

The wonderful thing about meditation is its simplicity. It is so simple it can be too difficult for people to grasp. Entering a meditative, or altered, state is so easy, so natural for us, we do it all the time without realizing it. The process of meditation is the ability to recognize and control it, so we can enter this state whenever we want. We enter it when things are good. We can enter it when we have problems, and that's the real "trick." Anyone can meditate when things are happy and peaceful, but we need it most when we are in turmoil. Going within helps us process the turmoil, release it, and trust the Goddess and God to lead us to the solution.

You don't need anything special to meditate, but you might find certain things aid the process. First, pick a place where you won't be disturbed. If you are inside, and you live with other people, tell them that you want some privacy and ask them to take messages if anyone calls. Otherwise, if you're alone, turn off the phone and other equipment that might break your concentration. Get into comfortable clothing. Witches usually wear either black or white robes when doing ritual, or go "sky clad," meaning naked, with only the sky clothing them. You don't need to have special clothes for meditation, but as we get into ritual, they may serve you better. If you have something you wear only for meditation and ritual, when you put it on, you are subconsciously preparing yourself to focus on your spirituality.

Witches also build altars as magical workplaces and for a constant focal point and reminder of the craft. They are embodiments of sacred space. As we continue through this book, you can gather the various tools you need for ritual. For now, all you need is a white candle and a place to put it. If you have any natural incense you like, you can burn it. Frankincense and myrrh, lavender, sage, and copal all work well for meditation. Many witches-to-be realize they have already gathered up some special power items without realizing why. Crystals and stones, feathers, seashells, and the like can be used on the altar. For now, arrange it however you like, but put the candle in the center.

To do the following exercise, you can memorize the steps, have a partner read it in a soothing tone and guide you, or make a tape of yourself reading it and listen to that. The instructions in parentheses are to be carried out by the reader, and not actually read aloud. Light your candle and incense to begin, and get in a comfortable position.

Exercise 1. Basic Meditation Technique

1. Take deep, cleansing breaths. As you inhale, you breathe in peace and tranquillity. Let out a sigh. Feel any tension, worry, or fear in your body release with each exhale. Continue to breathe deeply and relax.

2. Feel waves of relaxation move from your crown down your entire body, including your arms and legs. Relax with the waves. Feel free to gently stretch as needed.

   First, relax all the muscles in your head, neck, and the face.
   Relax your shoulders and arms, down to the tips of your fingers; feel waves of relaxation flow through you, clearing away all tension.
   Relax your back and chest.
   Relax your waist, hips, and abdomen.
   Relax your legs, starting with your thighs, down through your knees, calves, and shins, to your ankles, feet, and tips of your toes. Feel the waves of relaxation move through you, releasing all stress.

   If you feel any remaining stress, breathe into the area, imagining your breath goes deep into your body, and as you exhale, exhale the last remaining stress. (Pause a few moments.) You are now completely relaxed.

3. Gently turn your gaze to the white candle. Soften your gaze and look into the flame, and even past the flame. The image may get blurry, and that is normal. As you breathe deeply, in and out, stare past the flame. If your eyes are tired or are bothered by the light, close them and pretend you are staring at the flame, visualizing the candle in your mind's eye. (Pause for a few minutes.)

4. Now, close your eyes if you haven't already done so, and prepare to enter a deeper meditative state. You will count backward, from twelve to one. As you count, you may visualize you are walking down stairs, one by one, with the count. The stairs are leading you down to your deepest meditative state. If you don't see anything, that's fine, too. Simply count along. (Count slowly from twelve to one.)

5. You are in your deepest meditative state, completely relaxed, yet aware. Imagine the stairs have led you to your favorite place, anywhere in the world, a place of peace and tranquillity. It can be outside, like a mountain, beach, or forest, or a sacred space indoors. You may have never even seen it before, but you realize now it is a special place. It has everything you would want in a location. Simply invite, imagine, and allow the place to

manifest around you. You may hear it, feel it, smell it, or simply know it more than see it. Go with your first impressions.

6. Look for a reflective surface in your inner sacred space. It can be a pool of water, a mirror, crystal, or piece of glass. It doesn't matter, but find someplace where you can look at yourself. Here you will reprogram your consciousness with the following affirmations. Repeat each one silently three times while looking into your own eyes in your favorite place, your place of power. Feel the energy of these words.

Everything I do is for the good of all involved, harming none.
I am happy.
I am successful.
I am completely healthy.
I release all that does not serve.
I love myself.
I love all others.
I am open to give and receive love.

7. Let your attention turn from the image and back to your place of power. If there is anything you want to change, do so now. The environment will respond to your thoughts, but it will also reflect your own state of mind. You may return to this place and find it very different.
8. Count upward one through twelve. Imagine the stairs taking you back to where you began, back to your physical body. (Count one to twelve.)
9. Feel your physical body. Wiggle your fingers and toes, then your wrists and ankles. You may need to ground yourself a bit. Start by bringing your hands above your head and sweep them downward, from your crown, down to your belly, releasing all unwanted energy.

   If you still feel light-headed, press your palms against the floor, imagining unwanted energy flowing out of your palms like faucets and grounding into the floor and the earth below.

   If still you're still feeling ungrounded, imagine your legs and feet are the roots of a great tree, digging deep into the planet. Feel yourself fully anchored. Eating or drinking something can also help ground you in the physical state.

❊   ❊   ❊

This basic meditation helps you develop skills to induce an altered state and return fully grounded. If you practice it often, you will have no problem with the other exercises and experiences. You will use these techniques in most of your meditations. Unlike many Eastern forms of meditation, this technique seems similar to hypnotherapy, but will be further developed into deeper magical experiences as your practice grows.

Feel free to vary the imagery if you find something else that works better for you. Instead of stairs leading down into a special power place, you can use other images. Another powerful image is the cave. The cave leading deep below the Earth's surface is full of the Goddess's mysteries, the mysteries of emotion and healing. In many shamanic traditions, you climb a tree or mountain to the sky realms, much like Jack and the Beanstalk. The tree/mountain imagery is phallic, and has association with the sky god, although most traditions believe the tree/mountain holds caves and tunnels at the base, to reach the underworld mysteries.

If you don't remember your experience, don't be concerned. It is common for meditative experiences to slip away like a dream in the beginning of your practice. You know something happened, but almost wonder if you fell asleep. You are walking between the physical and dream worlds, so such perceptions are ordinary. When you start, affirm to yourself that you will remember your meditation, and after you count up and ground, write down everything you can remember. This technique also works for remembering normal sleep dreams. I suggest you keep a journal for your meditations, dreams, and daily life events.

The affirmations are a powerful way to program your consciousness. The power of positive thinking has gained a lot of attention recently, but affirmations you make while in a meditative state are even more powerful, because they go deep into your consciousness. They may sound corny, but they really are effective. Self-esteem is a big issue in my own life, and saying "I love myself" every day for quite a while gave me the self-esteem I needed to continue the craft. If you didn't like these affirmations, try writing your own. You may still not like affirmations, but you know what you need to shape your consciousness.

Practice this exercise at least three times before trying the next meditation or experimenting with the other paths. As you continue with it, remain aware, yet relaxed. You might find the meditation takes on aspects that are not scripted. Always be open to your first impression. Then, meditation moves from the realm of simple visualization to a direct interaction with new worlds of consciousness.

5

Meet the Divine Couple— The Goddess and the God

*From the Goddess and God all things come,
and to the Goddess and God, all things return.*

Witches recognize the many faces of the divine, accepting the multicultural aspect of each archetype. All gods lead back to the God. All goddesses lead back to the Goddess. Together, the Mother and Father, Goddess and God, consist of all creation, the divine mind, or Great Spirit. All the deities are shadows cast from the same eternal flame.

Belonging to a polytheistic tradition, witches have recognized some basic divisions of the divine. Each individual practitioner or tradition can focus on a specific deity from a culture. Such deities are called "godforms." Each is one form of the archetype, one cultural expression of the many-faced being.

Like our Paleolithic ancestors, modern witches often take a matriarchal view of deity, focusing on the Goddess, but the majority of traditions do recognize the God as having a pivotal, if not equal, role. For many gay and lesbian practitioners, this is greatly welcomed. Most of us had to deal with a stern patriarchal father figure, often sitting above in judgment, in our early religious experiences, so for many of us, the feminine energy of a personal, loving Mother Goddess is simply more welcoming and inviting. The Goddess generates a sense of coming home. In my own practice, I feel it is important to recognize and balance both the Goddess and God energies, lest we, as a society, go out of balance again. The God is also kind and loving, and not at all like the stereotypical images of God the Father from mainstream religions.

The Goddess is most often recognized as the Triple Goddess. Triune goddesses existed in many ancient cultures. The Moon phases are usually the source of this division, with the waxing Moon embodying the Maiden Goddess, the full Moon symbolizing the Mother Goddess, full like the pregnant womb, and the waning Moon representing the Crone Goddess. The dark, new Moon is for the cycle of death, where the Goddess is reborn as the Maiden.

The manifest world marks the Triple Goddess in another style. She Who Is Above Us is the goddess of the Moon, stars, and night sky. She Who Is With Us is the goddess of the Earth and grain, the giver of bounty and harvest. She Who Is Below Us is the goddess of the underworld, the queen of death and destruction. You can also divide the three who are one into the past, present, and future, as the Norse did in the embodiment of the Norns, or the Fates.

Maiden, Moon, and sky goddesses found in cultural triplicities include Artemis, Kore, Athena, Anu, Astarte, Inanna, Aphrodite, and Aradia.

Godforms of the Full Moon, Mother, and Earth are Diana, Selene, Luna, Cerridwen, Babd, Isis, Demeter, Ninhursang, Quan Yin, Sedna, Tiamat, and Gaia.

Hecate, Persephone, Kali Ma, Morgan, Macha, Arianrhod, Tlazoteotl, and Ereshkigal are goddesses of the underworld.

Many creation goddesses were androgynous or bisexual in nature, making love with themselves to bring the universe into being. These individual aspects of one being bore the universe out of the principle of love and their own gender; in this, we can see the divine, creative aspect of the lesbian life—women honoring the divine within themselves and all other women, emulating the Great Goddess's act of creation through their everyday life.

The God is seen as dual in nature, having two aspects, a light side and a shadow side. The god of light is both a solar god and a deity of the growing vegetation. He rules over the living half of the year. He is the divine child who grows into the young king. Gods of the Sun, sky, creation, vegetation, and divine inspiration are the waxing gods. Gods such as Apollo, Dionysus, Lugh, Mabon, Bel, the Green Man, Freyr, Balder, Ra, Horus, and Shamash are in this category.

The dark god is the shadow self, the horned god, king of the underworld, bringer of death, lord of the hunt, and trickster spirit. He rules the waning half of the year, when the vegetation is harvested, withers, and we enter the winter season. Hades, Pan, Hephastus, Adonis, Chronos, Cernunnos, Pywll, Set,

Osiris, Tammuz, Tezcatlipoca, Baron Samedi, and Ogun are considered dark gods.

The god of light and the god of shadow are two sides of the same coin. One aspect is in control at any given time, but they maintain a shifting relationship. One becomes the other, and then is reborn. In a sense of inner divinity, they represent the divine marriage, the alchemy of light and shadow to create a being who is neither and both simultaneously. For those who only see the divine marriage in terms of female and male aspects being brought together, here we have a model of two male energies, of light and dark, coming together to form the sacred union. For gay men, it is an engaging model of sacred sexuality. The two gods can be seen as lovers, passing on the torch of power at appropriate times of the year, yet remaining partners through it all.

The result of this alchemical union is mythically evidenced by a number of gods who do not fit the mold of either the lord of light or darkness, just as many gays do not fit the classical model or masculinity and femininity. They walk the edge between two worlds, like a shaman. Likewise, these gods are shamanic in nature, often the gods of magick, transformation, learning, art, or androgyny. They are messengers between the worlds, living in all, but truly belonging to none but their own. Hermes, Mercury, Thoth, Ganesha, Gwydion, Baphomet, Loki, and Odin are of this archetype. They wander between worlds, gaining wisdom and power from their travels and the very differences that set them apart. These beings are perceived as trickster spirits and shape-shifters because they are not what they appear to be.

In modern queer pagan mythology, the Goddess, in her many aspects, births the God into being. The Goddess is recognized as the Great Mother, having many other faces, all lovingly creating together. The God, her son, is divided into light and dark, and the two are lovers, yet sometimes rivals. At times they are paired as Earth and sky gods. The divine is recognized as having both heterosexual elements and homosexual elements, and attributes far beyond our physical understanding. Aspects of the Goddess and God unite to form the cycles of physical life and creation, honoring the heterosexual, while other aspects unite honoring the homosexual nature of the divine. Both are important aspects of creation. Even science is now recognizing that both orientations, and bisexuality, have always occurred in nature, in the animal kingdom. Modern witches look to the wisdom of the animal kingdom, those who have not lost their way and connection with the divine, to lead us back to our true roots, our true nature.

As Aleister Crowley suggested, whereas heterosexual relationships help keep the cycles of life going in the physical plane, homosexual relationships—

not directing their energy to physical conception—directs energy to magical pursuits, perhaps continuing the life cycles of the magical realms, such as the collective unconscious. Although the magical realm is very energetic, I believe that it requires less energy to maintain than the dense, physical world, so the population of homosexuals is smaller, because less are needed to maintain the spirit worlds.

Inner Divinity

Witches believe in the concept of inner divinity. God and Goddess are not outside of yourself, beyond your reach and available only to you through the words of prophets or priests. Deities are all around you. They are in the trees and land, the sky and water. The deities are also within you. You are part of the Great Spirit. You are a part of nature and super nature. You contain both divine masculine and divine feminine traits, regardless of physical gender, sexual identity, or sexual orientation. Through pathworking, you can have an inner, personal experience of the divine, as embodied by the gods and goddesses.

In psychological terms, these inner divinities are like sub-personalities, aspects of your own being, like your inner child or inner warrior. Jungian psychologists see the feminine in every man as his *anima* and the masculine in every women as her *animus*. The anima/animus reflects our ideal self of the opposite gender. Witches believe that we each have both an anima and animus, regardless of our gender. In the Silva Method of Mind Control workshop, a plan for psychic development with elements common to many Wiccan practices, workshop participants visualize a male and female helper in their inner "laboratory" where problems are solved from a gender-balanced perspective.

Others would swear these experiences to be contact from a realm beyond, not within, that these beings are guardians, spirit guides, ancestors, angels, or patron deities. They seem absolutely real, with personalities very different from the individual, giving information previously unknown, or synthesizing knowledge into a wise choice. The process of going within, through meditation and journeying, opens up the gateway to these worlds and allows for communications, though sometimes the message is more symbolic, and needs to be decoded, like a dream filled with personal symbolism.

To the witch, there is no distinction between outer world and inner world, or between parts of yourself and another being. All is connected. All is one spirit with many faces. Modern witches embrace both the spiritual and psychological models as holding a version of a truth beyond name and form.

Contact with our own inner gods move us beyond traditional masculine stereotypes, even the stereotypes that may be pervasive in historically accepted myth. As you can see, the gods have more than one side to them. The inner gods bring us in touch with our own masculine side of sensitivity and tenderness. Expression of grief, shame, love, creative style, and emotional maturity is found in their myths, and part of our spiritual heritage, even though these concepts in a man are denied in the overt, patriarchal world. We are swinging the pendulum from the masculine back to the center, where the rough-and-tumble warrior coexists with the sensitive artist in one god, and within one person.

Contact with the inner goddess brings us closer to the divine creative force, the source of all life. For gay and transgendered men, the beauty of the inner goddess helps us accept our own feminine sides that are usually scorned by mainstream society, and even in some segments of the gay community. The inner goddess helps us celebrate our own queerness. True self-acceptance is a difficult hurdle for us all. Within each of us is a goddess. Drag queens, transvestites, transgendered individuals, and other wonderful diva sisters have been living this bit of wisdom as a part of their own personal path. No wonder so many tribal shamans held a tradition of cross-dressing and gender ambiguity. They, too, were living this goddess wisdom.

Study of the archetypal goddesses and gods in mythology help us create a bridge to the collective world. The more you know of a particular goddess or god, the easier it can be to contact that particular godform. Under certain circumstances, they will pick you first. As you read and research, one being in particular may catch your attention. Perhaps you've always felt a connection to the image or story. In ritual, I felt a connection to the goddess Macha whenever my teacher called upon her. I felt a powerful presence and love. Then she started popping up in my meditations unbidden to give me messages and guidance.

In the many classes I have led, people will return from a pathworking and say they met someone with a particular deity's name, but until that point, they had never heard that name. As I describe the deity from classical mythology, I see the shock on their face as I describe someone they think they have made up. The gods are real, and a part of us, though we don't always get that outside verification. Think of how many divine images have not been recorded in societies that did not write. Think of the records lost as ancient libraries were burned. Think of how many new forms of divinity are waiting to be expressed!

For this next exercise, we will contact aspects of the Goddess and God. You never know what shape or form they will take. Some come from classical myths. Others are vividly unique and personal. Remember, each individual and society dresses the archetypal being in comfortable images.

Exercise 2. God and Goddess Meditation

1. Do steps 1 through 4 in Exercise 1 (page 60) to get into a meditative state.
2. You are in your deepest meditative state, completely relaxed, yet aware. You are in your place of power. There are two paths before you, one to the left and one to the right. One will lead to a goddess, and one will lead to a god. Don't worry about making decisions between the goddess and god. Simply pick the direction that you are intuitively drawn to walk toward. It will lead you where you need to go.
3. Take notice of the path, and all you see, particularly plants and animals. Is it outside or inside? Is it day or evening? Is it light or dark? The environment can be giving you subtle clues to your own spiritual well-being. Do not ignore them.
4. At the end of the path, you reach a being of great power and love. Greet this being and introduce yourself. The deity will introduce itself. Ask it any questions you have, of a spiritual nature or of a personal and practical nature. Listen for the answer, but be aware it might not answer with words. Be open and go with your first impression. (Pause for a few minutes.)

    Ask this spiritual being if it has a message for you, or a gift of some kind. Be ready to receive it. The deity may ask for a gift or pledge in return.
5. When you are done, thank this god or goddess, and say farewell. Return back to the path and back to where you began. Return back to the staircase, leading you up and out.
6. Count from one to twelve. Imagine the stairs taking you back to where you began, back to your physical body. (Count one to twelve.)
7. Feel your physical body. Wiggle your fingers and toes, then your wrists and ankles. You may need to ground yourself a bit. Start by bringing your hands above your head and sweep in a downward motion, from crown, down to your belly, releasing all unwanted energy.

    If you still feel light-headed, press your palms into the floor, grounding unwanted energy, or visualize your grounding roots. Write down your experiences in your journal. Try to recapture the messages word for word because sometimes our ego and interpretation muddles the purity of the message.

※   ※   ※

If you had difficulty with this experience, do not be alarmed. Some people see, others hear, and some simply feel or know. It is quite common to do one and not the others. When you see a wonderful goddess and can't hear the message, it can be frustrating. Until we start trusting our own intuition, gathering nonphysical information is extremely hard. Give yourself time.

My first experience with spirit guides was to see, but not hear them. I could see lips moving, but the sound was turned off. I finally asked them to speak up, or give me the message in a way I could understand, and suddenly the mute button was turned off and I could hear everything. Sometimes asking is the hardest part. The answers do not always come right away, or in the manner you expect. Sometimes messages are visual and symbolic, rather than direct communication. That is just as valid a form of information.

If you are having difficulties connecting with the goddess or god in your meditation, do the best you can and relax. All will fall into place with relaxation and practice. Take longer counting down. Play some relaxing music as you meditate. Say a prayer to the Goddess and God before you start to ask for their help. Learn what works for you to set the mood.

Before moving on to the next lesson, repeat this exercise, but choose the second path, and visit the other god or goddess. Build your relationship with these beings, and visit as often as you like. More may manifest to guide you, or one may take precedence over the other. You have many spiritual beings waiting to assist you. All you need to do is ask for them.

6

Animal Wisdom

To the Tribe of the Bear, we call your strength,
To the Tribe of the Wolf, we call your cunning,
To the Tribe of the Hawk, we call your vision,
And to the Tribe of the Dolphin, we call your song.

Because the gods and goddesses embody the forces of nature, the fundamental forces of the universe, their agents are many. In this worldview, all things are living, imbued with spiritual awareness, if not human intelligence. All beings of the natural world represent the power, design, and will of the deities. The spirits of the plant world bring healing and medicine, both physical medicine and spiritual medicine, as do the mineral spirits. Witches, shamans, and mystics from all Earth-honoring cultures recognize these spirits. Most important, they pay homage to the animal spirits. And so should we, for their wisdom is eternal.

Out of all of these natural forces, the animal spirits are the ones we relate to the most in the human experience. Animals eat and sleep as we do. They quest for food, hunting, gathering, or grazing. They mate, and many form families or even communities. We can observe playfulness, contentment, pain, fear, and even anger in animals. You could say humans have a very distinctive animal nature, sharing all these traits. If current evolution theory is to be believed, we evolved from the animal kingdom, so it is only natural we would share many traits. And through domestication, we observe an almost human quality in our pets. Dogs and cats become members of the family. The differences are not so distinct between humans and animals. The main difference, from the shaman's or witch's point of view, is the attunement animals have with the natural world, the will of the gods. Many animals are considered the sacred symbols and protectors of specific gods and goddesses. They act as messengers and guides to the followers of these deities. Several gods, particularly Native American and Egyptian, are often portrayed as animals or with animal heads, marking the close connection between the two.

Animals live in the moment. They follow instinct. They don't debate, reason, or play games with themselves. They follow what they know to be true. They follow the inner urges of their instinctual self. They have all the answers and information they need. The only time they become perplexed is when humans take them out of their natural habitats. We have this instinctual self, too. One might call this part of our consciousness the "animal self," others, the "intuition," or "psychic mind." In certain practices of modern shamanism, the lower self refers to the intuitive faculties, but people often confuse the word "lower," meaning below the conscious ego, with "bad" or "evil." Your lower self is not bad any more than your feet are bad because they are below the rest of your body.

Unfortunately for us, humans tend to forget about the instinctive self, in tune with the natural forces and through this attunement, connected with the divine will. Our personal divine self is called the higher self, and is the source of our spiritual wisdom. We tend to ignore both the divine self and the intuitive self, who are really partners. We favor logic in this society. Logic is great when needed, but sometimes the mind can fool us into thinking things we know not to be true. The mind and logic are great tools, but many people serve the mind rather than having the mind serve them. The mind often works to preserve its ego, the limited identity based on personality, rather than identify with the divine self.

Direct messages from the divine, from our higher selves and the goddesses and gods, can be difficult to hear. The ego wants to remain. It fears the change spiritual messages can bring. Sometimes we hear what we want to hear, not always what we need to hear. This is the great trick of the mind, and we have programmed the mind to act this way, whether we realize it or not. The only other way we receive the message is through a messenger, and through the symbolic wisdom of the animal world.

Native American traditions refer to each animal's wisdom as its medicine. Animal medicine will not tell you intellectual knowledge, but rather modes of behavior that bring you balance, harmony, and happiness. Their messages point out what we are lacking or doing too much of, and what example we can follow to remedy the situation.

Each animal has particular characteristics that set it apart from others. By observing an animal's behavior, characteristics, color, shape, and habitat, you can discover the wisdom this animal embodies and the message it is giving you. Sometimes we ask for the message, meditating upon a question, praying to the divine for a "sign" indicating what to do. Other times we are simply open to the message, and it comes without warning or a specific question.

You receive the message in two main ways. The more mystical of the two is to envision the animal spontaneously in a meditative state, usually during a visualization or spiritual journey exercise. That is why meditation is so important. Not only does it relax, heal, and clear the mind, it gives the divine a chance to send messages and messengers. If you don't slow down long enough to listen, you will never hear or see what you need to bring balance.

The second method is to encounter the animal in the waking, physical world. Traditionally, the animal would cross your path in some way. Tribal people across the world had a more intimate contact with nature, living in the fields, forests, and mountains. They had greater opportunity to meet a variety of animals. In the modern world, an animal might come across your path in the physical, but also in nontraditional ways. You may see the animal in a book, magazine, television, or movie. Even without knowing the "meaning" of the animal, it will stir something in you, even just for a moment, that makes you pay attention. Pay attention! Our first habit is to say, "Oh, that was nothing. My mind was playing tricks on me. I'm just imagining it." Follow your intuitive wisdom, not your mind, when it comes to animal magick.

If you have an attraction to a particular animal, you may be intuitively working with the wisdom of that animal. The signs of the zodiac, both Western and Chinese, are mostly based in animal symbolism and you work with a particular energy for your whole life because of the day you were born; animal medicine works in much the same way. One or more animals can be with you for your entire life, representing the wisdom and spiritual challenges you seek to master over the course of a lifetime. Other animal messengers come and go as needed. Some stay for a period of time, representing a particular challenge in life. Others simply deliver their message, make sure you understand, and then leave, forming no lasting relationship.

Long-term animal helpers are usually called totems, or power animals, while short-term ones are simply allies. You can work with more than one totem at a time. The energies of Crow and Spider remain with me constantly, but I've also had experiences with Dolphin, Butterfly, Cow, Snake, Horse, Owl, and Lion. Each came when I needed its lessons most.

We access this wisdom in several ways. The first, if encountered in a visionary journey or meditative state, is to ask the animal what its message is, if it's not obvious to you. Some spirit animals will speak, but most will show you, guiding you on a journey. Guidance is the first function of animal spirits, and visionaries around the world report being guided by animal spirits on their spiritual quests. The journey itself contains the message.

Often, you will only get a glimpse of the animal in meditation, or you encounter it in the physical world. You don't have an opportunity to ask. You can always meditate on it, and try to create an experience, or you can delve into the animal's symbolism. The mere presence of the animal has given you everything you need to decode the instructions.

Look to the animal's behavior and habitat. How does it live? What are the dominant characteristics? Does its behavior remind you of anything in human life? Does the animal have any unusual colors, shapes, or symbols associated with it? If you were to act more like that animal, how would your own behavior change? Also look to any myths or deities connected with the animal. These timeless stories will give you clues to the deities and archetypes speaking to you.

Tribal people are well versed in the animal meanings, as our ancient ancestors were. Animal, plant, and mineral wisdom, along with mythic stories with spiritual meanings were as well known as the alphabet is to those of us in the modern Western world. So we have to do a bit more digging to discover the intuitive messages of the animal world. You must trust your own intuition, because there is no absolutely right or wrong answer. Opinions vary from story to story, tribe to tribe. The important thing is to follow your own feelings and sense of synchronicity to lead you to the perfect answer for you. Outside advice can help. Tribal people would go to the wise one, the informal ancestor of the modern witch, for interpretation of symbols, visions, and dreams. Those well versed in symbol and myth can offer suggestions, but ultimately you must follow the path, yourself.

With the message firmly in hand, you must then heed the message of the animal spirits. Good advice helps only if you follow it. Meditate on the animal's message. Pretend to be the animal. Tribal dances and ceremonies often revolve around animal imitation, quite often including dancing with animal masks. Dancing your animal is a way to understand its power within your own body. Shamans would not only pretend to be their animal power, but spiritually transform into it while visiting the spiritual realms in trance. The act of becoming your animal, or merging with it, is called shape-shifting. It allows your energy to become one with the animal's spirit, seeing things through new eyes, giving you new advantages, lessons, and a fresh point of view. You may feel your arms becoming paws, claws, hoofs, or wings, as you grow fur, feathers, or scales. You know you are still human, but physical sensations with an almost lucid dreamlike quality are common.

With this new understanding of the animal, be mindful of your own behavior and how to incorporate its lessons in your life. If Turtle visits to teach patience, and you are constantly on the run, look for opportunities to slow down before your body forces you to slow down through illness or injury. If Snake visits to shed its skin, encouraging you to shed your outer skin, and reveal the inner you, then do so. The time is right. Failure to act upon the messages can result in less frequent messages. Like a good friend, the animal world wants to support you in claiming your true identity. It doesn't want to support your crazy schemes and self-sabotaging behavior. If you ask a friend for advice, and do not listen, the friend may continue to be supportive and listen, but will no longer offer advice. Only when you are ready to hear the message will a friend again speak, and only when asked.

Animal Instincts and Sexuality

By looking at nature, we find homosexuality in the animal world, particularly among "higher" or more intelligent mammals. It exists and thrives without guilt. Many animals have individual herds, some male, and some female, only coming together for mating season, such as reindeer, elk, moose, elephants, bats, and certain primates. Their other adult companionship is satisfied with same-sex companions. Our Stone Age ancestors, living in tribes and more in tune with nature, probably had more in common with these animal tribes than the traditional, nuclear, heterosexual family model we use today.

Some cite animal totems as having an influence not only with our orientation and choice of partners, but on our "style" of love relationships. Polyamory and polyfidelity is also evident in the animal world, and many cite it as evidence that such lifestyles are more natural than monogamy. But there is also evidence of monogamy in the animal world, too. We may be attracted to a particular lifestyle in terms of partners, or simply feel that like being GLBT, it is a part of our identity, of who we are.

I have a bisexual friend and student who strongly identifies with Wolf, and the wolf clan, as her main spirit helper. She feels polyfidelity is a natural part of her makeup, regardless of what other people accept or understand. She finds commitment in the clan, in the larger group of partners. We can look to our animal allies for support and inspiration, but ultimately we are the combination of many animal spirits and beyond, and must make the decisions that are right for us. I work with many insect and arachnid spirits, but it is not acceptable for me to devour my partner after mating! Animal energy can help us on the path, but we must decide for ourselves the direction in which we wish to go. Polyamorous and polyfidelitous relationships are possibilities to explore if you feel drawn to them for your highest good, just as monogamy is an exploration of life.

Animal Medicine

Animal medicine is not only a symbolic name, but also a spiritual truth, for the animal spirits can be used to directly heal on the emotional, mental, spiritual, and even physical levels of existence. When one undergoes shamanic or spirit healing from a nature-based practitioner, often the spirit of an animal whose medicine is sorely needed will be spiritually "injected" into the energy body of the one in need. South American shamans believe each child is born with a totem, or spirit animal, that acts as a protector. This spirit protects one from sickness, injury, and ill fortune. If the animal power is ignored, dishonored, or forgotten, it will go away, leaving one open to these misfortunes. The shaman enters a trance state to either retrieve the original animal spirit and coax it back to ward off illness, or to find and convince a new animal spirit to act as guardian for the patient. The shaman blows the spirit into the patient's body via the crown and/or heart, restoring this needed power. Many traditions feel the animal power is actually a component of the individual's own personal power, or perhaps a facet of the lower, intuitive self. Loss of such power creates an opening for illness and imbalance.

How many people do you know who honor and acknowledge their animal? Not many, I would imagine. Although modern Western society has great medical knowledge to fend off physical illness and injury, I fear it leaves us open to more subtle spiritual illnesses and injuries—individually and as a community. Luckily, by turning to the language and spirit of the animal kingdom, we can seek to restore our natural balance and honor both types of healing, medical and spiritual. During your experiences, you may feel you have retrieved an animal ally or totem. You body, energy level, emotions, and thoughts may change, energetically integrating the message into your whole being.

The Animals and Their Messages

The following is a list of animals that may cross your path and grant you their wisdom. The list is by no means complete, but it offers you a good springboard for understanding the mechanics of the intuitive animal language. Most important, several of these animals have associations with queer myth and history.

Ape: The ape and its extended family of species are the animals most strongly associated with the intelligence of humanity. We believe they are genetic relatives of ours, having a similar body shape and structure, and demonstrating a great deal of intelligence, reasoning, and language skills. Ideally, the ape represents the double edge of intelligence. On one hand, ape medicine represents wisdom. On the other, trickery. The patron to the ape is the trickster archetype, demonstrated by Thoth and Hermes/Mercury. One of Thoth's guises is as a man with an ape head. Tricksters trick us into seeing our own folly and ego traps. They trick us into seeing the simple truths, and from them, the great wisdom. For the Aztecs, the ape is associated with the flower god Xochilpilli. With his association of performance and art, he also shares several trickster attributes. Because of this, ape indicates a need or talent for performance, art, music, or comedy, to see the wisdom played out in such arenas. Ape urges us to see the truth, and to look to our deep wisdom rather than become caught in our supposed sophistication or intellect.

Bear: The totem of the bear has been adopted by many men in the gay community as part of their identity, both their physical and, to an extent, personal qualities. Bear as a heavyset, hairy man is an aesthetic of beauty. The bear is associated with Goddess energy as well, viewed as an embodiment of the Mother archetype, nurturing and protective on one hand, and bringing death through the hunt on the other. Most important, the bear cave is the womb of the Earth goddess, symbolizing going within for a period of regeneration—a death and resurrection experience. The cave is also associated with the center of the brain, finding balance in hibernation and reclusiveness. Bear medicine asks us to quiet the mind, come to stillness, balance, and to listen to the unconscious. As the bear lives off its stores of fat, it teaches us to be self-reliant and go within for our resources. Bear cults are some of the oldest of the ancient religions. Some Stone Age men would consume the semen and cerebrospinal fluid of the male bears as a part of their rites, believing them to increase life energy and vitality. Bear is associated with Athena and the huntress Artemis/Diana. Artemis's lover, Callisto, and her son Arcas are transformed into constellations, with Callisto forming Ursa Major, the Great Bear. Odin of Teutonic religion held Bear sacred, particularly to his warrior berserks. Odin exemplifies both the wisdom and potential danger of Bear. Bear also tells us that everyone must leave the cave at some point. Bear teaches us to find the honey of life, and some priestesses of Artemis were associated with bears, others, with bees. Bear mothers give birth to their children in winter caves, and nurture their playful spirits, reminding us about being joyful, taking care of ourselves and family. Finally, bears are known as great tree climbers. Trees are a sign of wisdom, and climbing them gives one a greater view, connecting to higher, divine consciousness.

Bull: Bulls and cows are ancient symbols of fertility and are associated with both gods and goddesses. The cow is seen as feminine and lunar, while the bull, in contrast, was often seen as masculine and solar. The Egyptian god Osiris sometimes was pictured with a bull's head, while his wife, Isis depicted as Hathor, wore the cow's horns. The bull played a prominent role in worship, often used as a sacrifice. The horns of the bull were also seen as lunar symbols, like the crescent moon, and were associated with Goddess worship. The myths of the Minotaur, the man-bull of Greek myth, living in the maze and demanding the sacrifice of virgins may simply be a corruption of the ancient Goddess fertility rites of the labyrinth. Bull medicine asks us to balance our masculine and feminine attributes or, more likely, bring our masculine "bullness" to the feminine Goddess. The sign of Taurus the bull, is ruled by the planet Venus, named after the goddess Aphrodite/Venus, and although a masculine symbol, astrologers denote it as a feminine sign. Stubbornness is an aspect of Taurus's negative traits. This sign is also associated with our resources, or body, talents, home, food, music, creature comforts, and material wealth. All are signs of fertility blessings. Going beyond growing crops or having children, modern associations with fertility include the fertility of creativity, imagination, music, prosperity, knowledge, and wisdom. Bull medicine asks us to rekindle our inner fertility through a balance of inner masculine and feminine energy.

Butterfly: Butterfly medicine's key is the act of transformation. The butterfly is in a constant state of change and transformation, from the egg, larva, chrysalis, to the true butterfly form. As a spirit, it petitions us to see what changes are going on in our life, and if such changes are being born (egg), taking action (larva), going within for contemplation and reflection (chrysalis), or complete and ready to be shared with the world, as the butterfly. As a symbol of the soul in early Christianity, it harkens us to look for our own inner and outer changes, realizing the beauty on the inside ready to emerge. Butterfly is not all serious change, but fun, play, and dance, as it flits from flower to flower, reminding us to enjoy life. The color of the butterfly is also significant, as each color relates to a different element or chakra. (See chapter 7.) Mythologically, this totem is associated with Eros, Tlazolteotl, and

Xochiquetzal. Later, the lavender, or rainbow, butterfly became a symbol of gay rights and liberation.

Cat: Cat is the animal of mystery and of magick, particularly black cats, who were later known for causing bad luck. The superstition only arose because of the cat's association with magick. As Christianity rose, all magick was feared. Early cultures honored the cat as a bringer of good luck and divine fortune. Bast, the Egyptian goddess, was often portrayed with a cat's head, and she is a patron of the Moon, magick, divination, and love. Cats are aware of the spiritual realms, and urge us to look with them into the astral. Though modern domesticated cats are symbols of a life of luxuries and sensual enjoyment, cat medicine is also that of the survivor, one who will overcome, like the crafty alley cat.

Crow: Crow is the bird of the dark goddess, sacred to Macha and the Morgan, and the keeper of the sacred law. Sacred law is not necessarily what is legal, but what is right, according to the Goddess, to Spirit. Crow asks us to do the right thing, to follow the honorable customs of our society, and to respect our elders. Crow is also the symbol of the shaman, the shape-shifter, bending the laws of nature to open to new realities. Crow knows how to walk between the worlds with honor. Like the triple goddesses, Crow is beyond time, looking at the past, present, and future. Crow asks us to reflect on our past, be in the present, and move toward the future. When crows shows up, this spirit is an omen of change or potential challenges in your life.

Dog: Though many traditions tell us domesticated animals cannot be totems, I disagree, simply based on the experiences of my students. If you tell someone you can't have something, they won't see it in a vision. If you let them have their own experience, they will get the perfect totem for them. Many report that a family pet who has passed on returns to be a spirit guide. Dog is the most common, connecting to our sense of loyalty, trust, friendship, playfulness, and unconditional love. In The Fool card of the tarot, the dog is usually the companion of the fool, giving unconditional support on the road before them both. Dog asks us to appreciate and cultivate these qualities.

Dolphin: Longtime mythic and magical associations come with Dolphin. It is the sacred totem animal of Eros and Hyacinth. Ranging from Christian salvation to sexual union, the dolphin symbol speaks to everyone. Its most powerful lessons come in the form of breath and sound. Dolphins, as mammals, must surface to breathe. Their specialized breath opens one to the new rhythms of life. Their language is made of pure sound and rhythm, having intricacies found in, and perhaps surpassing, human language. Breath and rhythm are keys to reaching altered states of awareness. Dolphins are linked to the magical mind state, balancing male and female and connecting to the dreamtime, the higher consciousness. Dolphin medicine asks you to be aware of your own breath and rhythms, and search for the answers within you.

Eagle: Eagle is of the world, yet soars high above, flying in the realm of Spirit. Eagle is a creature of power, close to the sky gods, and brings lessons and tests to claim your spiritual power. It beckons us to a higher viewpoint, to see things from Spirit, from above, and see the whole picture, yet remain part of the Earth. Look with the sharp eagle eyes. Sometimes the challenges of Eagle are difficult, but they always allow us to grow in power and wisdom. Eagle feathers are used by shamans for healing. (Unless you're a Native American, possession of an eagle feather is a federal offense.) Zeus took the form of the eagle when he abducted Ganymede, as the eagle is associated with storm, sky, and father gods such as Zeus.

Fox: Fox energy is the lesson of invisibility, or blending with your surroundings so as to appear invisible. Go unnoticed. Camouflage yourself. Adapt to any situation as a fox adapts to each season, shifting the colors of its coat to better match the available foliage or winter snow. Be in the world, but not of it. Fox asks us to step out of the limelight and observe, silent and unseen like the wind dancing through the trees. Take this time to observe. Observe yourself. Observe others. Seek to understand. Be aware of all the actions around you. Don't try to figure out another person's motives, but simply observe and follow your intuition. Watch actions more than words. The color of the fox gives us subtle hints of its meaning for us. Red calls for more fire and passion. White is like the snow of winter, water frozen, asking us to cool our emotions and reflect. Brown foxes link to earth, grounding and being practical.

Frog: This spirit denotes some of the most sensitive people in the world. Frogs interact with their environment through their skin, and when an environment is polluted, the frogs are often the first to feel it. They absorb toxins through the thin skin, and mutate. Frog medicine asks us: When are we being sensitive, or thin-skinned, particularly emotionally? When are we being sensitive to the environment around us? Some toxic environments are purely in the form of "negative" psychic energy from unhappy, angry, or sad people around us. Those who are learning frog lessons take on those energies, but don't need to do so. Frog medicine is about cleansing, clearing, and healing. Their song is the song of water, of healing and purification. The cleansing can take place only when a person with frog medicine sings their own song, and speaks their own truth to clear the air and waters around them.

Goat: The goat is the symbol of the climber, sure-footed and stable before taking the next step. Goat is associated with the astrological sea goat,

Capricorn, related to the god Pan, and later to Dionysus. Goat was also the favored sacrifice of Aphrodite, and later became the image of Baphomet. The dark and light sides of these gods represent the dual aspect of goat medicine. On one hand, it is cautious and well prepared while climbing to the heights, spiritually, physically, or career-wise. The skeleton supports the goat's prepared movements. Their fur keeps them warm as they climb into the cold. Their horns protect them from adversaries. Goat medicine asks us if our footing is stable. Are we supported in our climb? It is far easier to fall than to climb. The other side of the goat is the wild, passionate, animalistic side, found in the ecstasies of Dionysus and Pan. Goat is fun-loving, playful, and sexual, enjoying life and the climb up. Beneath the veneer of all respectable Capricorn-influenced people is the wild one itching to let his or her hair down.

Horse: Power and freedom are the watchwords for horse medicine. Mythologically, magical horses pulled the chariots of the gods. Horses pulled Apollo's chariot of the Sun. Odin rode an eight-legged steed to which his blood brother Loki actually gave birth. The goddess Macha was forced to race against a horse, and many Celtic underworld goddesses, like Epona and Rhiannon, are associated with horse magick. We still define mechanical power as horsepower. Other powers are more subtle. Chiron the centaur, half man and half horse, was a scholar and physician. While he was Hercules' teacher, he was wounded with a poison arrow, but because of his divine nature he continued to live with the unhealed wound. Chiron traded positions with Prometheus, whom Zeus had chained and tortured in the Greek underworld (as punishment for stealing the divine fire), and the gods rewarded him for this altruism and courage by releasing him from his pain and wound, and putting him into the heavens as the sign of Sagittarius. Power can be mental, spiritual, or compassionate. The journey of the horse is akin to the shamanic journey within. As a faithful guide and companion, Horse often carries brave adventurers into the spirit realms. Horse has been associated with both male homosexuality and lesbianism in various cultures, and is sacred to Artemis, Athena, and Poseidon of Greek myth, and Astarte of the Middle East. Horses also represent untamed freedom that we as humans seek to master. Horse is our wild nature, our sexuality, and our desire to roam. Horse medicine may ask you to run free, feel the wind in your hair, and go wherever the moment takes you. Sagittarius asks your mind to roam free, exploring higher education and philosophy. This totem asks you: Where are you fenced in, where and when do you feel limited? When Horse visits, reflect on your use of power. Do you use it with wisdom? Do you need to explore other cultures, lands, and viewpoints? Such visits are not always physical, but can represent a journey of mind and spirit.

Ibis: The ibis is the sacred bird of Thoth, the Egyptian sage and scribe god. Thoth often took the form of a man with an ibis's head. This bird's medicine has all of the same attributes as Thoth, as a wise one, magician, and somewhat of a trickster or traveler spirit, as was Hermes/Mercury. The ibis itself is associated with anal intercourse, enemas, and cleanliness. Its medicine is that of the trickster, and also asks us to look at our own cleanliness—physically, emotionally, mentally, and spiritually. Chapter 7 contains techniques for purification and balance before a ritual.

Jaguar: Jaguar is the animal of initiation. The Aztecs associate the jaguar with Tezcatlipoca, the Smoking Mirror and Father of Witches. Initiation experiences are not simply magical or ritualistic. Any rite of passage—anything that forever alters your worldview, that changes you completely, usually by overcoming a traumatic situation—is an initiation. The coming-out process is such an initiation, as are first loves, losing virginity, and your first experience with magick or psychic ability. Initiations often force you to examine your shadow, your darker half, and make peace with it as you reclaim your power. The jaguar involves straddling the line between the spirit and material worlds, relating to shamanism, healing, and shape-shifting, particular animal/human hybrid shapes, and gender-variant forms. When jaguar medicine rears its head, reflect on recent initiations or those that are yet to come. Such experiences may be coming sooner than you think.

Lion: The lion is the totem of the astrological sign Leo. Lion is the king of the pride, ruling as a strong father figure would. Lion spirit is about having courage in the face of adversity. Male lions actually do little for the pride, while the female lions do most of the hunting. Lion spirit can ask if you are doing too little or too much in a relationship or community. The Egyptian goddess Sekhemet is often pictured with a lion head, as a destructive solar goddess and great protectress. Leo characteristics involve doing something well and being recognized for it, and often the energy is put into entertaining. Lion gives us related lessons and warning about pride and ego. As we ask for recognition, we can often base our self-image on the thoughts of others and become wounded easily. Lion embodies sensitivity to friends, family, and lovers. This totem asks us: When are we being sensitive, where is our ego, and where is our kingdom? Think about your own kingdom. Where do you shine?

Lizard: Lizard's key medicine is perception. Perceiving every subtle movement, Lizard asks us to observe and act only when necessary. Lizards watch the movement of insects, their food, to better catch their prey. They also are aware of the vibration of the Earth through their feet. Their spines and crests associate their sensitivity to the body and the chakra system. (See chapter 7 for more information on chakras.) Like the snake, the lizard is associated with kundalini, the rising life force at the base of the spine that is sometimes activated through sexual practices. The lizard itself was an ancient Greek symbol of the penis and associated with Apollo. He is a "lizard killer," now thought to slay, with his warming light, the serpent and reptiles representing winter, but certain scholars see the erect penis as the lizard awoken, and Apollo "slays" it by achieving orgasm and returning it to a flaccid state. Lizards also teach detachment and regeneration, as many species can leave their tail behind if a predator grabs it, allowing the lizard to escape and regrow the tail. What are you holding on to that keeps you in danger or unhappiness? Can you shed it and create something new? Finally, as keepers of perception, lizards are associated with dreams and the spiritual realms. They feign sleep while in the sun to allow insects to come in close and be eaten. They perceive in the awakened and sleeplike states, asking us to pay attention to the messages of our dreams.

Owl: Owl is a powerful animal of the night. Our nocturnal animals bring the lessons of mystery, dreams, psychic powers, astral travel, divination, and facing our own shadow, our darker half. Owl totem is associated with the Moon, the goddess, fertility, and mystery. The Greeks in particular connected the owl with the goddess Athena. Owl medicine lets us see and hear acutely, both physically and spiritually, knowing the thoughts and inner darkness of others. People with strong owl medicine will not be easily deceived by others, and are often seen as unsettling to other people. Owls devour their prey, usually rodents, head first, swallow it whole, and then regurgitate the bones and hair, symbolically teaching us how to absorb the wisdom while releasing that which offers no sustenance. Take what serves you, and leave the rest.

Peacock: In Western alchemy, the art of transmutation, the peacock is a symbol of androgyny, the hermaphrodite containing a balance of male and female energies. Although most believe alchemy to be the art of transforming lead into gold, the actual practice was spiritual, not necessarily material. Laboratories and chemicals were outward manifestations of the spiritual work. Alchemists were attempting to transform their own inner lead into pure, spiritual gold, or enlightenment and immortality. Part of the process was uniting, balancing, and ultimately merging the inner masculine and feminine represented by the peacock. When this bird appears to you, look and see if one side is out of balance or favored heavily in your life. How can you get into balance? In Hindu myth, the peacock took ugliness and turned it into beauty, as in the familiar ugly duckling/beautiful swan archetypal fairy tale.

Ram: Ram medicine is the basis of the astrological sign of Aries. Ram qualities are leadership, straightforwardness, and dedication. Ram asks us to be brave. A ram charges forward, using its horns to batter through any obstacles. Ram is obviously associated with the various horned pagan gods. Horns are also a sign of perception, to observe and be aware of where you are going. Ram medicine also urges us to not be too headstrong or brash, and be a bit more sensitive to our companions and surroundings as we charge up the mountain.

Rooster: Rooster is the animal of vigilance, heralding the Sun's rising each morning, and bringing fire and solar associations to this bird. Rooster medicine tells you to be more vigilant, aware, and observant, possibly putting the "light" before everything else. Rooster is the sign of passion, often associated with male sexuality and virility, which brings us to the rooster's other name: cock. One rooster fertilizes an entire hen house. Roosters are associated with the great goddess faiths of the Middle East and their homoerotically inclined priesthoods, as they were often sacrificed in those rites. They are also associated with Ares, Dionysus, Eros, and Ganymede. Roosters were exchanged as gifts between gay lovers. In Chinese astrology, the rooster is a symbol of humor, enthusiasm, and eccentricity. A visit from this spirit may be telling you to be yourself and enjoy life.

Spider: Spider is the cosmic weaver, writing our first letters and alphabet in its webs. Spider is the totem of the artist, the writer, the creator. Associated with Goddess imagery through the Native American Spider Grandmother, Spider spins the web of life, connecting us all through space and time. We all walk the web. Spider medicine ask us to look at where we are going. Spiders know which strands are sticky traps, and which ones can be walked. Are you stuck in a trap of your own making? We also learn patience, to sit in the center and observe the vibrations of the web. Spider spirit helps us conquer our fear, overcoming the arachnaphobic reaction to those things we find alien or repugnant. Ultimately, spiders are protectors and guardians, defending the home from other insects. That is why it's unlucky to kill a spider.

Turtle: Turtle is the messenger of Mother Earth, the great Goddess welcoming us all home. Turtle is a symbol of the planet itself, and many Native traditions speak of the turtle who carries the world on her back. Turtle is associated by its very nature with the feminine elements, earth and water, spending time at both. Turtle asks us to be grounded and centered, yet aware of our emotions, and to go within to process our feelings. Turtle is the symbol of protection, to retreat within when necessary, and to snap defensively, too. Turtles have slow metabolism and take a slow-and-steady pace, as in the fable of the turtle and the hare. They enjoy the ride, think before reacting, and are patient.

Wolf: Like Bear, Wolf is another strong archetype of the gay community because it is associated with both male and female characteristics. Wolf is the protector of community—the pack—and someone with Wolf medicine will fiercely protect their family and tribe, be it blood family or adopted spiritual community. In Native American traditions, Wolf is the teacher of life and its mysteries. Someone with strong wolf medicine may be a teacher of important wisdom and lore.

❋   ❋   ❋

For further resources in animal wisdom, I highly recommend *Animal-Speak* and *Animal-Wise*, both by Ted Andrews (Llewellyn Publications) and the *Medicine Cards*, an animal card divination and book set by Jamie Sams & David Carson (Bear & Company). Most important, learn all you can about your animal spirits. Look in encyclopedias and scientific sources for information on their habitats, feeding habits, and natural talents. Then use your symbolic interpretation to understand the animal beyond the scientific, and really speak to the spirit guide making contact with you.

Exercise 3. Meeting Your Power Animal

Start by thinking of your intention to meet your power animal. Do not try to control what animal it will be, but keep a general focus of meeting a power animal as your goal. We do not try to control the experience, but simply follow it, and allow the spiritual worlds to speak to us intuitively, through symbol.

1. Do steps 1 through 4 in Exercise 1 (page 60) to get into a meditative state.
2. Now you will count backward, from twelve to one. As you count, you may visualize you are walking down stairs, one by one, with the count. The stairs are leading you down to your place of power. (Count slowly from twelve to one.)
3. You are in your deepest meditative state, completely relaxed, yet aware. You are in your place of power. Waiting for you will be an animal spirit. The animal may be familiar to you, or a creature you have never seen. Simply go with your first intuition.
4. Ask the animal what message it has for you. Ask the animal its purpose with you. Is it your totem animal, guide, and protector? Or is it just here to give you a specific message and leave?

5. Observe the animal spirit. It may communicate with your directly, or take you on a journey. You may feel yourself merge with the animal, or shift your shape into an identical animal shape.

6. When you are done, thank your animal, and say farewell. Take your own human shape back if you have changed at all. Simply will it to happen and it will. Return to where you began. Return to the staircase, leading you up and out.

7. Count one through twelve. Imagine the stairs taking you back to where you began, back to your physical body. (Count one to twelve.)

8. Feel your physical body. Wiggle your fingers and toes, then your wrists and ankles. You may need to ground yourself a bit. Start by bringing your hands above your head and sweep in a downward motion, from crown, down to your belly, releasing all unwanted energy.

Ground yourself as needed, and write down your experiences in a journal. Reflect upon them. If you did not understand the message, learn more about the animal you experienced.

❄   ❄   ❄

After you have experienced meeting an animal guide once with no specific intention, you can repeat it when you have questions and concerns in life, looking for advice from the divine. An animal may be the messenger, or, as in the previous chapter, you may meet with the gods and goddesses directly. Your question could go unanswered in the meditation, only to be answered in the appearance of an animal in real life, or through the words of a loved one in your life. The gods choose many messengers to get their love and guidance across to us.

7

Building Your Temples

Blessed Be the Temple of my Body, may I be fit and strong
Blessed Be the Temple of my Heart, may I be open and loving
Blessed Be the Temple of my Mind, may I be clear and sharp
Blessed Be the Temple of my Soul, may I be bright and wise
Blessed Be the Temple of my Spirit, may I be the center
of all sacred space, now and always.

Witches have no churches. We have no lodges or hallowed halls. In the ancient civilizations, temples were devoted to the gods and goddesses, but there are virtually no remaining, actively used temples from the ancient world. Modern witches realize the church of the Goddess and God is all round us. Every place is sacred, to be respected. Nature is our cathedral. The world is our temple.

All places are sacred and flowing with life, but there are particular power spots and locations that are popular among Wiccans. Natural settings are greatly loved, be they the clearing in the woods, mountaintops, flowery fields, or beaches. While those locations are great, not all of us have the good fortune of living near such a picturesque setting. City-dwelling witches and pagans often gather in public parks, but they often find they need a permit, and depending on the city, such gatherings might not be welcome by the community at large. Most rituals take place in the privacy of the home. The home is the first temple. The location is no problem. You don't have to go anywhere to practice witchcraft. Sacred space is all around you, all the time. The act of the ritual recognizes the space as sacred. The ritual known as the

Magick Circle, or Witches' Circle (details in chapter 8), creates sacred space anywhere you are.

Temples and churches are created to hold energy that will nourish a certain state of mind, a connection to the divine. Witches, as walkers between worlds, work on consciously controlling their energy and state of mind in order to enter this spiritual communion with the divine. Since Wicca is a spiritual tradition that honors nature—the land, animals, stars, and sky—outdoor settings are ideal to help us generate this state of mind, but the true test of faith is to recognize that all those forces are around all the time, even if you can't see them. They are omnipresent, encompassed in everything, just the like the divine mother and father.

The Altar

Although you don't need anything to recognize sacred space, certain tools help you achieve this awareness. First among these tools is the altar. An altar brings up many connotations through history, from the altar of traditional Christian sects, to the bad horror movies featuring sacrificial altars. Both have similar roots, since the ancient religions of the world, including Judaism, from which Christianity built its foundation, conducted sacrifices. Some were animal sacrifices, and many were grain and harvest sacrifices. Sheep and lamb were common offerings in Old Testament sacrifices. Such practices were part of the culture of that time, and appropriate for those people, but it is not appropriate for this place and time. Modern witchcraft has no more to do with sacrifice—animal, human, child, or otherwise—than modern Judaism or Christianity does. Sometimes we make offerings of grain, flowers, or wine.

For now, we are stripping back to the basic function of the altar. The altar is a magical workspace. Ceremonial tools, candles, incense, and other objects of power are placed on the altar for use during a ritual. Traditionally, altars were made on wooden surfaces, but modern altars can be created on any available space. Most witches cover the altar with a cloth to match the season or spell work. Some altars are shrines to various deities, while others are simply functional. They can be permanent altars left in a home, or even an outdoor shrine, or altars built for a specific ritual or occasion. Covens will build an altar for a ritual. Each member will contribute items necessary for their time together, and then claim their items at the end of the gathering. Although I highly recommend building a permanent altar in your home, even if it is hidden among other personal objects, I realize that is not feasible for everyone, due to living arrangements, home life, and whether you are "out" as a witch or not.

Wiccans see the altar as a microcosm of the forces of nature. Each item on the altar represents a fundamental cosmological force called upon for celebration and magick. Although items are symbolic, they also serve a functional purpose. The altar is a microcosm of the Magick Circle, which in turn is a microcosm for the universe, all of creation, the body of the Goddess and God.

Altars most often face the north or east. North is for the power of the Earth, closest to the magnetic north pole when in the Northern Hemisphere. You can use a compass to find magnetic north. If you are in the Southern Hemisphere, you can face south. East is used for the power of the rising sun. Each direction has different correspondences and meanings, so if you want your altar to face another direction, learn about that direction first.

Gathering and Arranging Your Magical Tools

Upon the altar are several items, though they vary from witch to witch. Traditionally one must have at least four items, each to represent one of the four elements: earth, air, fire, and water.

Earth is represented by a stone, crystal, or bowl of sea salt or kosher salt, and placed in the north. Earth also embodies the energies of the Goddess, so sometimes a rounded, feminine stone, perhaps a crystal ball, is appropriate. The colors of earth are obviously earthen tones such as brown, black, tan, and green. The energy of the earth element represents the physical world. Everything material is of the earth element, including anything you sense with your physical senses, your body, your home, and all your possessions. To create anything in the physical world, you work with this powerful element. Magically, earth relates to all physical concerns, including health, money, job, pain, pleasure, and sense of comfort.

Air is represented by incense, a bell, chimes, or a blade, which you put in either the east or south, depending on the tradition you choose to follow. A witch's blade is called an *athame*, and is double-edged, like a dagger, with a dark handle. You don't use this blade to cut anything physical; it represents the male aspect of the God during ritual. Cutting blades used for harvesting herbs are white handled and called *bolines*. Air symbolizes the mind, logical thought, communication, and creativity. When we speak about the mind, we often use sword and metal imagery. We say, "Get to the point," like the point of a sword. Other phrases include, "Her mind is sharp," and "His words stabbed me in the back." All are blade images to describe the powers of the mind. The colors of air are blue, gray, and yellow.

The symbols of fire include candles, matches, and, most important, the wand. The wand is another symbol of the God and is used to direct energy in ritual, to channel the will of the user. Fire is all about willpower, energy, and vitality. Being a transition state between matter and energy, fire is the most difficult of the elements to describe. It means different things to different people. Wherever you put your energy is where your fire element is. The passion of a romance, lust, career drive, exercise, and artistic expression are all provinces of fire. Fire colors are red, orange, and yellow. Like the blade, the wand is usually put in the south or east, depending on the style of magick. Fire and air have much in common. Fire needs air to consume, and will needs the mind to express itself. Both the wand and blade are considered phallic tools of the God.

Water is the last element, placed in the west. The west is the land of endings, the place of the setting sun, and, in many world mythologies, the land of the dead. The underworld lies beyond the western sky, in the depths of the ocean. Oceans and islands have a strong association with the land of the dead. Water is an element of the feminine, of the Goddess, the giver and taker of life. Water and earth are both symbols of the womb and tomb. The main symbol of water is the vessel, usually a chalice or cauldron. All vessels are symbols of the gateway of the Goddess, and the gateway of womanhood. Drinking the waters of the Goddess brings you into divine communion with her. Water is also the realm of emotions, feelings, and the astral plane. The seas represent the changeable waters of emotion, sometimes tranquil and sometimes churning. The highest expression of water is the waters of unconditional love and healing. The color of water is blue.

Most traditions recognize a fifth element, combing the previous four. You can call it spirit, ether, or akasha. I place a cauldron, a tool that can represent each of the four elements at various times, in the center of my altar, to represent spirit. It also serves the function of containing burning spells. Spirit is also represented by a peyton, a ritual pentacle, or five-pointed star in a circle, used to invoke the elements. The pentacle is most strongly associated with earth, but each point represents one of the five elements.

You can have more than one tool for each element, since some tools serve other purposes ritually. I have both an athame and incense for air, and a wand, matches, and a candle for fire.

Other items on the altar include representations of the Goddess and God. Though they are embodied by the four elements, many witches have statues to represent the divine couple. I use a black candle on the left side for the Goddess and a white candle on the right for the God. The two candles also represent the pillars of consciousness. Some reverse it, or use two white candles.

Altar

You could also use a crystal point for the God and a crystal sphere for the Goddess. If you have chosen specific deities from chapter 3, you can put their pictures or statues by your altar.

Anything that reminds you of the divine can be used on the altar, along with any other power object you have collected over the years. Many aspiring witches realize they have a whole drawer full of odds and ends that they saved for some reason, and these objects work nicely on their altar. Crystals, stones, feathers, shells, bottles, statues, special jewelry, and pictures of passed loved ones can be placed on the altar.

I recommend building a home altar. By making a space in your home for the Goddess, God, and four elements, you are making a space in your life for this practice. The altar is a reflection of your life and your spiritual world. Caring for the altar symbolizes care for your spiritual life and your own inner balance of the four elements. Make building an altar a quest, and a great excuse to visit flea markets, antiques stores, and yard sales. Most cities have specialty pagan and witch shops, usually listed under the heading "occult" or "New Age," that will carry many of the materials you may want, but I find questing for tools off the beaten path is more fun. As soon as you decide to build your altar, you may find people giving you strange gifts, even if you do not tell them about your interest in building an altar. They have no idea why they are giving you such strange things. They are simply going on intuition. Think of them as gifts from the Goddess and God to help you on your path. You may have most of your tools already in your home, never knowing they were meant for an altar.

Of all the tools, the wand is one of the most important. You will use it to mark the boundary of sacred space, and to direct your will in various ways, including healing. Although commercially made wands of glass, silver, and crystals are available, most practitioners prefer to make their own. Wands are traditionally the length of the middle finger to the elbow, but that is not a hard-and-fast rule. I have larger and smaller wands. They can be made of any-thing, as long as they conduct energy. Natural substances such as wood or metal are the best. Copper and silver are the favored metals, and more afford-able, although a gold wand would work quite well. Woods such as oak, ash, hawthorn, apple, and willow are also popular. Each has a magical association. The Celts had a tree language based on the magick and symbol of special trees. It's an excellent subject to study prior to building a wooden wand. Edred Thorrson's *Book of Ogham* (Llewellyn Publications) is an easily accessible and understood work. You can also have more than one wand and they don't nec-essarily have to be made of Celtic woods. My first wand is bamboo, with crys-tals glued and wired to it. Quartz crystal points are good for energy direction. I have a wand that is simply a long crystal point. I have a five-foot red oak staff with wood-burned designs, wrapped in copper wire at the base. I have a willow wand with a simple painted design, and a copper tube filled with crys-tal chips and magical fire herbs, capped with a quartz point. Wands can be as simple or as elaborate as you like.

CHARGING YOUR RITUAL TOOLS

Whenever using a ritual tool for the first time, you must cleanse and charg it. *Charging* is another word for "consecration," or "blessing," but witches know they are putting a magical energy, a charge with an intention, into each ritual item. When you do the magick circle ritual for the first time (see page 107), you will have to consecrate all your tools prior to use, starting with the wand. You will also use this process for herbs, oils, and other objects you use in your workings.

To purify an item, hold it over some incense, particularly frankincense and myrrh combinations, sage, cinnamon, or copal. You can anoint it with salt water or a protection potion (see page 145) and then clean it off or pass it over an open candle flame. All four elements purify and cleanse. Or simply visual-ize it filling with white light, burning away all impurities.

Then hold the item, feeling your pulse and energy mingle with it. Bring your attention to your heart, and the Perfect Love and Perfect Trust of the Goddess and God. Fill the object with that energy, and any other intention you have for it. What does it represent on your altar? Tell it. Charge the black candle for the Goddess and the white candle for the God. Charge the chalice for water, and so on. Charge the wand to create sacred space through a magick circle, to represent fire and the force of the God. Items can have more than one use or intention.

You may periodically cleanse and charge your ritual items. Some people are more obsessive about it, particularly if anyone else has touched their altar, while others are more laid-back. Again, it is a personal decision. I cleanse and rededicate my altar about once a year.

Your Home

As the altar is a reflection of your inner balance, the home is another microcosm for your soul. The home is a temple. It houses your altar, but most important, it houses you. The state of your living space is directly related to your well being. Homes reflect the personality and health of their occupants. If you do not care about your own living space, you cannot care about sacred space very much.

Many books are dedicated to the art of *feng shui*. In Chinese, it means "wind and water," but it relates to the harmonious balance between home, land, and the energy flowing between the two. Although feng shui is a complicated and wonderful art to study, many of its basic principles can be understood intuitively. The concepts are found in many traditions that pay attention to the energy of the Earth. Feng shui uses a different five-element system, but the concepts behind the symbols are the same. The basic watchwords are balance, simplicity, creativity, and a sense of the sacred.

First, clear the mess, clutter, and dirt from your home. As you do, you sweep clear the mind and emotions of unnecessary clutter. Clear out the things that no longer serve you. If you have something you do not use or like, get rid of it. Magick is a matter of exchanging energy. If there is no room in your home or your heart for new blessings, then such changes will not come. You have to make room for them. When you try to hold on to the past in the midst of changes, you only invite sorrow. You are only losing something you no longer need. It may serve everyone's best interest to remove it.

When you spend time in a room, how do you feel? Does it bring peace, happiness, joy, or relaxation? Does it bolster your spirit, or make you feel uneasy or uncomfortable? Is there something in the room that bothers you? Then perhaps you have to change it. Intuitively rearrange until you come to a harmonious balance of styles and elements. Balance aspects of the elements.

In the Wiccan elemental system, earth is in the north, fire in the east or south, as is air, with water in the west. Use the symbols and colors I mentioned earlier to help bring balance to your living space. Perhaps rooms in the north side will be more earthen tones. Your fire rooms can be brighter in color and design. A water room can be more reflective, like a library or sitting room. Don't completely redo your house if you don't want to; simply find the balance in what you already have.

Generally, rounded corners and a moderate number of twist and turns in the house break up the energy, letting it flow smoothly like rocks in a stream. When energy runs in a straight line, say in a long hallway or room, it often needs to be broken up to promote health. Hang chimes and lead crystals to diffuse the energy. Shelves and furniture can also disperse the vital life force; too much, however, will make the energy of the room stagnant and sluggish. Good energetic health incorporates a flow, and exchange in moderation. Most important, watch how you and others feel in the room. Make your home reflect your personal tastes, current place in life, who you are, and what you are doing in the present.

Your Body

The last of the temples discussed here is the temple of your body. This temple is always with you, from birth to death. The body is your first magical tool, capable of representing all the energies on the altar. You have an inner masculine and feminine, the God and Goddess. You contain the elements within you. You body—muscles, bones, and minerals—is earth. Your blood, the liquids making up over 70 percent of your body, as well as your emotions, is water. Your lungs, and the oxygen and carbon dioxide they constantly exchange, along with your mind, is the air element. Your metabolism, your inner fire and life force, along with your very soul, is the element of fire.

The care and maintenance of your body should be a priority, although it represents a challenge for many. Nutritious diet, exercise, and rest are as important to a witch as lighting candles and incense, and doing spells. Wicca is a religion of the manifested. Witches believe the divine is manifest in everything, everywhere, particularly our bodies. While some religions look to the flesh as a temple of sin, or the material plane as a prison to escape, witches view the body and world as the divine manifest, a paradise of the Goddess and God and a gift to us all while we have our human experience.

Some people can take health practices to an extreme, because they hold themselves up to a godlike ideal like that of the mythical Adonis or

Aphrodite. Wicca teaches balance and moderation, and that we are all divine by our very nature. We do not have to do anything to earn it by looking a certain way. Although we are familiar with the divine statues of physical perfection, particularly from the Greco-Roman period of art, there are as many statues, both from the classical period and dating back to the Stone Age, depicting the divine in many body shapes and sizes, starting with the classical archetype of the Earth Mother with rounded belly and including the love-handles of Bacchus. Witches seek balance in all activities, and make friends with reality. Contrary to popular belief, witchcraft is not an escape from the real world. One of the key components of good magick making is self-love and self-esteem. That means loving and accepting yourself and your body.

Your Aura and Chakras

Health is not restricted to the physical body; it also involves the energy bodies. Metaphysicians the world over believe in a subtle field of energy, most likely connected to the electromagnetic spectrum, that surrounds and permeates your body. In addition to surrounding the body, it provides a template for the body on all energetic levels. Witches have adopted the term "aura" from esoteric practices to describe this energy.

The health and well-being of the aura reflect our own health, on the physical, emotional, spiritual, and mental areas of life. Psychics and witches look at the aura to see the roots of imbalances. These imbalances can eventually become illnesses in the physical world. Caring for the aura maintains health on all levels, not just the physical. The aura itself is usually visualized as an egg shape, or sphere, slightly larger than arms reaching all around your body.

The aura is divided into several layers, called subtle bodies. They are not physical bodies—they surround and permeate the physical body. Some are close in size and structure to the physical, but the farther you get from the physical level, the more nebulous each layer becomes in shape and characteristic. They relate to the four elements, which is another way to divide the layers of the aura. They also relate to seven spiritual "organs" found within the energy bodies, called chakras. *Chakra* is Sanskrit for "spinning wheel," and they are usually observed by psychics as spinning balls of light at the base of the spine up to the crown. Each chakra holds the energy of each level of consciousness in the human experience, from our basic needs to highest spiritual aspirations. The seven chakras also correspond to the seven colors of the rainbow and the seven notes of a major scale. Patterns repeat themselves all

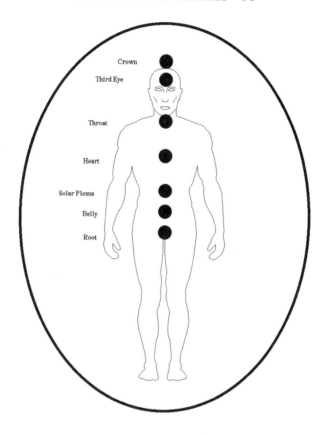

Aura and chakras

through the universe, and witches know to watch the patterns of creation to understand better themselves and the world.

At the base of the spine is the root chakra, forming a red ball of light at the perineum point, between the genitals and the anus. The root is related to the physical body, because it deals with physical needs. The ability to be grounded and present in the physical world, along with survival instincts, pain, pleasure, and procreation relate to the root. This first chakra is your base and foundation, rooting you to the world. Earth is its element, but because of the red color and intensity surrounding it, fire is also appropriate.

At the belly, at or slightly below the naval, is the second chakra, colored orange. No one can seem to agree on the name, as it has been called the spleen, sexual, naval, abdominal, or sacral chakra in various traditions. I simply call it the belly chakra. The belly relates to the etheric body, an energetic template of the physical body, hugging closely to the physical. Some see it as a white, hazy outline surrounding the body. Physical illness must manifest in the etheric before becoming physical. The belly deals with our ability to reach out to and make contact with another. Trust, instinct, and relationship are the realms of the belly, along with sexual contact, since it, along with the root, is connected to the sexual organs and reproduction. Both earth and water are linked to the second chakra.

The solar plexus is located right below the diaphragm muscle, above the naval and below the sternum. Colored yellow, the solar plexus is our place of power, vitality, and life force. From here, we exert control, both in a helpful and harmful sense. Here is the consciousness that controls others inappropriately, and where we give our power away to be controlled in harmful relationships. The solar plexus also contains our self-image, fears, and angers, and connects to the adrenal glands. The astral body, a finer duplicate of the physical, related to our spiritual self-image, is the subtle body of the solar plexus. Mystics project this energy outward for the purpose of astral projection and remote viewing. Things must take shape and form on the astral to manifest in the etheric and physical, but the form is fluid and easily changed, like the element of water. All physical things have an astral duplicate, but not all astral beings, including spirits, ghosts, and deities, have a physical body.

At the sternum, you find the heart chakra, a glowing orb of green light, like the color of fresh grass or an emerald, although pink is also associated with the heart. This chakra is the bridge between the lower body and upper body, a connection from lower needs and desires to higher reasoning, intuition, and spirit. The thymus gland, along with the heart, circulatory system, and immune system, is associated with the chakra of love, empathy, and higher relationships. When we think not of ourselves, but of others, when we feel empathy, love, and understanding for another, we connect through the heart chakra. We are using the emotional body, which is also connected to the astral. Several traditional esoteric schools of thought call the emotional plane the upper astral.

The throat chakra is located at the larynx, colored blue, and rules over the power of communication and expression. The thyroid gland, lungs, and throat, itself, are the physical tools of this chakra, and it relates to the mental body. The mind is not simply in the brain, but surrounding the entire physical body. Your cells listen to your inner dialogue, and respond accordingly, creating health or illness, depending on the conscious and unconscious programs you give them. The mind is a great, creative tool, allowing us to manifest our will through our words, express our ideas, and form our creative pursuits. Unfortunately, most people create from the unconscious mind. The process of healing includes cleansing the unconscious mind and emotional body so we can create from a place of knowing. The mind and emotions—air and water—interact like the ocean and sky. Thoughts create feelings, and feelings lead to thoughts, though most people don't recognize the process when the internal storm is brewing.

At the brow is the most talked-about chakra, the third eye. For the work of the witch, an intimate familiarity with the third eye is critical, because this chakra rules our psychic abilities and our psychic body, the subtle body that gathers intuitive information in the form of pictures, sounds, or deep knowing. Visualized as purple or indigo, between and above the physical eyes, it is said to open whenever we use our intuition. The pineal gland, speculated to be either a vestigial or a newly evolving eye, is the gland of the brow chakra. When you talk about picturing something in your mind's eye, you are using the third eye, even if the experience doesn't feel magical or psychic. All imagination is a part of magick.

Culminating this upward system is the crown chakra, at the crown of the head. Pictured as a violet, orchid, or dazzling white sphere radiating light, like a crown of white fire, it regulates our divine connection to the universe. Spiritual experiences, epiphanies, and very moving moments come to us through the crown and the divine body. The divine body is connected to the divine mind of the entire universe, the Goddess and God, as well as everybody else's divine body. We are all one. This subtle body goes beyond the boundary we perceive as the auric field. The divine body is another name for the higher self, super consciousness, or god self, and relates to the pituitary gland, the master gland for the crowning chakra.

Purifying Your Outer and Inner Temples

Part of magical energetic health, and preparation for the deeper rituals and meditations in subsequent chapters, is the balance and purification of these subtle bodies, chakras, and your magical workspace. First, magically cleanse your home, and in particular the room with your altar in it. You can do this ritual cleansing as often as you like, but it should be done prior to most major workings.

Certain incenses, when burned, release purifying energies. My favorite of these incenses is a combination of frankincense and myrrh, but other substances include sage, sweet grass, copal, lavender, cinnamon, sandalwood, and clove. I like the frankincense and myrrh combination because they are considered masculine and feminine, respectively. It brings a good balance. Look for all-natural incenses when possible, and get an incense burner to prevent ash from scattering. A heat-resistant bowl filled with sand works nicely.

Start by blessing the incense. Ask that the incense be used for purification, and feel your intent go into it as you hold it. You are catalyzing its power, charging and consecrating with intent. You can do this with any-thing—food, medicine, herbs—to bring out their natural powers. Then, take the burning incense to each of the four quarters—north, east, south, and west—asking Spirit to "purify all harmful unwanted energies." It's that easy.

If incense bothers you, you can mist your space with rose water by mix-ing a few drops of rose essential oil with spring water and spraying it from a misting bottle. You can also get cheaper rose water and glycerin from a drug-store. Or simply visualize the room filling with violet or white light, purifying it of all harmful energies.

You must also learn to purify yourself. Meditation, clearing the mind, walking outside, and relaxation are all ways to let go of the worries of the day. One of my favorite techniques is ritual bathing. Ritual bathing is a wonderful way of purifying the body, mind, emotions, and spirit. You can steep herbs in the water, to add some magical energy to the ritual. You can also add salt, which absorb harmful energies and is great for purification and cleansing. Magically I prefer sea salt or kosher salt.

One of my favorite herbal bath recipes comes from *The Complete Book of Incense, Oils and Brews* by Scott Cunningham (p. 153). His formula is adapted from *The Key of Solomon*, an ancient magical text.

Ritual Purification Bath

4 parts lavender
4 parts rosemary
3 parts thyme
3 parts basil
2 parts fennel
2 parts hyssop
1 part mint
1 part vervain
1 pinch of valerian root

I also like to add 4 parts sea salt to the formula. Charge each ingredient as you mix it into the formula. Feel the power of the herbs. Place the mixture on a square of cheesecloth and tie the corners to form a little bag. Soak in warm bathwater. You can make several of these bath bags at time so you will always have one on hand as needed. I highly suggest Cunningham's book for more bath and bath salt recipes, handmade incense, and a plethora of other exciting magical formulas.

While in the bath, visualize all your aches and pains, worries, fears, and stress entering the water. Release them all. Let the water take them. When done, let the water drain out, taking your problems with it.

✳   ✳   ✳

If you don't like baths, take a shower, and visualize the water as a shower of light. Go through the colors of the rainbow: red, orange, yellow, green, blue, indigo, and violet. End with white and let the shower of water and light cleanse your aura and chakras.

After a cleansing bath, you put on special clothes, such as ritual robes. Witches traditionally favor black robes and cloaks, though some work sky clad, or naked. These clothes are used only during ritual, and the very act of putting them on continues the purification process. Other traditions call for working sky-clad. Some people are nervous about working sky clad because of their self-image and feelings about the body. The idea behind being sky clad is to be unashamed of your nude body, and that the Goddess and God love us all, in a diversity of shapes, sizes, and body types. Sometimes we fall under the illusion of society's image projections. It would be wonderful if we could all have the bodies of models and movies stars, but the reality is that we all have different body types and different commitments to physical health. You shouldn't compare your intensity of exercise and diet to someone whose very job is to look good. Even if that's your job, too, comparison making is just a waste of energy.

Although sky-clad group workings are not for all of us, if you are uncomfortable with the very idea, I suggest getting sky clad and standing before a mirror. Look at every part of your body, from head to toe, and tell each part of your body that you love it and thank it. Do this as part of your regular meditation and affirmation experiences and notice the change in your thoughts and feelings.

You can use simple meditation, visualization, and energetic exercises to maintain balance, centeredness, and purification. I find the Chakra Tree Meditation extremely helpful, not only prior to ritual, but to maintain daily health and stability.

Exercise 4. Chakra Tree Meditation

1. Do steps 1 through 4 in Exercise 1 (page 60) to get into a meditative state. If you are easily getting into a meditative state, you can omit the candle staring if you want.

2. Feel as if your feet are the roots of a great tree. Feel your roots dig deep into the Earth, connecting you to the heart of the planet. You are grounded, rooted, and stable. Raise your arms, and feel as if branches are growing up from your arms and crown, reaching high into the sky. Feel the wind rustle your branches.

3. With each breath, imagine you are drinking up the energy of the Earth, up through the roots as if they were great wooden straws. You are drinking the waters of Mother Earth like a tree. Ask for her love to fill you.

4. The energy reaches the base of your spine, turning red and opening your root chakra. Feel the power of survival, of one grounded, and of the physical. (Pause for a few moments.)

5. With your next in-breath, the energy moves up to your belly, turning orange. Feel your instinct, intuition, and connection to all life. Feel your etheric body. (Exhale and pause for a few moments, breathing normally.)

6. With your next in-breath, the energy moves to your solar plexus, turning yellow. Feel your sense of personal power and your astral body. (Exhale and pause for a few moments, breathing normally.)

7. With your next in-breath, the energy travels up to your heart, opening the green chakra. Feel your sense of love, empathy, and healing. Feel your emotional body. (Exhale and pause for a few moments, breathing normally.)

8. With your next in-breath, the energy moves to your throat, opening the blue chakra and your own powers of communication and the mind. Feel your mental body. (Exhale and pause for a few moments, breathing normally.)

9. With your next in-breath, the energy moves to your third eye, opening the psychic center of purple or indigo light. Feel your intuitive powers blossom. Feel your psychic body. (Exhale and pause for a few moments, breathing normally.)

10. With the last in-breath, the energy moves up to the crown, the lavender-white chakra of divine connection, and flows up through your branches, reaching the heavens, connecting the Earth to the sky. Feel your divine body connected to the universe. (Exhale and pause for a few moments, breathing normally.)

11. Above you, you feel the air and wind. You feel the light—the Sun, Moon, and stars. With each breath, you draw down this sky energy through your leaves and branches. It flows down easily to reach your crown, down through your third eye, down through your throat, down into the heart, filling your body and moving down to the solar plexus, down to your belly and down to your root chakra. The energy travels down through your legs and roots, down to the center of the Earth. The energy takes along with it whatever does not serve your highest health, and sends it into the ground for transmutation. The Earth breaks down and reforms all.

12. Pause a few moments, feeling the energy of the Earth moving up and the sky moving down, balancing, purifying, and grounding you.

13. When you are done, thank the Earth and sky.

14 Feel your physical body. Wiggle your fingers and toes, then your wrists and ankles. You may need to ground yourself a bit. Bring your hands above your head and sweep in a downward motion, from crown, down to the belly, releasing all unwanted energy.

Ground yourself as needed. If you would like, write down your experience in your journal.

✳   ✳   ✳

Now you have the temple of your sacred body. Now you are prepared to work deeper in the mysteries.

8

The Magick of Being Your Own Priest or Priestess

We need no intermediaries. We need no institution.
Every one of us has a personal and intimate relationship
with the gods. We are all priestesses. We are all priests.
We are all equal in the eyes of the gods.

Witchcraft as a religion is not delineated into priest and parishioners. All members of the craft are clergy in a sense. Each becomes their own intermediary to the divine world of the gods and spirits. No one else is required. Each takes on the role of priest or priestess.

Covens

In the old tribal cultures of Europe, certain members of the community were the witches, acting as wise ones, healers, and spiritual leaders. Individual families often took roles within the community. One family would be black-smiths, another provided the community with weavers. And there was the family of witches, giving rise to the belief that the power of the witch is passed on through the blood. Like an aptitude for any talent, including art, music, and athletics, you can inherit the power of the witch, but it is not a prerequisite. Ability, knowledge, and practice are the true signs of the crafts-man. If the children did not want to learn the family craft, or did not show an aptitude, then the family would "adopt" someone who showed talent and a willingness to be apprenticed in the arts. This custom included all traditions, not only healers and ceremonial leaders. While one family acted as spiritual guides, the rest of the community, although pagan in religious belief, would not be considered witches. At certain times, these families may have gathered together, but for the most part were a loosely organized structure, not a formal order. In ancient civilaizations, these family traditions existed side by side with the formal orders of priest and pristess found in the temples.

The classic image of the witches' coven probably arose from the early days of the Holy Roman Empire, when families had to keep their religious practices secret among a group of select people in order to survive and preserve their traditions. Household items, things everyone possessed, the broom, the pot, and the knife, among other utensils, became the tools of the witch. If everyone had them, you could not be persecuted for simply owning them, as you could with more ceremonial tools. Magick hid deep in cooking, herbalism, and simple folk charms. Most forgot group worship and the religious aspect entirely, keeping their craft where it was safest, in the household. They passed the traditions along family lines, from parent to child, using simple folk custom. No one was as trustworthy as your own children. This harkened back to the origins of the craft, with the magical family, those families kept in hiding for the most part. Modern family tradition, or "fam trads," revealed themselves in modern history and claim an ancient lineage, although scholars and witches debate the veracity of their claims.

As witchcraft reemerged, due greatly to these families, their acquaintances, and the work of Gerald Gardner, witchcraft again focused on the small group as the core structure. Covens of no more than thirteen would gather, each with high priest and high priestess. The coven assigned to their members ranks indicating their level of experience and ability, and passing through the ranks was marked by initiation rituals. Generally, one starts as an initiate, an aspiring member of the group, and then moves on to the first degree. At the second degree, one is considered a priest or priestess, and many stop there. An adept of the third degree is considered a high priest or priestess, who has earned the authority to start his or her coven. Some traditions even mandate that the high priest or priestess depart from the "mother" coven.

This rising through the ranks is a traditional model, but since its initial resurgence, Wicca has taken many twists and turns. Other traditions, many much less formal, have arisen, along with the practice of solitary and eclectic witchcraft. But the gift of this initial structure was given to us forever more, for good and bad, like Pandora's Box. By fusing the titles witch and priest/priestess, the term "witch" now generally means one who claims the roles and responsibilities of clergy.

Witches learn to conduct entire rituals, as well as actively participate. Solitary witches must, by definition, take on all roles, acting as high priest and high priestess, even if only for the duration of the ritual. Because we claim this role, ultimately we are our own clergy. No one acts as intermediary for us. We may share in ritual with our community. We may seek out elders and teachers for advice and healing, but we need no cleric to absolve us or aid in our communion with the divine. Our relationship with the gods and goddesses is individual and personal. We are all our own Hierophants, or Popes, the ultimate authority on our spiritual tradition and personal practice. With that authority comes responsibility. No one can damn us and yet no one can save us. In fact, as witches, we don't believe we need saving. For me, that was such a refreshing yet frightening thought growing up gay and Catholic. Such responsibility is no easy burden to bear, but if we keep in mind the Wiccan Rede as the guide, "Do what thou will and let it harm none," then we carry the ultimate personal freedom, as well.

It is important to note that many who ascribe to the practice of paganism, but do not consider themselves witches for whatever reason, sometimes claim the role of priest or priestess on a pagan path. Other pagans do not claim such roles. Though many witches see themselves as the new clergy of the neopagan population, many pagans are not looking for clergy, but simply want to practice in their own way, and on their own terms, without the title of witch or priest/ess. You do not have to be Wiccan, or even pagan, to claim the responsibilities and freedoms of clergy. In the end, we are all responsible for our own beliefs and the actions based on them.

Key Concepts in Ritual

Ritual is one of the key components of the clergy. A priestess or priest can be defined in many ways as one who has the knowledge and ability to perform the rites of a religion. But in a broader sense, we all perform basic rituals, whether we know it or not. Mundane rituals are often called habits, but some serve a higher purpose. A ritual is a repeated action used to create a change in consciousness, to open you to greater awareness. If every day after work, you come home, change, put on some music, and sit down with a magazine to relax and unwind, you are doing a ritual of sorts. The combination of the set time of day, music, dress, and action relaxes you. Relaxation brings greater awareness after a stressful day. As you hear the first few notes, or start to take off your work clothes, your awareness already begins to shift. These acts are part of the ritual preparation, leading to the expansion of the mind, emotions, and body, unwinding you. These acts are symbolic, as symbols help unlock the doors of awareness. Though this is a mundane example, all rituals work in a similar manner, if not the same technique.

The initial purpose of a ritual is simply relaxation. As part of the preparation, not the means in and of itself, relaxation opens the doorways to the deeper self. Spiritual rituals connect the finite self, the conscious personal self, with the vast spiritual self, the super consciousness, or realm of the Goddess and God. From this point of awareness, we touch the unending fountain of unconditional, divine love. Witches call this Perfect Love and Perfect Trust. Here, our souls are refreshed and replenished. Here, we heal and know the infinite love and wisdom of the universe. Here, we experience the divine, and we do not need faith, after experience. Here, all things are one. Here, we make magick.

All rituals have symbols. Symbols are the tools of the ceremony, and can be literal or metaphorical. Symbols are the language of our unconscious self, and act as a bridge between our personal self and this super consciousness, what some call the higher self. Most of the time, it is difficult to directly and easily connect with this higher realm. Telling someone to simply connect to the super consciousness is like asking someone without wings to fly. Those who are most successful at it learn inner technologies, patterns to make such contact easier. Scriptures, religions, and spiritual paths are usually patterned after a particular person's techniques, though all the world's religions tell most of the same basic truths, such as "go within."

A tried-and-true method is to go lower, through what is called the lower self, to get to a higher consciousness. Hermes Trismegistus, a mythic teacher, gave us the Hermetic Principle, "As above, so below; as below, so above." All patterns repeat. If it is easier to connect with the unconscious, what shamans call the lower self, then it will lead to the higher self. Witches often call it the psychic self. The lower self is simply the intuitive self, when its voice is honored and recognized. The purpose of developing the psychic self and magical abilities is to connect with the divine and experience it, not to simply have faith.

SYMBOLS AND RITUAL

Symbols are the way to access the psychic/lower/unconscious self. Symbols are how the unconscious gives us messages in dreams. It is actually relaying messages for the higher self. Psychic visions, hearing spirits, and feeling energy are all symbolic ways to interact with this realm. The gods and goddesses of mythology, and their archetypes, are symbols. They are masks that the divine wears. They are facets of the one Goddess/God/Great Spirit running through us all, making it easier to connect and experience the divine greatly. Although many would disagree, all gods lead to the source of all life.

Witchcraft has several symbols at the heart of the practice. The most well known is the pentacle, a five-pointed star in a circle. When drawn without the circle, it is called the pentagram. Although popularly depicted upside down as a sign of Satanism, it is no more Satanic than the cross, which Satanists turn upside down. The star represents many things, but is primarily the symbol of the elements, earth, air, fire, water, and spirit on top. To invert it is to put spirit last, or at the bottom. The pentacle is also a symbol of humanity, of physical incarnation. Its points represent our two arms, legs, and head. In ancient Greece, the pentagram was called the *pentalpha*, a symbol of Pythagoras and his students. The geometry represents musical and architectural proportions. It also stands for the five senses surrounded by the sixth, or psychic, sense.

Although not as popular, the six-pointed star, or hexagram, is also used in modern magick, by both witches and Judeo-Christian magicians. King Solomon, a great Hebrew sorcerer, reportedly used both the pentagram and hexagram in his magical talismans. The two triangles of the hexagram, in union, can represent the harmony or merging of two forces, particularly masculine and feminine, or projective and receptive.

The hexagram also represents the merger of all four elements. Four special triangles denote the four elements, and combine to make the hexagram. The triangle itself has become a prominent symbol in gay culture. Pink triangles were used by Hitler's regime to mark homosexual men. A black triangle marked women who were deemed unusable, including lesbians and prostitutes. The triangle was adopted in the 1980s by the activist group ACT-UP and now has generally been used to denote gay pride and gay rights. Colors include pink, black, lavender, and rainbow.

The most important symbol in Wicca and other Earth religions is the circle. It surrounds the five-pointed star, but is a symbol in its own right. The circle is the first symbol, and cultures around the world use it as the basis of many

Pentagram and pentacle

Hexagram

sacred drawings, and mandalas. The circle is the planet, the world as our Earth Mother. The circle is seen in all the planets, and the ring of stars known as the sidereal zodiac. The circle is the cycle of life, continually following pattern, be it the cycle of the seasons, Moon, or our very own lives—birth, life, death, rebirth. The circle is sometimes viewed as the *uroboros*, a serpent devouring its own tail, with no beginning or end. Snakes are another symbol of the Goddess. The circle is the womb of life and the tomb and cave of death. The circle is the cauldron of the Goddess. And most important, the circle is the basis for the magick circle, the foundation ritual of the modern witch.

The Magick Circle Ritual

The function of the magick circle is the creation of sacred space. To a witch, every place is sacred space, but through ritual, we energetically create a living temple, inviting in the fundamental forces of the universe to our space. The circle is a microcosm for the universe. As a symbol, we can use it to commune more easily with the divine and manifest our intentions in the world. As we look to the altar, our other microcosm for the divine forces, we see the basic pattern of the circle. Prior to the circle are any purification rites, of both the physical space and the participants. (See chapter 7.)

CASTING THE CIRCLE

First, the circle is cast, starting in the north, and usually with a wand or an athame, both symbols of the projective god force. A ring is traced three times in the air, and visualized in white, blue, or violet light, marking the boundary

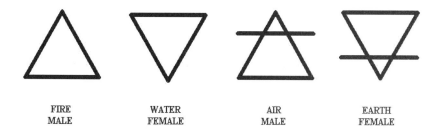

| FIRE MALE | WATER FEMALE | AIR MALE | EARTH FEMALE |

Triangles

of the temple. Traditionally circles are nine to thirteen feet in diameter, but for the small group or solitary, the size of your room is fine. You can imagine the perfect circle etherically passing through walls and furniture, rather than create a circle that is too tight. The north is considered a great reservoir of energy, pointing toward magnetic north, as magnetism is associated with the Earth goddess.

Medieval magicians would talk about the circle's boundary for warding off "evil" spirits, but actually the circle is a container and amplifier for the energies gathered. It protects by raising the energetic vibration of an area, blocking out all harmful lower vibrations, including "evil" spirits. The main function, however, is to create and contain sacred space.

QUARTER CALLS—EVOKING THE ELEMENTS

Next, the four elements are invited into the space, as anchors in the four cardinal directions; this is known as "calling the quarters." One by one, starting in the north, the element and a patron of sorts is invited in to manifest the energy of that element. Ritually, salt may be sprinkled for earth, a candle lit for fire, and incense smudged for air. If outside, water may be used for a libation, poured into the ground, as an offering, or aspersed, taking a branch such as pine, dipping it into the water, and shaking the water out into the circle.

Table 1 on page 109 gives a list of elemental correspondences with animal spirits and queer-positive deities, which you can use when devising your quarter calls. Some gods will have more than one elemental association. Others embody a realm of power not really associated with the elements and their energy. Ideally, at least in initial practice, if you are going to choose deities to call upon to anchor and guide the quarters, you should use those from one culture. If you choose Aphrodite for water, then choose all Greek deities, such as Zeus for air, Apollo for fire, and Gaia for earth. In many cases, you will have to research additional gods of that culture to get a set of four. Always educate yourself and then meditate upon deities or animals before you call on them, to make sure they resonate with you. Eclectic practitioners often mix deities from several cultures they know well, but if you are just beginning, stick with one cultural energy.

As the elements are secured, the symbol of the circle takes on the form of the shield, a circle with a cross, the astrological symbol of the planet Earth itself. Energetically, it can feel more like a sphere than a circle, taking on a three-dimensional life. Into the center of the circle, as the element of spirit, the Goddess and God are invited. They may be specific cultural godforms, or generalized deities. They embody the creative play between masculine and feminine as the polarity of the divine spirit.

As you grow in your magick, you'll notice your relationship with the four elements. Some will feel comfortable in your life, while others are distant. When you invoke them, you may really feel one element, but not another. Witches strive to know and balance all four. You can bolster your relationship with an element by partaking in its activities. To improve your relationship with earth,

TABLE 1. ELEMENTAL CORRESPONDENCES.

Element	Direction	Animal Ally	Deities
Earth	North	Stag, Bear, Goat, Bull, Turtle	Adonis, Tammuz, Astarte, Cernunnos, Pan, Dionysus, Ereshkigal, Freyja, Freyr, Isis, Tlazoteotl, Xochilpilli
Fire	East, South	Fox, Lion, Horse, Ram, Jaguar, Rooster	Apollo, Bran, Eros, Hercules, Horus, Kali Ma, Loki, Set
Air	South, East	Crow, Eagle, Ape, Ibis, Butterfly, Owl	Artemis, Diana, Athena, Inanna, Ganesha, Gwydion, Hermes, Indra, Isis, Macha, Odin, Thoth, Zeus, Jupiter
Water	West	Dolphin, Fish, Whale, Lizard, Snake, Frog	Aphrodite, Venus, Damballah, Dionysus, Ganymede, Osiris, Sedna, Tezcatlipoca, Yemaya

work on your body. Nutrition, food, exercise, dance, yoga, martial arts, ritual, and touch are ways to get in touch with the earth element, as well as being practical, planning ahead, and being careful with your finances. To improve your time with fire, tap in to your passions, creativity, career, and sexuality. To work on water, turn inward and reflect with meditation, relaxation, rest, dream work, and build strong, loving relationships. To develop air, communicate with yourself through writing and with others through speaking. Take a class. Stretch your mind and perceptions. Explore the unknown.

THE GODDESS AND GOD

The Goddess and God are celebrated in ritual communion, through an act called the Great Rite. The Great Rite refers to the greatest act of magick, creation, as the creation of the universe through the Goddess and God. Through their union and love, as the Great Mother and Father, all things come into being. Like all rituals, there can be an element or repetition or reenactment. Their union is reenacted. Some traditions did this physically, as ritual sex between the high priest and high priestess, both embodying the God and Goddess, respectively. Most covens now usually reserve that intimate act for couples already in a sexual relationship, and usually in private.

More often, the ritual is symbolic. Traditionally, the chalice, or cup, represents the Goddess, and the athame, or blade, is the God. Some traditions use the wand or cauldron in place of either, but I learned with the chalice and athame. The priestess holds the chalice while the priest draws the blade. The athame is blessed, often calling upon the power of the Moon, or "drawing down the Moon," for the ritual, and thrust into the chalice, energizing the water or wine with the powers of the Goddess and God. The priest and priestess drink the liquid and usually share it with the coven.

Here is where some perceive a heterosexual fertility bias in traditional Wicca, the pairing of male to female that is sometimes upsetting to homosexual initiates. But this is a limited perception.

Solitary work has given us a profound gift, a realization many forget. When working alone, a witch must embody both God and Goddess, holding the chalice in one hand, blade in the other. We all contain God and Goddess together. Our roles and energy can be fluid as needed. A woman can embody the God. A man can embody the Goddess. One individual can embody both at the same time. We usually do. The gods and goddesses from myth are usually not gender stereotypes, unless their myths were recorded badly. As we are made in their image, the gods themselves contain masculine, feminine, and transgendered elements, as demonstrated in chapter 3.

Alan Moore, critically acclaimed, groundbreaking comic book writer, and noted ceremonial magician, shares many esoteric insights about magick and initiation in his work, particularly in his ongoing series, *Promethea*. (See vol. 1, no. 10 [America's Best Comics], pp. 18–19.) Promethea's magick teacher describes the path of spirituality as the path of the chakras, rising up in consciousness, and how gender and the ritual tools apply to this spiritual awareness. Ceremonial magicians often use the wand to represent the god force where a Wiccan would use the athame. They are both male tools, symbolizing projection. Each tradition simply has different associations and uses for the tools themselves, but the ideas remain constant.

The teacher says, "This is because magicians . . . irrespective of their gender . . . are male. Their symbol is the wand . . . the male member . . . because they are that which seeks to penetrate . . . the mystery. . . . But once they succeed . . . then they become magick . . . they become the mystery . . . become that which is penetrated. . . . They become female. And we become each other . . . become hermaphrodite . . . as we climb towards the godhead . . . of the [crown] chakra . . . the blissful thousand-petaled lotus . . . above the crown of the head . . . that pure white, diamond brilliance where we can step out of time . . . or just . . . as easily. . . step . . . back . . . in."

Magick as a spiritual path is one filled with transgenderism. A magician of any sort must fluidly shift shapes between genders—like a shaman shifts shape in the spiritual realms with animal allies—and leave behind complete attachment to one side or the other. Here is the fundamental reason, at least in the opinion of most queer-positive mystics, why gays, lesbians, bisexuals, and transgendered people were recognized as potentially talented in the mystical arts. Our recognition of the inner masculine and feminine and our ability to balance, heal, and bring this inner relationship out into the physical world are the driving forces behind such talents. They are the source of our spiritual power.

THE WORK

As we continue the Magick Circle Ritual, usually we have a purpose, "the work," to carry out, so we declare it in the ritual space. This is an announcement of intention. The work can be healing, spells, divination, celebration of a seasonal/lunar holiday, or a spiritual journey to seek guidance from the gods. The ultimate work, in the long term, is called the Great Work by many, and is the process of enlightenment and oneness with the divine. Our smaller works in the circle help us on that journey.

Part of actually doing the work is raising the energy necessary to reach and maintain these altered states. The circle is a container, like a cauldron, containing the powers gathered and raised. The ritual adds fuel to the fire, but the energy must be directed. Methods for raising power vary according to a practitioner's aptitude and preferences. Most people use pure intention, concentration, and visualization to direct the intent to the working of the ritual. The training involves simple concentration to access psychic power. Meditation techniques are helpful. Breath work, chant, song, and dance are other more physical methods. The "Charge of the Goddess" and other poetry is used to raise energy and open awareness. (See chapter 9.) Sexual activity is another physical way of raising power; yet another is pain.

Energy, like fire, is neither good nor bad until programmed with intent. The energy is raised for a purpose, and must be infused with that purpose and directed out to the world to manifest the work of the ritual.

Once programmed, the energy is released in the cone of power. All participants raise their hands up, visualizing a cone of light bursting out of the magick circle/sphere. This is the position of the Goddess, hands raised up, almost like the crescent Moon. It can be seen in many of the Paleolithic Goddess statues, particularly the Nile Goddess. When the group releases the energy, the members lower their arms, cross them over the heart, and bring their feet together, forming the God position, like the Egyptian god Osiris (see figure on page 113).

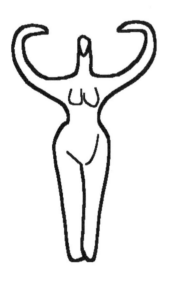

Left: Nile Goddess. Right: Goddess position.

Left: Osiris. Right: God position.

The remaining energy is "earthed," or grounded. The most common way to do this is to put your hands on the ground, or get on all fours, and visualize yourself pouring the remaining energy back into the ground. If bending is a health issue for you, point your wand, athame, staff, or sword to the ground and release the energy through the tool, or press your hands to the altar, and let it flow to the ground through your magical workspace. Wheat or corn cakes are often blessed and eaten to aid in grounding your consciousness back to the physical. Eating activates the physical body and prevents the lightheadedness common after ritual.

RELEASING THE CIRCLE

The circle is released by starting in the north and moving counterclockwise, releasing and thanking all the elements. The God, Goddess, and any other invited spirits are thanked and released. Some think of it as dismissal, but many Wiccan groups find that insulting to their patron deities. "Stay if you will, go if you must" is the usual parting phrase. The circle is then released, tracing or dissolving it in a counterclockwise motion, again starting in the north. I visualize it expanding out, like a ripple in a pond.

You must make sure to release the circle. As you are building with the universal forces, you must dismantle it when done. If you simply walk out of the circle, you disrupt the natural balance of energies in the area. Candles are snuffed out, not blown, as both a sign of respect, and to maintain a balance with the elements of fire and air. All ritual tools are cleaned as needed and put in their proper place on the altar. The cakes, wine, and water are often left out as offerings to the nature spirits and animals of the area.

Exercise 5. Casting the Circle and Creating Sacred Space

Preparation

1. First, follow the simple instructions on pages 145–46 to make some protection potion if you don't already have some.
2. Ritually cleanse yourself. Get into any ritual clothes you use such as a black robe or cloak. If you desire, you can work sky clad.
3. Cleanse the space. Use incense, salt water, and/or candlelight. Visualize the space filling with cleansing white or violet light. Many use a besom, or ritual broom, and sweep the space while visualizing.
4. If this is your first circle, charge each ritual tool before you use it.

The Ritual of the Magick Circle

- Stand before the altar. Do steps 1 through 4 in Exercise 1 (page 60) to get into a meditative state.
- Starting at the north, take your wand, and going clockwise, draw a perfect circle of light around you and the altar three times, big enough to be comfortable, while saying:

  I cast this circle to protect me from all harm. I cast this circle and invite in only the most perfect spirits. I cast this circle and create a temple between the worlds. So mote it be!

- Invite the four elements in, starting in the north and moving clockwise. Hold up a ritual pentacle, the peyton, in your left hand, or simply spread your fingers open, while facing each direction. This particular quarter call uses animals, but you can rewrite it to include different gods and goddesses.

  To the north, I invite the element of earth and the great Bear to join me.
  Hail and welcome.
  To the east, I invite the element of fire and the great Lion to join me.
  Hail and welcome.
  To the south, I invite the element of air and the great Crow to join me.
  Hail and welcome.

To the west, I invite the element of water and the great Dolphin to join me.
Hail and welcome.

- Face the altar and invite the divine into the circle. You can choose a specific god and goddess if you like and create your own poetry to honor them as you call:

    I invite the Goddess and God into this circle, to guide and guard me.

- Light the black and white candles.

    Light any other candles or incense you desire.

    Anoint your wrists and third eye with protection potions and say:

    Blessed be.

- Now you'll perform the Great Rite. Hold the chalice in your left hand, and the athame in your right. If outdoors, under the Moon, look at the reflection of the Moon in the chalice. Hold your blade up to the light and visualize drawing down the silver light of the Moon, even through the ceiling if indoors. The Goddess knows no boundaries. Say:

    As the sword is to the grail, the blade is to the chalice. I draw in the power of the Goddess and God, and feel their love.

    Take the light of the blade and project it into the water by plunging the athame into the chalice three times. I draw a pentagram in the water with the blade, take it out, and then drink from the chalice, feeling the power generated, feeling union with the divine parents. Say:

    Blessed be.

- Bless any cakes for ritual celebration by saying:

    "I bless these cakes in the name of the Goddess and God."

- Do any work to raise energy for the circle, such as poetry, song, or dance.
- Do any spell work, meditations, or ritual celebrations you have planned. (Spells are detailed in chapter 10. For now, simply do the ritual and skip the spells to gain a greater understanding of the magick circle.)
- Raise the cone of power after the *"So mote it be!"* of each spell, assuming the Goddess position with arms raised up.
- Reflect in the God position for a few moments, with arms crossed over the heart.
- When finished with all spells, ground the remaining energy.
- Consecrate any personal or ritual items for general use.
- Close with a circle of healing. Name anyone you know who is in need of healing, on any level. Place their name and image into the circle through your intent. Feel the circle fill with healing color and light. Ask that:

All those in this circle receive the healing they need, for the highest good, harming none. So mote it be!

Raise your arms up and feel the energy reaching those who need it. Ground yourself as needed.

- Release the quarters, starting in the north and moving counterclockwise. Rasie your right hand and say:

  To the north, I thank and release the element of earth and the great Bear.

  Hail and farewell.

  To the west, I thank and release the element of water and the great Dolphin.

  Hail and farewell.

  To the south, I thank and release the element of air and the great Crow.

  Hail and farewell.

  To the east, I thank and release the element of fire and the great Lion.

  Hail and farewell.

- To the center, facing the altar, say:

  I thank the Goddess, God, and all spirits who have joined in Perfect Love and Perfect Trust. Stay if you will, go if you must. Hail and farewell.

- Face the north, pointing with your wand, and release the circle, retracing it counterclockwise, saying:

  I release this circle. The circle is undone, but not broken. So mote it be.

- You can eat the cakes blessed at this time, to aid in grounding.

✳   ✳   ✳

Although most witches memorize the ritual, there is no rule saying you can't write out the steps or words you will perform or say, and have it with you during the circle. I learned the ritual by reading much of it out of my notes as I cast it, and later from writing it out several times, making my own versions. Eventually, the words became a part of me, and I more easily adapted and changed it on the spur of the moment. This is how you build your ritual skills.

The magick circle can be done by one lone priest/priestess, or by a group, dividing up the roles. Groups usually have a high priest and high priestess, even just for the ritual, who guide and direct. They usually cast and release the circle, and do the Great Rite. Other members will clear the space, call the four quarters while standing in that direction, and anoint the coven with potion. Ritual affirmations and greetings such as "So mote it be," "Hail and welcome," "Hail and farewell," and "Blessed be" are usually repeated by the group, to unify the group's consciousness and intentions. Statements with "me" and "I" can be changed to "us" and "we." I actually always use plurals myself, to align my actions with my higher self and spiritual guides.

When not holding any ritual tools, at the quiet moments between ritual acts, the members stand in a circle, facing in toward the altar, and hold hands. Traditionally, one held hands with the right hand over the left, since the right hand sends power out while the left receives, creating an energy circuit. For many, that position can be uncomfortable, so use what feels right to you.

Adapt the ritual to suit your personality and style, but understand that each part here serves a purpose. If you adapt or remove it, or add something new, understand the new purpose and how it adds to the ritual as a whole. Use the elemental correspondences to write new quarter calls. If these words seem too old fashioned for you, modernize them. They may not be formal enough. Fill them with purple prose. Make it more tribal. If you're still working with Christian elements, add them as you feel comfortable. I know some sects of witches who use Jesus and Mary as God and Goddess, or call Jesus the Sun of God, and call him as the fire patron, and Buddha as the air patron. Most traditional witches would be scandalized by it, but if you are drawn to do it, follow your own wisdom.

In the end, the altar tools and ceremony are simply a technology to allow you to access and acknowledge sacred space. They are not necessary. You can cast a circle through sheer intention. Your finger is your wand, your hand is the blade, your body, the pentacle and the chalice to be filled. The elements are within you and all around, in every direction. The ritual itself is a useful structure, but there are many others. I've found that once you are comfortable not only with the ritual, but the purpose behind each part, more creativity comes into play and you forge your own traditions.

Sometimes you will be forced to improvise. Sometimes lack of funds prevents us from getting the "perfect" ritual tool, but that doesn't mean we can't have a perfect circle. Don't have an athame? Consecrate a letter opener. Can't get a silver chalice? Use a wine glass. Necessity is the mother of invention. I've been in many wonderful, unprepared circles, out in the woods or fields. I did not have my robes or cloak. I had no wand, chalice, athame, or altar. But the ceremony was energetic, and internal, and just as effective.

9

Invocation— Welcoming the Gods and Goddesses Within

If you can't see the Goddess in all, then you can't see the Goddess at all.

In ritual, Wiccan priests and priestesses often invoke, or "aspect," a goddess or god. Invocation is the act of inviting divinity within the temple of your body. Invocation is distinguished from evocation, which is simply inviting a spirit or deity into your space, not your physical body. Primal forms of invocation include the Voodoo practice of riding. When a loa, or god, enters or "mounts" a participant during their ecstatic dances, the participant will often speak in the loa's voice, giving wisdom and prophecy. A more sedate version of invocation is the modern practice of trance channeling, during which a spirit will speak through a medium, or channeler, and give wisdom, or even write a book.

Invocation is often confused with possession, particularly by those from a Christian background, because that is the only context they know about in which something similar happens. Possession, in which a random spirit or entity takes over an unsuspecting person's consciousness, is a rare occurrence, contrary to the publicity Hollywood has given it. Invocation is a voluntary practice, performed under set circumstances. When you are done with the ritual, you release the spirit or deity, who returns to its plane of origin, with no lasting effects, other than leaving you feeling a personal empowerment and connection to the divine. You can invoke specific deities to help bolster their attributes in you. If you need to be a warrior for an upcoming court case, yet keep your head about you, invoking Pallas Athena to bolster those qualities in you would be a prudent choice. She is the goddess of wisdom and strategy. Once you identify those qualities within you through the invocation, you can more easily find them in your day-to-day life, by remembering the divine is always a part of you, in ritual or in the courtroom.

The difference between invocation and pathworking meditation is their metaphysical "location." In pathworking, you are going to the divinity, who welcomes you into the spiritual world. For invocation, or even evocation, you are asking them to come to you, into your body, or your ritual space.

Identifying with the divine is an important aspect of the practice of witchcraft, but it is not something to take lightly. Exercise 6 serves as a brief meditative experience of invocation. You will further develop this skill through ritual use. Do it only when you feel intimately comfortable with the Magick Circle Ritual. It is not a mandatory part of the magick circle, but can be part of the experience. You may intuitively experience this invocation in a general sense during the Great Rite with the chalice and the blade, as you draw upon the energy of the Moon or Sun. If this practice is new to you, wait until you are more comfortable and confident. Master the magick circle and then return to Exercise 6.

First repeat Exercise 2 on page 68, and go to either being you wish, or you may find a different being on a different path. Continue to build your relationship with these deities through conversation and pathworking. Ask the deities you meet if you can invoke them at a future date. Even if you do not hear an answer or see anyone, you will get an intuitive "yes" or "no." It will feel correct or not. If you get a "yes," continue with Exercise 6. If not, skip it and try it at a later date, again asking permission first. Only do so if you desire it and it feels comfortable for you. It will come with time and practice.

If you would like, cast a magick circle before doing Exercise 6.

Exercise 6. Invocation

1. Do steps 1 through 4 in Exercise 1 (page 60) to get into a meditative state if you are not in one already.
2. Silently, or aloud, invoke the goddess or god. Simply say:

    I, (state your name), invoke (state the deity's name—if not sure, visualize him or her) now, for the highest good, harming none.

3. Visualize the deity in front of you, moving closer and closer with each breath. Feel the deity step into your body, and merge with you, looking out through your eyes. Each breath stabilizes the connection. You can feel their energy and wisdom within you. Your thoughts become their thoughts. The little voice in your mind, what some see as the conscience, takes the qualities of the goddess or god. Your body, even your gender,

feels different, taking on proportions, at least on the spiritual level, of the deity. Feel the power of this being.

4. Simply be at peace with this new identity and energy for a short time. If it is uncomfortable, go to the next step and release. If you're okay with it, simply explore your new level of awareness. Notice your new thoughts and qualities. How is your outlook changing, taking on the characteristics of this aspect of divinity? Each goddess and god has an individual outlook. Now you are in a greater partnership with him or her. How does it affect you?

5. When done, release the entity by saying:

   I, (state your name), thank and release (state the deity's name), for the highest good, harming none. Hail and farewell.

6. Feel the deity step out of your body and, with each breath, fade away. Do not forget to thank it and say farewell. Feel it return to its side of the veil.

7. Release the magick circle as usual. When done, count from one to twelve, and ground yourself as necessary. Even if you still feel physically oriented, you may need grounding.

❋   ❋   ❋

Invocation is most commonly performed as part of the Great Rite. Traditionally the high priest invoked the Goddess into the high priestess, and the high priestess, as Goddess invoked, invokes the God into the high priest. They often identify with the primal mother and father rather than focus on specific godforms or deities from specific cultural myths. Certain covens will focus exclusively on specific divine couples as the primal mother and father. Other magical practitioners will use the technique of invocations outside of a traditional ritual, to bring the qualities of that god to them in times of need. My book, *City Magick: Urban Rituals, Spells, and Shamanism* talks more about nontraditional uses of invocation, including invoking spirit forms in dance clubs and other social situations.

Using the same process above, but in a much more fluid manner, invoke deity as part of the Great Rite. Identify with the divine within you as you drink from the chalice. Feel your will merge with the divine will, the will of the gods and goddesses. Adapt the technique when working alone and when working with others. The same basic principles apply, and you have the same experience, but the perspective is different.

The Charge of the Goddess

To connect with the divine, and continue to strengthen that connection, many priestesses and priests read what is considered sacred poetry. The Charge of the Goddess is the piece cited most often. It is used to identify with the divine through words attributed to the Goddess, and to help understand more about invocation/aspecting. It is also used to raise energy for spells and other workings, but you don't have to be invoking the Goddess to read it and make it a part of your ceremony. It is a form of worship, celebration, mystery, and means to raise power.

The original version of the Charge of the Goddess was transcribed by Charles Leland from an Italian witch named Maddalena. He published it in 1897 in *Aradia: Gospel of the Witches*. It has been modified several times, first by Doreen Valiente and later by Starhawk. The following is a version I learned from my teacher.

CHARGE OF THE GODDESS

Listen to the words of the Great Mother, Who of old was called Artemis, Astarte, Dione, Melusine, Aphrodite, Ceridwen, Diana, Arianrhod, Brigid, and by many other names:

> *Whenever you have need of anything, once in the month and better it be when the Moon is full, you shall assemble in some secret place and adore the spirit of Me Who is Queen of all the Wise.*

> *You shall be free from slavery, and as a sign that you be free you shall be naked in your rites. Sing, feast, dance, make music, and love, all in My presence, for Mine is the ecstasy of the spirit and Mine also is joy on Earth. For my law is love unto all beings. Mine is the secret that opens upon the door of youth and Mine is the cup of wine of life that is the cauldron of Ceridwen that is the holy grail of immortality.*

> *I give the knowledge of the spirit eternal and beyond death I give peace and freedom and reunion with those that have gone on before. Nor do I demand naught of sacrifice, for behold, I am the mother of all things and My love is poured out upon the Earth.*

Hear also the words of the Star Goddess, the dust of Whose feet are the hosts of heaven, Whose body encircles the universe:

> *I Who am the beauty of the green Earth and the white Moon among the stars and the mysteries of the waters, I call upon your soul to arise and come unto Me. For I am the soul of nature that gives life to the universe. From Me all things proceed and unto Me they must return.*

Let My worship be in the heart that rejoices, for behold—all acts of love and pleasure are My rituals. Let there be beauty and strength, power and compassion, honor and humility, mirth and reverence within you.

And you who seek to know Me, know that your seeking and yearning will avail you not, unless you know the Mystery: for if that which you seek, you find not within yourself, you will never find it without. For behold, I have been with you from the beginning, and I am that which is attained at the end of desire.

There are also modern inspirations called the "Charge of the God." My own coven has found and modified a version—the Charge of the Goddess and God—which fuses both Goddess and God concepts into one charge.

CHARGE OF THE GODDESS AND GOD

Listen to the words of the Great Goddess, who of old was called Artemis, Astarte, Diana, Gaia, Freya, Ceridwen, and many other names. Listen to the words of the Great God, who is Apollo, Ouranous, Dagda, Wotan, Cernnunos, and many more:

Whenever you have need of anything, once in the month, and better when the Moon is full, assemble in some secret place and adore us, the Queen and King of the universe. Sing, feast, dance, make music, and love, all in Our presence, for Ours is the ecstasy of the spirit and Ours is the joy of the Earth. Our law is love unto all beings. Ours is the secret that opens the door of youth, and Ours is the cup that is the Cauldron of Transformation and the Grail of Eternal Life. We give knowledge of the spirit eternal and grant peace and freedom, and reunion with those who have gone before. Nor do We demand aught of sacrifice, for behold, We are the mother and father of all things and Our love is poured upon the Earth.

We who are the beauty of the green Earth, the night sky, the white Moon, the shining stars, and the mysteries of the deep, call upon your soul to arise and come unto Us. For We are the two who move as one in the love of the Great Spirit. We are the soul of nature that gives life to the universe. From Us all things proceed and unto Us they must return. Let Our worship be in the heart that rejoices, for behold—all acts of love and pleasure are Our rituals. Let there be beauty and strength, power and compassion, honor and humility, mirth and reverence within you all. And you who seek to know Us, know that your seeking and yearning will avail you naught, unless you know the Mystery: for if what you seek, you find not within yourself, you will never find it without. For behold, We have been with you since the beginning, and We are that which is attained at the end of desire.

❋   ❋   ❋

Use either of these charges to inspire your own magical prose to raise energy in ritual. One of the most appropriate forms of magick and worship is creativity!

Part III

Empowerment—
Love, Sexuality,
Healing, and Ritual

10

Make a Wish: Spells and Magick

Every thought, every word, and every deed are acts of magick!

Witches make magick. Witches do spells. It's part of the craft or art of the witch, though many people practice the religious aspect of Wicca without doing spell work. In fact, some refer to the religious and spiritual practices as Wicca and the use of magick and spells as witchcraft to differentiate the two disciplines, but most Wiccans I know practice some form of magick and usually claim the title witch as well as Wiccan.

The bending or shaping inferred by the root word *wic* most likely relates to shaping the natural patterns to make magick. All artisans bend their raw materials into something new. Weavers take yarn and thread and make cloth. Blacksmiths take metal and forge it into tools and weapons. Potters take raw clay and make vessels and art. Witches take the forces of life and make magick.

The principles of magick could be several volumes all on their own, but the basic concepts of spell work, both technical and moral, can be boiled down to some extremely simple ideas. Aleister Crowley defined "magick" (on page xii of *Magick in Theory and Practice*) as "the Science and Art of causing Change to occur in conformity with Will." His definition has stuck, although others have added to and abridged it on occasion. Magick is simply putting intent out into the universe to cause change. We all do magick. Life itself is magick, and we partake in it whether we realize it or not. When we manifest something through creating an intention and follow it up with hard work, we are still doing magick. It may not be as flashy as the entertainment industry has led us to believe, with special effects of light and sound, but magick is based on results. When we focus on the power of the mind-body connection, use positive thinking, or creative visualization, or even say a prayer asking for healing or answers, we are doing magick. Whenever you make a wish and it comes true, you are doing magick.

Basic Components of Spell Work

While we are all magick and do magick to a certain extent, not everyone does spells. Spells are magical formulas. You can follow the formula in a spell book or improvise one, as long as you keep some basic rules in mind. Magick is very similar to cooking in that respect. There is a foundation to work from, but much creativity can be injected into the process. Just as there are many schools of cooking, there are many traditions of spell casters, each with a different method and philosophy. Each may borrow a bit from the other, but ultimately sticks to their own style. Witchcraft represents one tradition of casting spells that encompasses many styles, but there are other paths.

While those who pray or visualize understand that the universe, God, Goddess, Great Spirit—whatever you choose to call higher spiritual intelligence—responds to their intent, but many who use these techniques don't quite understand how they work. And you don't need to; it still works. I don't understand the finer points of my car, but it still works when I put the key in and step on the gas. Witches and other spell casters understand how spells manifest and, like a good mechanic or racecar driver, use that knowledge to make their intentions more powerful.

THE LADDER OF THE ELEMENTS

Witches use the model of the five elements as the model of creation. By casting a circle, they are unifying all aspects of the creative process, making their wishes clear on all levels. They create a container to build their intent and the energy to manifest their intent, until it reaches a critical point. Other techniques of magick do not contain and build the energy in quite the same manner as a magick circle, though in the end, if you get results, use what works.

When you do a spell, think of reality as a ladder. You are on the bottom rung, on the level of the earth element. As you cast your circle and get into a ritual space, you reach up to connect to the top rung, Spirit, as manifested by the gods and goddesses. You make contact with the highest level of creation and your own divine essence.

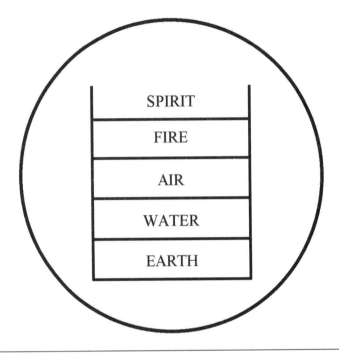

Ladder of the elements

It is important to realize that the spiritual level viewed at the top rung actually envelopes and permeates all the other levels. Spirit runs through all the elements.

Through your will, your fire element, you send out your intention. You must have the necessary will to manifest it. Then you form the idea completely in the mental level, using the element of air. You think about exactly what you want. Then you bring it into form on the astral level. You can do this through visualization, or strong emotional response, since the astral is the realm of water, the emotions. Witches focus on Perfect Love and Perfect Trust, unconditional love, by casting the circle. Only when an intent takes root in the astral/emotional level will it precipitate into the physical, earthly level.

SPELLS WORK—IF YOU DO, TOO

The spell itself, though seeming very esoteric and occult because of the ritual, usually manifests in a very mundane manner. The channel by which it reaches you could be so mundane, you would be tempted to chalk it up to coincidence. If you've been hunting for a new job with no luck, and you do a spell for a new job, and soon find one, the effect may not seem that magical.

If you continue with spell work, you can find your life to be a series of lucky coincidences. The first few can be easily dismissed, but soon you realize something else is at work. Such simple success may never convince a true skeptic, and if you go into a ritual with overwhelming doubt, you reduce your chances of success. Magick responds to your thoughts and intentions. If you think it is nonsense and it will never work, it won't, because those are the instructions you've given it. You will only get what you project.

A healthy amount of skepticism with an open mind is fine when you start. I think you even get a bit of beginner's luck from the Goddess and God. I wasn't convinced of this whole spell idea when I started. I thought of it as somewhat delusional, but since a few of my good, respected friends felt it was valid, I tried it with an open mind, and got some amazing and consistent results.

Although we don't like to hear it, we are responsible for allowing the spell a pathway to manifest in our lives. We have to be willing to open the door when we hear a knock upon it. Sometimes that means following up magick with real, commonsense work. Here is where we lose people, and why many spells fail. People want life to come in one quick, easy-open package, but it doesn't always work that way. It doesn't make life any less magical. Sometimes our subconscious fears are at work, and that is why it is so important to do our previous meditations on a consistent basis. A witch must know him- or herself intimately, and clear the subconscious, to wield magick effectively.

If you are doing the job spell mentioned above and you do not send out any résumés, answer any ads, or make any contacts, you are not giving the spell a chance to manifest. You are not opening the door to it. It is possible someone will just knock on your door, but less likely. If you open the door, the spell can bring many more opportunities.

Spells, meditations, and psychic phenomenon give us experiences of the divine—direct, personal experiences. We work in the realm of ideas, knowledge, and experience. We do not need faith, because we experience things that change us deeply. That's why it's unnecessary to preach to skeptics. No amount of conversation will convince, but if you have a personal experience, you can choose as to how to interpret that experience. When you consistently enter a meditative state and intend to make something happen in your life, and it consistently does, it is hard to doubt the existence of some form of higher intelligence and interconnectivity.

A Word about "White" vs. "Black" Magick

Many people who are ignorant about magick divide it into white and black categories, respectively, indicating good and evil magick. Although there are those with less than helpful intentions, most witches do not label themselves as good or evil. The traditions of Wicca are based in healing and working with the flow of natural forces rather than against them. If you encounter a black, evil, or Satanic witch, they are probably playing with movie stereotypes or using traditions that have nothing to do with modern Wicca. Many witches wear black, but they do not do so because they identify themselves as black or evil witches. Nor do good or white witches only wear white. Black robes are a tradition from the Burning Times, when one needed to hide in the forest. Black as a color also draws in energy. Some hermetic magick traditions divide their craft into white, black, and gray magick, though most witches do not.

Spell-casting Ethics and the Laws of Magick

Many people fear the power represented by magick, or fear it will give them an unfair advantage against people who do not use it, or don't believe in it. Others feel it goes against fate, or the will of the universe, and is ultimately harmful because it disrupts what is meant to be or in their natal chart. Although there are spiritual patterns and inclinations, we all have free will. Witches make their own fate. We all do so, but witches actively acknowledge their part and pursue their own happiness.

Spells do not usurp divine will. They work within the divine laws. As physical life follows the laws of physics, spiritual energy follows an equally stringent, if less equally defined, set of laws. The principles of magick are based on them, and many esoteric systems have tried to define them as a science. If the divine did not allow this manifestation, we would not have it.

The first ingredient to any spell casting is to connect with the higher consciousness, the divine, and our own divine identity. We work within the frame of higher will. Most spells have a disclaimer affirming this, asking this spell to "be correct and for the good of all involved, harming none." Other traditions simply ask that it be "in accord with the will of the Goddess and God." Only through connecting with higher will do you find your role and place in the world. Only through active partnership with the divine do we develop a relationship with it.

Witches strongly believe in balance and harmony on all levels. We do not renounce the physical world with vows of poverty or chastity, yet do not work excessively for material gain. A balance must be reached between physical and nonphysical needs. We don't seek to renounce all attachments and desires, but use spell work to actively reflect on our needs as well as our wants. If we feel our life is lacking something, we must ask why. If spells are not working to manifest what we need, perhaps there is something more appropriate in store for us, from the Goddess and God. Discover what the root of the desire is. Perhaps our human will is not quite in harmony with divine will.

THE WICCAN REDE

You are responsible for all that you do, and all your magical intentions. We believe in the Rule of Three, meaning all that you do comes back to you three-fold, or three times as strong as your original intent. This is the core concept of spell work. You send a nonmaterial intention out into the universe. The universe sends it back to you stronger than you sent it out, in a boomerang-like effect. The extra energy is the energy that allows it to manifest in the physical world. Likewise, all intentions, even if directed at someone else, eventually return to you, so keep your intentions with the highest of morals.

Witches have no set philosophy regarding moral conduct. We have no commandments or scriptures telling us how to live, only our own personal responsibility demonstrated in the Wiccan Rede. A rede is simply a motto or good saying, so it is not even considered a law. You have ultimate responsibility as to even choose to follow the rede. The basic intent is "do what thou will, and let it harm none." The Wiccan Rede is a variation on the Golden Rule, "Do onto others as you would have done onto you." If you follow that simple advice, no more is needed.

WICCAN REDE

Bide the Wiccan Law ye Must
In Perfect Love and Perfect Trust.
Eight words the Wiccan Rede fulfill:
An' ye harm none, do what ye Will.

What ye send forth comes back to thee
So ever mind the law of three.
Follow this with mind and heart,
Merry ye meet and merry ye part.
Blessed Be.

A simplified version of Aleister Crowley's take on the ethics of magick is: "Do what thou wilt shall be the whole of the Law. Love is the law, love under will." Many people misunderstand that, too, not realizing we are talking about Divine Will and Divine Love. Our spiritual development is based on finding our true will, or divine will, through love. Llee Heflin, author of *The Island*

Dialogues, has his own version of "The Law" as a take off on Crowley's version: "DO WHAT THOU WILT IS THE WHOLE OF THE LAW. LOVING IS THE LAW. THERE IS NO WILL BUT LOVING."

Scott Cunningham, one of the most influential modern authors on Wicca, whose writings inspired the solitary and self-initiated Wiccan community, made a wonderful and truthful statement about the heart of magick. "Magick is love. All magick should be performed out of love. The moment anger or hatred tinges your magick you have crossed the boarder into a dangerous world, one that will ultimately consume you" (*Cunninghams's Encyclopedia of Magical Herbs,* p. 8). His words are wisdom I carry with me always.

AVOIDING HARMFUL MAGICK

Witches do not do curses because we know what we send out will come back to us. We never seek to harm another, striving to keep in balance. Magick can be used for many things, but never to cause the misfortune of another. If we do any harm on any level, intentional or unintentional, we actively work to make amends for our wrongs. Some texts about older traditions of magick, from the Dark and Middle Ages, often recorded by the witch hunters of the Burning Times, would mention curses and "black" magick, but this is ancient propaganda and has nothing to do with us now. Even if certain past traditions dealt in curses and magical wars, they reflect the consciousness of the time. There is a reason why it was called the Dark Ages. They do not reflect on modern witchcraft any more than the sacrifices of the Old Testament reflect on modern Judaism and Christianity.

If you feel you are sending out harmful intentions without even meaning to, there are ways to correct that. Our slang is filled with jibes and put-downs that may not carry strong intention, but the words themselves are pretty powerful. Our thoughts and words are another way of manifesting ideas into form. The word "spelling" comes from the concept of magical spell. The wise ones, the priest and priestess in charge of the magical symbols, were the first to learn language. When we name-call, judge, gossip about, and insult others, we are sending those harmful thoughts back to us, threefold. We can never take anything back, but we can send intents out to prevent them from manifesting. By saying or thinking "I neutralize that" after such unconscious intentions, we prevent it from manifesting or returning, and eventually program ourselves to be more conscious.

Gossip and barbed play talk is even more prevalent in the gay community, and it can be hard to retrain ourselves in the midst of what has become normalized behavior. In these cases, we have to understand the power of our words even more. If we claim our power to do magick, then we must claim the responsibility to use it wisely at all times. Every thought, word, action, and moment is magick when we live our true magical lives.

Working with the Moon

Traditionally, witches look to the Moon as a guide to the flow of the world, particularly for planning ritual. As the Moon governs the ocean tides through gravity, it also governs the tides of magical energy. Notice how many people feel and act differently during the full Moon. Those who work in emergency care units and law enforcement know to mark their calendar and expect trouble. The Moon pulls on the fluid in our brains and bodies, causing us to open psychically or go a bit crazy, reminding us of the root word of lunatic and lunacy—*luna*, the Latin for "moon."

Because of the relationship the Moon has with the Sun and Earth, it goes through several stages of reflecting light, from our viewpoint on Earth. While astronomy divides it into four quarters, witches often align the Moon with the image of the Triple Goddess. The Moon is usually considered a feminine energy, as the Sun is masculine. The Moon cycle is twenty-eight days, like the menstrual cycle. The Moon influences the subtler, emotional, and psychic aspects of life.

When the Moon is waxing, the light is growing stronger and brighter with each night, starting in the first quarter, as you see a sliver of light. When the Moon is half full, it moves from the first to the second quarter and continues to wax until it reaches the full Moon. When the Moon is waxing, the time is right for drawing things to you, manifesting things in your life, and making plans. The closer to the full Moon, the more powerful the energy and quicker the manifestation. That is why witches are known to worship under the full Moon. The earlier waxing stages are for long-term plans, to manifest further in the future. The waxing Moon relates to the maiden goddess, huntress with the silver bow. The full Moon is the Mother Goddess, full of life and power.

As soon as the Moon goes full, it starts to wane, and enters the third quarter. Some traditions say the Moon is full for a number of days, but technically, it is always waxing or waning. There is still a lot of energy under the waning full Moon, but the energy is different. The waning Moon is a time for banishing and removing obstacles in your life. Anything you want to release and leave behind—both physical obstacles and internal mental and emotional ones—should be released on a waning Moon. When the Moon goes half dark, it moves from the third to the fourth quarter, until it goes completely dark.

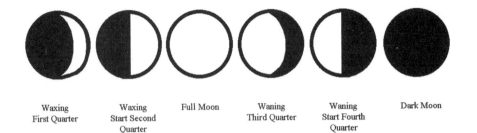

| Waxing First Quarter | Waxing Start Second Quarter | Full Moon | Waning Third Quarter | Waning Start Fourth Quarter | Dark Moon |

Moon phases

Astrologers and astronomers call this the new Moon, but witches call the short time it goes dark prior to reentering the first quarter the "dark of the Moon." This is the most powerful time for banishing and protection magick.

As the Moon wanes and enters the dark, this is the time of the Crone Goddess, the dark underworld Goddess, filled with power and wisdom. The Crone goes into the dark totally, and returns again as the Maiden, as the Moon enters the first quarter and shows a bow of light. The cycle begins again.

Although you can see the Moon and its cycles, and learn to feel them intuitively, you will not know the exact shifting of the quarters unless you have an astrological calendar that includes the time the Moon changes phases. If possible, also get one that tells you what astrological sign the Moon is in. As you grow in your astrological knowledge, such information will come in handy for planning spells. Each zodiac sign also carries a flavor and personality. Most astrological calendars will list short descriptions of the signs. Always check the Moon phase before doing a spell.

Witchcraft is all about paying attention to the cycles and patterns of life, including the seasons, the Moon, and the cycles within each person. We all have cycles and patterns in our emotions, mind, body, and soul, and a good witch follows the wise advice given to us by the ancient priestess of the Temple of Delphi in Greece, originally a temple to the Earth Mother Goddess Gaia: "Know thyself."

Petition Spells

Petition spells are the simplest. With them, you are simply petitioning the Goddess and God to manifest your will. No fancy equipment is needed other than the standard altar setup and some paper.

Before you enter a ritual space, reflect on what you want to manifest. Think long and hard about what you want. Be careful what you wish for, because you just might get it. Magick is a powerful tool, and spells shouldn't be used without definite thought and reflection. What you want now, in the heat of the moment, may not be the best possible solution to your current situation. Think about what you want, and focus on the results. How would you feel, think, and live if this spell result occurs? Meditate on it, asking your divine patrons and animal allies for guidance.

Magick can usually be divided into several broad categories, such as protection, love, healing, prosperity/money, inspirational, purification, divination, psychic development, spirit work, and spiritual union. Usually the goal is either tangible and concrete, like obtaining money, or more nebulous in nature, like connecting to a spirit guide. Think about how your intention may fit into one of those categories.

Once you have decided, write out your spell on a blank piece of paper. Look to the Moon phase to determine how to word it, as attracting or banishing. If you want to attract something, and the Moon is waning, you can ask to banish all obstacles that prevent you from attaining it. You can use colored paper, to match your intent. (See "Candle Spells" on page 137 for more information on colors.)

CREATING THE PETITION

Using my tradition, I write out spells in the following format:

I, [write your name], ask in the name of the Goddess and God to be granted/freed of [name your intention]. I thank the Goddess and the God for all favors, and ask this be your will, for the good of all involved, harming none. So mote it be!

"So mote it be" simply means "it is so" and makes the request an affirmation in the present. When you focus on a desire and repeat it over and over again, such as "I want money" all you do is create a greater want for money. If you affirm "I want money and I have money now" you create your own prosperity.

After you write out this spell, read it aloud before doing a ritual. Make sure it sounds and feels right to you. Did you leave any loopholes in it? Be specific about your goal, but not about how the goal manifests. If you desire a new job, be specific you want a job you will enjoy, in whatever industry you feel qualified, that will pay you within a range that will meet your needs. If you simply want a new job, you may see a "help wanted" sign at a fast-food restaurant and not in the computer industry, when you had originally intended a high-tech job in your field, but did not verbalize it. If you said, "a job as vice president at IBM, with a corner office and third parking spot from the door," you narrow your chances of getting it, and shut out many other opportunities with which you would be quite happy. Or you can give up the details to higher will and simply state, "a job that is correct and good for me on all levels." I might write the spell on a waxing Moon like this:

I, Christopher, ask in the name of the Goddess and God to immediately grant me a new job, in my chosen profession, that is completely acceptable to me. I thank the Goddess and the God for all favors, and ask this be your will, for the good of all involved, harming none. So mote it be!

Make the petition fit your personality, but remember the important points noted above. Wicca is not a craft of rules, but suggestions. A witch discovers what speaks to his or her own soul, and uses those elements, but pays homage and respect to the wise ones who have gone before.

When you are ready to cast the spell, cast a magick circle to create a sacred space, as outlined in chapter 8. After the Great Rite, feel the power of the circle. Feel the energy you have gathered. Think about your intent. Read your spell. I like to read it three times, once for the conscious, once for the lower self, and once for the higher self. As you read, you are building energy. Burn the paper in your cauldron or other heatproof vessel. Visualize your intent and raise the cone of power, assuming the Goddess position and releasing your spell. Assume the God position and meditate and visualize your intention. Psychic information may come to you at this point, such as a vision or impression of the results, or someone who will help with your situation. If you have anymore spells, do them now. You can do up to three per person in the circle, but you cannot "share" spell credits. If someone in the circle doesn't do a spell, that doesn't mean you get their spell potential and can now do six. Then ground the energy, release the quarters and the circle.

When you practice in a group, the group should echo your "So mote it be," adding their intention and help for your spell. It is considered good manners to read your spell to the group prior to the ritual, so everyone knows what they are contributing to in ritual, and if someone is uncomfortable with your intention, to do it alone rather than in that group.

If the spell is for the good of all involved and you raised the energy and released it, it will manifest soon. Typically, results can occur a day or several months later, depending on the circumstances. The best advice I have is to let go of the intention once you've done the spell. If you talk about it, think about it, and obsess over it, you are actually drawing the energy back and are not letting it fulfill its programming.

Spells with Poetry and Verse

A long-honored tradition in magick is writing a spell in the form of poetry and verse. You can use any form of poetry, though simple rhyme is most often used. Melody can also be used in the spell crafting, along with other musical instruments. Many chants and mantras are actually magical songs. Make sure to still be clear in your intent while being creative. A good rhyme means nothing if the spell doesn't work.

With a job-seeking intention, I might create a verse like this:

By the light of the full Moon,
I banish all my fear,
Asking the God and Goddess for a boon,
To bring me a new career.
A job I love and appreciate,
With all the things I need,
I ask this to be my fate,
And will go where you lead.

You would recite a spell like this in a magick circle as I previously described, though you can repeat it more than three times if it's in musical form. Be creative and have fun writing your own spell poetry.

Candle Spells

The power of candles is undeniable. Candle magick is one of the simplest, yet most effective forms of magick. The candle is a microcosm of the altar. Fire is evident in the wick. It needs air to consume and keep the fire burning. The wax is the physical element of earth, and the melting wax and condensation is the water element. All it needs is your intention to infuse it with spirit.

CHOOSING YOUR CANDLE AND ITS COLOR

Choose a color that is in harmony with your intention. The following is a list of traditional magical correspondences to color, but if you are intuitively drawn to use another color, then do so. I also prefer unscented beeswax taper candles, but use what you like. Since you want it to burn quickly and completely, I don't recommend large, pillar candles, unless you are working a long-term spell.

Red: Power, energy, lust, sexuality, protection, warrior spirit, aggression
Orange: Memory, mind power, logic, creativity, travel, healing
Yellow: Solar energy, health, power, wealth, illumination, revealing truth
Green: Love, attraction, money, comfort, art, music, food
Blue: Peace, tranquillity, communication, expression, creativity, prosperity, opportunity
Purple: Intuition, psychic ability, spirituality, awareness, guidance, prosperity
Violet: Cleansing, clearing, releasing, spirituality, higher awareness, ritual
White: Union with God/Goddess/Spirit, all-purpose, enlightenment, banishing, protection
Black: Grounding, centering, relaxing, nature, facing the shadow, attracting, protection

You can do candle magick without a magick circle, particularly if you're in a pinch, but I've found them far more powerful inside the magick circle. You create your intention as you would for a petition spell. You can even write out your petition in addition to performing the candle magick. Hold your candle and feel your energy mingle with it. Through intent, fill the candle with your spell. I visualize the candle as an empty glass, and fill the glass with water, or energy, until it can take no more. Speak, think, and/or visualize your spell. Raise the candle in the cone of power, and then light it before assuming the God position, or grounding the energy. If you wrote a petition, either burn it as usual, or place the paper under the candleholder.

Let the candle burn as along as possible. It is the engine for your desire. If you can't let it burn down at once, snuff it out and re-light it at the next opportunity. Don't blow it out. Breath imbalances the element of air in the candle. Snuffing seals in the power until lit again. Don't leave candles unattended.

While burning, the candle will continue to make magick, even when your attention is focused other places. This is particularly good for healing magick. The spell is not complete, however, until the candle burns down completely. Candle spells can add an extra component of energy, color, and fire to standard petition spells, for those drawn to them.

Natural Magick

The province of the witch is in all natural forces. The elements, animals, Earth, sky, and Moon all play a part. Another important aspect of the craft is the relationship with nature and nature spirits, as represented by the land, trees, and plants. The old wise woman and cunning man were great herbalists, knowing the secrets of the plants not through trial and error, but through communication with the plant spirit itself, learning how the plant was to be used and prepared for maximum effectiveness. Pharmaceutical companies go to the jungles of Africa and South America to speak with shamans, to learn their herbal knowledge and synthesize new drugs, yet they don't have the same relationship to the nature spirits as the shamans, and are not able to reproduce the same results.

Each plant has a specific vibration, and its energy is harmonious with certain intentions, and not with others. Choosing plants and using them in magick can greatly add to the energy raised, if you research your plant thoroughly. The clues of the plant's magical purpose are found in its color, shape, habitat, traditions, medicinal use, and mythology, as well as by speaking with the plant spirit directly.

PLANT WISDOM

Here are some plants and their correspondences. Some even play a part in gay-positive myths.

Apple: Apples are the fruit of Aphrodite, and associated with female companionship and lesbian love. Apples are a powerful symbol of the divine Goddess in her many forms, but also associated with Dionysus. Apples are the food of the dead in Celtic mythology, used in many Samhain, or All Hallow's Eve, rituals today. Apples, and golden apples in particular, are associated with immortality. In magick, apples are used in communion with ancestors, love spells, and healing. They can help heal the relationship between the body and spirit, when the mind feels the body is betraying it in illness.

Apricot: Apricots are a fruit of love, as their flowers, stems, juice, and pits are used in love charms, to make the love more "sweet." It has associations with androgyny, mixing the flavors of peach and plum, and associated with both gays and lesbians.

Cinnamon: Cinnamon is an herb of spiritual expansion, used for raising the vibrations of any area or person. This wonderful spice is used in money potions, purification incense, and the development of psychic powers. All this, and it tastes good, too.

Copal: Copal is a resin used in South America for protection and purification, to sanctify a temple space when burned like frankincense. Mexican magick workers also use copal in love spells.

Dragon's Blood: No dragons are harmed in the harvesting of dragon's blood. Actually, it is another resin, found in a palm tree and dried into a bright red powder. Dragon's blood is power, used for protection, exorcisms, and enhancing the power of any other spell or incense. It smells particularly good when burned. Dragon's blood is also used in love spells to ignite the fire of passion and lustful intent.

Fennel: Magically, fennel is used for healing, fertility, and virility, as well as protection and in purification rites, for removing unwanted spirits. The witch trials uncovered a possible surviving shamanistic cult called the Benandanti, or "good walkers." In their visions, these healers would "fight" spirits of illness and withering during the change of seasons. Their spiritual weapon of choice was the fennel stalk. Fennel is also associated with Dionysus, whose followers used wands of fennel with pinecones on the top, an obviously phallic symbol. Interestingly, the Italian word for "fennel," *finocchio*, can also be associated with homosexuality.

Frankincense: Frankincense is an herb of the Sun and Jupiter, two powerful planets bringing light, awareness, and success in many areas of life. The Sun's vibration works on the more physical levels, while Jupiter works on the spiritual. Frankincense is used for protection and prosperity spells.

Ginger: Gingerroot is a powerful herb, used for almost everything, including protection, prosperity, and healing. As a fire herb, ginger, when eaten or taken as a tea, heats you up, adding to your personal power and bolstering your immune system.

Grape: Grape is the sacred fruit of Dionysus/Bacchus and of many other resurrected vegetation gods. It is a symbol of fertility, of multitudes, both physical fertility and the fertility of the creative spirit. Grapes are now associated with the planet Neptune. The highest form of Neptune is unconditional, spiritual love, and divine psychic experience. Unfortunately, Neptune also rules over illusions, delusions, and addictions, as you can imagine with the product of grapes—wine. Both should be used in moderation.

Hyacinth: Hyacinth flowers are named after a mortal lover of Apollo's, who transformed his shed blood into the beautiful flowers. Hyacinth is used in gay love spells and to cure nightmares and obsessions with unhealthy relationships. The herb also symbolizes beauty, peace, and spring rebirth, and is used to ease pain in childbirth.

Ivy: Ivy is another plant sacred to Dionysus. It is used for luck, love, and fidelity.

Jasmine: Jasmine is an herb of psychic abilities, dreaming, and prophecy. Using jasmine before going to sleep will induce special dreams. It also can be used in love spells to focus strong emotions of love, and in money spells to aid in our psychic projection for wealth and prosperity.

Lavender: This is one of the great all-purpose herbs. The scent of lavender is calming and relaxing, aiding in reducing insomnia and stress. Lavender is associated with happiness, harmony, and long life, dispelling sorrow and darkness. Lavender can also help manifest peaceful, loving relationships. It has also been used in love potions by gay male witches.

Lettuce: Lettuce is sacred to the Egyptian god Set, and in both ancient Egypt and in modern Latin America, lettuce is associated with male homosexuality. Strangely enough, some use lettuce magically to induce chastity in those too tempted by the flesh.

Lily: Lily is considered to be an androgynous plant, containing both masculine and feminine qualities in the stem and flower parts, respectively. Lily is used to break love spells when cast between specific people, and in general used as protection, resurrection, and good-fortune symbols.

Mandrake: Mandrake's strongest association is protection. The root, usually shaped like a human, was believed to scream when harvested by age-old witches. They would use the human-shaped root as a poppet, like a voodoo doll. Obtaining a whole root is not always easy, but the powdered or chopped root is used for protection and purification. Mandrake is also said to aid in communication in matters of love and money.

Myrrh: This is the scent of the Moon and Saturn, releasing the powers of the Goddess and used for dream work, meditation, and psychic abilities. Myrrh is also used in healing magick, to purify the body of all illness or imbalanced energy. Mystics throughout the ages have paired myrrh with frankincense to make a temple incense of incredible strength.

Narcissus: Narcissus is named after the Greek youth who fell in love with his own image in a pool of water. Here we have the origin of "narcissism," but many feel this was originally a homoerotic theme. Narcissus didn't know it was his image, but that of another male, though some tell the story of Narcissus's androgynous good looks indicating he thought it was a young woman. The flower is used in love spells, especially those for self-love. It is also used to connect with higher spiritual vibrations, viewed as a "trumpet of the gods" to hear the inner voice.

Pansy: Pansy is now used as a slang for effeminate men, but originally they were flowers of love and tenderness called heart's ease. Magically, pansy can be used in love spells, but also in spells to heal a broken heart or an ended relationship. The plant spirit, when used in a remedy known as a flower essence, is said to be antiviral. I've used it quite well in my healing work with people who have STDs.

Papaya: The papaya is a symbol of male homosexuality in modern Chile, and also symbolic of female genitals and lesbianism. Papaya is used in manifestation spells of any kind, for granting wishes, love, and protection spells. Its enzymes are also very good for digestive disorders.

Peach: In ancient China, the peach symbolizes immortality and relationships between men. They also used peaches, twigs, and pits in exorcism, protection, and healing rites. Peach is the fruit of wisdom and love, used in spells to gain a wise and mature relationship.

Rose: Rose is the premier flower for love spells and potions, sacred to Aphrodite/Venus, Adonis, Dionysus/Bacchus, and Eros/Cupid. In alchemy, the rose is linked to androgyny and Hermes/Mercury. Roses are a symbol of love, passion, fire, and life. In ancient Greece, male lovers gave each other roses, and they were also associated with priestesses of Aphrodite on the Island of Lesbos. In modern times, roses are used in all manner of love spells, gay and straight, representing the sweet flower of love, as well as the danger of the thorns. Magically, roses are also used for psychic abilities, peace, prosperity, and purification. Rose water can be used like incense to cleanse a home or ritual space.

Sandalwood: Another favorite incense, sandalwood can be combined with most other woods and resins for a pleasing smell. By itself, sandalwood is a plant of spiritual awareness. One knows and understands the spiritual energies behind life when using sandalwood. In healing magick, it is used to get to the spiritual root of the manifested illness. Sandalwood is also used for love spells invoking spiritual partners and to manifest wishes.

Solomon's Seal: With six-pointed flowers, Solomon's seal is a plant of protection. Usually the dried root is used, both herbally and magically. You can use the root in protection charms, or bury it at the four corners of a home to create a shield of protection around it.

Vervain: Vervain is the witch's herb, used for everything. Traditionally, you gather vervain on the summer solstice, and use it for purification, protection, love, healing, sleep, dreams, peace, prosperity, and prophecy.

Yarrow: Yarrow is a fire and water herb of passion and love, and of protection and attraction. Yarrow is used in fidelity spells and in marriage and partnership blessings. Yarrow teaches us about healthy boundaries, as it grows on the side of roads and at the fence edge in gardens. Yarrow helps you define your own personal space and relationships, for the good of all involved.

❊   ❊   ❊

For more specific information on magical herbalism, I suggest *Cunningham's Encyclopedia of Magical Herbs* by Scott Cunningham (Llewellyn) and Paul Beyerl's *Master Book of Herbalism* (Phoenix).

You can use these herbs magically in several ways. Herbs can be mixed together for a variety of effects. You can use them in magical cooking, aromatherapy, incense, herbal teas, medicines, and baths. If you are making any magical herbs to consume, please consult the above books or a good traditional herbal book to make sure none of your ingredients are poisonous. Some of the most powerful herbs magically are also the most deadly.

Charms

One of my favorite methods of herbal magick is a charm bag. Create your intention just as you would for a petition spell. Charms can be for more general intentions, such as general protection, health, or success, though they can be used, like candle spells, for specific events. Gather the herbs that fit your intention, or use a recipe from a spell book, and cast your magick circle. To raise energy, you will create a charm.

Hold each ingredient in your hands. You can keep them in bowls or other containers, especially when using sticky resins, but you want to feel connected to the herbs. Feel yourself attune to the energy and spirit of the herb, as you feel when you consecrate your ritual tools, as described in chapter 7 (page 91). Place your intention, visualization, words, and willpower into each herb, catalyzing its magical power. One by one, mix them together and consecrate the entire mixture. Place the mixture in a pouch with a color appropriate to your intention. You can simply get a square of cloth, roughly 5" x 5", depending on how big you want it, and tie the ends together to create a bag. I like fairly small charms so I can carry them in my pocket without anyone noticing. Place the charm wherever you feel it will do the most good. Here are some formulas to guide you.

Protection Charm

Make this protection charm during the waning Moon, and carry it in a black bag. The charm projects a field of protection and awareness to avoid injury and harmful energies. Keep it on your person, in your car, or in your home.

2 tsp. sea salt
1 tsp. frankincense

1 tsp. myrrh
1 tsp. vervain
1 tsp. mandrake
1 tsp. yarrow

Prosperity Charm

Make this charm under the waxing Moon, and carry it in a blue, red, or green bag.

2 tsp. cinnamon
2 tsp. ginger
1 tsp. jasmine flowers
1 tsp. dragon's blood

Health Charm

Make this charm on the waxing Moon to bolster your immune system, particularly during the winter months. It will ward off colds and flu, but you should empty it after the winter is over, bury the ingredients in the ground, and burn the cloth bag. Make a new one for each winter. Carry it in a green, yellow, red, or black bag.

2 tsp. apple blossom, bark, or dried fruit
2 tsp. ginger
1 tsp. myrrh
1 tsp. sandalwood

Potions

The witch's potion is another powerful and ancient use of herbal magick. Though most potions from fairy tales and myths are consumed, here you will be using potions like cologne or perfume, anointing your pulse points and chakras to absorb the magical vibrations. You can also used them to anoint candles and other ritual tools. Making them in an oil or saltwater base will help preserve them. A correctly made and stored potion, kept out of sunlight and high temperatures, can last many years, since you only use a few drops at a time. I like making small batches so I can always experiment with more formulas and ingredients. If you want to make edible potions, I suggest you thoroughly study traditional herbal medicine and add these magical principles to your folk medicine.

Potion magick is much like the herbal charms, except this time, they get a little wet. Formulate your intention and gather your ingredients and materials prior to making the potion. You can bring some altar tools to the kitchen and cast a circle around the stove. I prefer to do it in my altar room, and use a small aromatherapy potpourri simmering dish. It makes just enough, I use a candle flame for heat, and it feels more magical to me. Use what works for you, though most witches suggest not using steel or iron unless you are brewing a protection potion. Iron grounds magical energies. Fairies from Celtic folklore are said to be trapped only by prisons and chains of iron. Use glass or enamel.

Again, you will charge each individual herb with your intention, and then drop it into the base water or oil. If you use water, dissolve the sea salt in it prior to adding the herbs. The sea salt will help preserve the potion. A good proportion to use is at least one tablespoon per cup of potion. Stir in each ingredient. I like to stir each one nine times, because nine is a magical number of the Goddess, repeating through infinity. Take any multiple of nine and add the digits together, and you get nine again: $2 \times 9 = 18$; $1 + 8 = 9$.

If you are using oils, make sure you use essential oils for your ingredients, with a good base oil, such as grape seed, apricot kernel, or jojoba. Synthetic oils do not carry a magical energy. Use about equal amounts of base oil to essential oil. If you like a stronger scent, use more essentials, but consult a good essential oil book. Certain oils, such as cinnamon, do not react well with the skin and should be greatly diluted. When in doubt, dilute a drop and do a test patch before wearing any given oil. Swirl in each drop of the essential oil, as you add it to the base oil. Take your time and smell the oils. Connect to their power. Since you can't touch the oils as you would herbs, you have to connect to the plants mentally and through scent.

When all the ingredients are in, charge the whole mixture. Let it cool. Strain if necessary, and bottle it, keeping it in a dark, dry place. Make sure to label it. Once you have a few, it can be hard to keep track of your potions.

Here, I give you two versions of each type of potion: one based in salt water, the other in essential oils. The oils will smell better and stronger, but they can be expensive. The water potion will yield more and last longer. Use either one, or feel free to revise as needed. Potions are like cooking—the intent and basic ingredients count, but it's not chemistry. Nothing will explode if you don't follow the formula exactly.

Protection Potion

Protection potion is one of the first potions you should make, even if you don't plan to make many potions. It can be used as part of the Magick Circle Ritual, although some traditions use mixtures of sea salt and water instead of a protection potion. Make a protection potion under the waning Moon, as close to the dark of the Moon as possible.

Water Based
2–4 c. spring water
2–4 tbs. sea salt
1–2 tsp. frankincense
1–2 tsp. myrrh
1/2–1 tsp. vervain
1/2–1 tsp. dragon's blood
1/2–1 tsp. juniper berries
1/2–1 tsp. patchouli
1/2–1 tsp. iron powder or nine iron nails
1 pinch of wolf's hair

Oil Based
20 drops of base oil
10 drops of myrrh oil
10 drops of frankincense oil
1 drop of dragon's blood oil or 1 pinch of dragon's blood

Wolf's hair can be found in some witch supply shops, or maybe you're lucky enough to be near a wolf shelter that you can visit and collect some fur during shedding season. Harm no animals in the process of getting it. Some substitute the hair of a wolflike dog.

Psychic Potion

Make this potion close to the full Moon.

Water Based
2–4 c. spring water
2–4 tbs. sea salt
1/2–1 tsp. vervain
1/2–1 tsp. rose buds or petals
1/2–1 tsp. star anise
1/2–1 tsp. cinnamon
1/2–1 tsp. thyme
1/2–1 tsp. bay leaf
1/2–1 tsp. lemon balm
1 piece of silver jewelry
1 moonstone crystal

Oil Based
20 drops of base oil
10 drops of lavender oil
10 drops of sandalwood oil
3 drops of rose oil
1 piece of silver jewelry
1 moonstone crystal

After you have added all the plants, dip into the potion a piece of silver jewelry that you have cleansed and consecrated. Silver is the metal of the Moon, opening psychic abilities and intuition. I kept a small silver hoop earring in the bottle of my first psychic potion. Also, place a moonstone, cleansed and consecrated, into the potion. When you strain and bottle the potion, you can take out the jewelry and stone.

Making Your Own Spells

With the tools given in this chapter, feel free to make your own spells, following these guidelines, but using your natural intuitive abilities and creative talents. These are not the only methods of magick. You can use crystals, cords, and magical symbols. You can place your spells in the jewelry you wear, into the metal of your car, and in the wood or stone of your home. There is a whole world to discover. Put on your witch eyes, and look at everything in a new, magical way.

Exercise 7. Cast a Spell

Choose an intention and cast a spell in a ritual magick circle. Use the formats above as a guide, or be inspired to create something new. Start out with the basics, and as you do more spells, you can get more elaborate. The act of spell casting is the act of empowerment; understand that your thoughts and actions cause change, and you must take responsibility for the changes you desire in life. If you are unhappy or unfulfilled, only you can change your life.

Write down your formulas, experiences and results from each ritual and spell in a journal. Witches call this journal a book of shadows. It serves as both journal and recipe book, keeping all your magical works for future reference. If you find a spell that works, and want to do it again, it's best to know exactly what you did to make it so successful.

11

Love Magick

All magick is an act of love, Perfect Love and Perfect Trust.
Open my heart to the magick of love.

All magick is love magick. All magick and all healing, when done in the spirit of correctness, harming none, is love. What is magick, but change, growth, and transformation? Magick is birthing a new event, a new reality, into the physical plane. For witches, magick is an imitation of the creative union of the Goddess and God. Through their love, coming together in union, they created all of reality. They are the divine mother and father, parenting all of reality as their child.

Birthing a new reality is a miracle that occurs in each of us, not exclusively women or heterosexual couples. Modern fertility rites celebrate the fertility of the creative soul, the idea, the mind, and the heart, as well as that of the land and people. When an artist draws a new picture, a writer drafts a new piece, or a musician sings a new song, they all are giving birth in a sense, to a magick that comes from the spiritual quest, from yearning and searching for their own truth. The ultimate truth, the ultimate answer to any question, is love. Love is the answer to all questions, at least our spiritual ones. Love is the necessary ingredient to create something lasting. Other emotions and thoughts can fuel the process, get us to question and express, but when we create, we touch that divine spark, our highest aspect. The most wonderful creations come through us. We are the vessel, the instrument of creation, but not necessarily the author. The divine is the author of our actions. And to touch the divine, we move through a sense of unconditional love, a connectivity to all things, everywhere. This is the heart of witchcraft.

Unconditional love is not an emotion like anger, joy, envy, or sadness. It isn't even like romantic love and family love. Unconditional love is a state of being, a state of consciousness. Unconditional love, by its very definition, is unattached. You are not putting conditions to your love such as, "I will love you only if you act in a manner that is acceptable to me," or "I will return your love if you think the same things I do." No, unconditional love has no conditions. I will love you no matter what you do or say or think.

You can be in unconditional love, emotionally, mentally, and spiritually recognizing your connections to all others, but not be pleased with another. I used to think unconditional love was acting nice all the time, being in "sweetness and light," never thinking an unhappy, unkind thought, never disagreeing or causing problems. I had this vision of the saint or yogi, always smiling, always happy, and always at peace, regardless of the circumstances. I have discovered that the human journey is not always so, and we must honor our feelings, thoughts, and personal truths. Unconditional love does not mean unconditional relationships. You do not have to like someone to love them unconditionally. While you strive to remain in love, it does not mean you allow someone else to abuse you or take advantage of you and later deny your feelings. If you let others harm you in such a way, you do not love yourself unconditionally. You do not love yourself enough to get yourself out of harm's way.

If someone wants to cause harm, and others voluntarily play those games, then that's fine. We all have free will. Some think magick and spells go against the principles of free will, but they are the expression of ultimate free will and ultimate responsibility. You can learn quite a lot from "getting into the playpen" as my yoga teacher Stephanie says. But when you realize it is a game, you can walk away from it. You do not infringe on another's right to play, but you choose not to play yourself. You can become detached from results and center yourself in love and compassion.

Perfect Love and Perfect Trust

Perfect Love and Perfect Trust create sacred space. If we carry those ideals with us always, wherever we go and whatever we do is sacred space. Perfect Trust is trust in the Goddess and God. We do our part in partnership with the divine to create our reality, through listening to our intuition, affirmations, meditation, and spell work. But we also trust that if we find ourselves swimming up stream and get knocked back into the ocean it will lead us to where we need to be, even when we don't understand or desire it.

Perfect Love is unconditional love, a spiritual love with no bounds. It is the love we feel from the Goddess and God. They are our unconditional, loving parents and grandparents. Although that is the ideal parental model, we don't always receive unconditional love growing up, from family or friends, particularly when we are perceived as being different. Witches must pick up the torch of unconditional love to then give back this love to the Goddess and the God. That might sound easy to do, thinking of indistinct images of the divine goddesses and gods, but as witches, the divine is manifest in everything and everyone. Loving the Goddess and God is loving the Earth, sky, animals, trees, minerals, and all our brothers and sisters. Like the Native American traditions, all life is our relations; all life is family: the stone people, tree people, and sky people. If the divine is in everything, all must be loved. This is the spiritual quest. This is the witch's path.

The Energy of Self-Love

I am thankful that one of my first teachers, Laurie Cabot, stressed the need for self-love, self-esteem, and self-acceptance as an integral part of the craft. Perhaps I heard the stress on this teaching because I really needed to hear it, and I took it to heart. She didn't know I was gay and closeted—no one knew. If she did, she never mentioned it to me. She did mention that you must first find love in yourself if you are to ever attract love in your life. You must generate love internally before you create the vibration of love in a ritual circle.

All magick is energy, and one of the principles of energy is something hermetic magicians call the Principle of Vibration. The hermetic laws are fundamental principles of how the universe works, physically and metaphysically. In some ways, our science is just catching on to them. Everything vibrates. Everything moves. Even when matter appears to be standing still, its atoms are moving. More important, the energy animating it is moving. Similar vibrations gather together.

That seems to fly in the face of the well-known "opposites attract." Opposite charges are attracted electrically, and there is a certain truth to the attractions between people. Many have used this fundamental law to explain the "truth" behind heterosexuality, seeing gender in pairs of opposites, and to justify their view of homosexuals as aberrant because they lacked the opposing forces. The lesser-known spiritual truth is similar vibrations gather together. Think of the people in your life. We tend to attract those we relate to best.

They may have similar tastes, backgrounds, politics, or personal views. They are harmonious and gather together. They share a vibrational or energetic quality.

In the physical world, think of vibration as density. All matter has different densities. When a scientist takes a soil sample, he or she can put it into a centrifuge, which will spin the heaviest material to the end while the lighter material remains on top. The spinning motion forces materials of the same density to gather together. If you were testing for a lead contaminant, it would move to the end, being a heavy metal.

On a spiritual level, the universe is like a centrifuge. The planet spins. It orbits the Sun. The solar system orbits another point. The galaxy itself spins. Everything is orbiting, like the spinning of a centrifuge, causing similar vibrations to gather together. The principles of homeopathy, using "like to cure like," in small doses, instead of using larger doses of opposites to cover symptoms, contain a more holistic and less toxic view of healing.

Both the attraction of opposites and the attraction of similars are at work in the universe, even in regard to love magick. A heterosexual couple, opposites by gender, can meet on similar backgrounds and values. A homosexual couple, similar in gender, can come together with opposite dispositions and interests.

The laws of the universe, the attractive forces holding and governing reality, are the bonds of love between Goddess and God. Sometimes similars work best in a given situation, and sometimes opposites work best. Each situation is individual. To generate the love of a magick circle, it is easier to start with the vibration of love, to build upon that foundation of love. Love is simply the easiest and most effective way to do magick, and a healthier path of spirituality. Other methods exist, but they might not be the most appropriate and healthy. To learn magick is to learn more deeply about love, and love starts at home. If you cannot generate the vibration of love internally, for yourself, you will have a hard time feeling love, or being in the consciousness of love, for anyone else.

I knew I didn't feel these things, and I wanted to be a witch and do magick, so I had to learn how. Once you make that determination, it will be much easier than you think. I feel witchcraft saved me years of traditional psychotherapy. I still went to healers and therapists, but owning the paradigm of magick, change, and self-responsibility has allowed me to go further than many of my friends and peers. I didn't just discuss my problems with someone. I changed the energy.

Coming from a strong Catholic background, I spent much of my life thinking there was something wrong with me, that I was evil or less than human because I was gay. I felt that if I was bad, then I would assume that bad persona, and try to be uncaring, aloof, and self-involved, hoping to keep others from seeing what was on the inside. Fortunately a friend introduced me to Wicca. Though many people get involved because it's "cool" or "hip" to be a witch now, with many modern movies and television shows, I really delved deep into the spiritual concepts behind it, looking for something to tell me I was okay. Not only did I find that in witchcraft, I found the roots of a tradition tangled with the gay culture throughout history, and I found that people like me were honored at certain places and times in our history. No one ever told me that before.

I imagine discovering the secret history of witchcraft is as important to all women, lesbian or not, to find a time in our history when the divine was seen as woman, and cultures that honored women's values and leadership. It is important to know that you were not always persecuted or discriminated against. Wicca brings these bits of truth to the light. Witchcraft encourages you to love yourself first. You must honor yourself, and through it, love and honor all of creation. Love is the key to all magick.

The Ethics of Love Magick

One of the areas people are most interested in when starting the path of the witch is love spells and potions. This is what most people think of when I say the words "love magick." They don't realize that the foundation for it is in self-love. We all have a basic human desire for companionship, love, romance, partnership, and sex. Many believe that witches and pagans have it easy in the love department. If you desire someone, you simply put a spell on them, and they love you back. I hate to shatter that illusion, but it is not that simple. Love spells that force the will of another are not in Perfect Love and Perfect Trust, because they do not honor the free will and the choice of your "target." That's not to say it's not possible, but I don't recommend it. Remember, all magick starts with self-love and self-respect. Some would call violating the will of another black magick, but to avoid returning to archaic labels with racial undertones, I simply think of it as harmful magick.

If you feel the need to "make" someone love you, first examine how you feel about yourself. Making someone "love" you is not a love spell at all. At most, it will be illusionary. If you do feel you love and honor yourself, there is no reason you cannot do a love spell, simply do it with the proper ethics in mind: "Do what thou will and let it harm none." Would you want someone to force your will? I think not. If you don't want it done to you, don't do it to someone else, no matter how much you think it is "meant" to be.

Magick cannot change orientation. You cannot make someone straight become gay through magick. If a "straight" man or woman comes to you through your love magick, then at the very least, they wanted to experiment. Magick cannot change your own orientation either. I remember hearing a story a few years ago about a gay man who was stalking singer Stevie Nicks, claiming she was a witch and could cure him of his gayness. Although her music is bewitching and loved by many pagans, I don't know if Stevie is a witch, but even if she is, she couldn't grant that wish.

Choose Your Love Spell—Carefully!

On page 154, I offer two types of love spells. Both types should be done on the waxing Moon. Friday is considered the day of love, sacred to Aphrodite and Freyja, so love spells will be more powerful on a Friday. May and October, when the Sun is in Taurus and Libra, respectively, are wonderful for love magick. June is good for long-lasting partnerships and marriages, as it's named after the Roman goddess Juno, wife of Jupiter and benefactress of marriage.

The advantage of the first type of spell is that it allows the universe and its infinite number of channels to fulfill your spell. In your finite wisdom, in the middle/ego self, you do not know all the possibilities. When you work your spell, your perfect partner could have passed you on the street, but the open nature of the spell will give you opportunity to meet for the first time, under more ideal circumstances. Sometimes we end up with a partner we never would have imagined, but it works because the time and place are right. Love spells help increase the chances of a right-place, right-time meeting.

You can also add other conditions to the spell, such as a partner with a job, who is thoughtful, has blond hair, or whatever else you desire, but each condition closes the door to a possibility. If you want a blond and there's a great brunette, then you've shut yourself off from that experience. Use only the conditions that are most important to you, if at all. If you tend to attract interest from the opposite sex, and want a same-sex partner, you can put that condition in as well.

The disadvantage of the second type of spell is it must be done in a spirit of correctness, and a spirit of nonattachment. That's harder than it sounds. If you have a crush on someone, or any strong attraction, and want to be with them badly, you are not unattached to the result. You want it. You desire it. When it comes to the strong feelings of love and sex, often we are not thinking with our head, or even our spirit. We want what we want, and are absolutely convinced that it is correct and right and meant to be. We can justify a lot by thinking things are fated and meant to be, but if you truly feel that, then why do a spell? When you do this specific love spell, you really have to mean that you want it to be "correct and for the good of all, harming none." Not only do you say it, you must mean it, and back it up with intention. This means you ask for this relationship, but if it infringes on this person's free will or higher spiritual plans and is not beneficial for you both, then you ask this spell not to come true. I don't know about you, but when I've been tempted to do such magick, I want it to work out the way I desire, not for a highest good that might make me unhappy or unsatisfied on a personal/ego level. I've only used the first, nonspecific type of love spell because of this. I've seen the second type of spell go awry and create some unhealthy relationships. Remember what you do comes back to you threefold.

An Open Love Spell

The first kind of love spell you can do is by far the most preferred. If you are seeking a relationship in your life, form your intention without a specific person in mind, such as:

I, [state your name], ask in the name of the Goddess and God, to be immediately granted a romantic relationship with the partner who is correct and good for me, harming none. I thank the Goddess and God for all. So mote it be!

A Specific-Person Love Spell

The second type of love spell does focus on a specific person, but in a spirit that harms none. You are asking to have a relationship only if it is correct and for the good of all involved, without infringing on this person's free will.

I, (state your name), ask in the name of the Goddess and God, to be granted a romantic relationship with (state your intended's name), only if it is your will, correct and for the good of all, harming none. So mote it be!

Getting What You Wish For—How Love Spells Really Work

Sometimes we don't know the mechanics behind love magick, and let our subconscious get in the way. Before I came out, I was a witch. I desperately wanted contact with another man, and had great success with all my other spells, so I thought I would do some love magick. And I did quite a few spells and charms in college, wanting it so badly, but having difficulty letting my intentions go to do their work. For a while, I thought more is better, but it really isn't. In fact, the more I did love spells, the more difficulties they caused me until I could simply let go and relax, like I did with other spells.

During this particular batch of spells, I noticed one boy kept popping up in my life right after each spell. We had mutual friends and would run into each other. I was certain he was gay, and in fact, he was one of the few people I knew who I thought was definitely gay. I was also fairly certain that this was how the love spell was manifesting because I suddenly saw him on campus all the time when I rarely saw him before. I came out to him and he told me he wasn't gay and didn't understand how I had that idea. He was one of the first people I came out to and things between us went fairly downhill from there. Even after our conversation, I would still run into him after using love potions and charms, leading to several embarrassing moments. What I didn't realize at the time was the experience was preparing me for my "highest good" in ways I couldn't imagine. Within two months, I was dating my first boyfriend and came out to all my friends and family. The love spells worked, fulfilling my instructions once I let go of my obsessions to make them work, and let go of how I thought it should manifest. The spells manifested in a way I would have never guessed, drawing to me the first boyfriend who was right for me then. Your intention is always important, but do not be attached to the way it is fulfilled. My college acquaintance came out years later and, from all accounts, is quite happy. Perhaps our conversation was for his "highest good" in the end too.

Intention

My early love-spell experience was an important lesson in intention—we must be mindful of the intentions we carry with us subconsciously. The reason why we meditate and do affirmations is to know, understand, and clear our consciousness of all that does not serve our highest good. As I was doing my first love spells, I kept the intention in the back of my mind that I wanted a boyfriend to really be "sure" I was gay before I told everyone. I knew I didn't like kissing girls, but wanted to make sure I liked boys before going through this somewhat traumatic experience of coming out. Although that was never part of any of my formal rituals, I carried it with me subconsciously. After two months with my first boyfriend, I was really sure this was for me. I felt comfortable with myself and unashamed. Once I identified those feelings and came out to many of my friends, our relationship ended and I was single again.

I subconsciously intended one thing. Once I got it, I thought it was something else, a stable, long-term relationship. I hadn't intended on manifesting a long-term partner, just a fun, easygoing boyfriend. My needs and desires changed, but my old intentions were still manifesting. I hadn't put any energy into the new intentions. Afterward, I dated a lot, but with the intention of finding a stable relationship, a potential life mate, and I remained single until I found one a few years later.

Intention, conscious and subconscious, is everything. When mystics say we create our own reality, they are correct. Students question this, asking why someone would create disease, poverty, and unhappiness. Perhaps we are creating from a higher consciousness, and although it seems unpleasant now, the events are serving to prepare us for a new role, in this life, or another. But most often, we are creating unconsciously, from the baggage we carry around in our minds and bodies. That is why self-healing, introspection, and awareness are vitally important to the witch, because as our actions take place in sacred space, they manifest more quickly in the physical world.

Before doing any love magick, think long and hard about your intentions, short term and long term, conscious and unconscious. Do you carry the energy of self-love within you, or are you looking to find it through a partner? Do you need a partner to love you to love yourself? If so, then do not attempt love magick. The love must originate inside you first. If you can't find it, do love spells to generate self-love, self-esteem, and self-acceptance. Only then will you attract a loving partner and be able to have a healthy relationship. If you feel you are ready for love magick, here are some formulas and ideas to spark your own creativity. You can modify them for self-love spells if that is your focus now.

Love Magick Tools

The colors of love magick are green and pink, the colors of the heart chakra. You can use anything associated with those colors and the heart in love magick, such as crystals like rose quartz, green aventurine, pink calcite, morganite, emerald, and malachite, which you would cleanse and then consecrate for romantic or self-love. Blue-greens, including turquoise, are considered more spiritual love colors. The planet Venus is named after the Goddess of love, and most material used in love spells and charms is "ruled" or influenced by the energies of this planet. Copper is the metal of Venus, and another color associated with love and attraction. It turns green over time. Plants associated with love and Venus are apple, apricot, bleeding heart, catnip, columbine, crocus, foxglove, geranium, heather, hibiscus, hyacinth, orris, passionflower, peach, raspberry, rose, strawberry, vanilla, and yarrow.

Surprisingly enough, Venus is also associated with money. Venus is really the power to attract whatever we value, and two things we value greatly in our society are love and money, and they are the two areas that also cause some of the greatest pains.

When doing a love spell, you may want to call on the Goddess and God as embodied by a specific homoerotic deity. Certain ones were considered patrons of homosexual love in the ancient world, such as Adonis, Aphrodite/Venus, Apollo, Artemis/Diana, Ereshkigal, Eros/Cupid, Hecate, Hermes, and Hyacinth. As you invoke the Goddess and God in a ritual circle, name one of these deities, asking their favor in your work. You should make a connection to them through meditation prior to the ritual and be comfortable with their energy.

It's also good to get into the habit of thanking the gods for all favors, those that manifest and even those that don't. Specific deities often have certain incense, flowers, oils, and foods sacred to them that you can leave out on your altar, burn, or place in an outdoor shrine. You can also offer your time and services to the greater community in honor of the deities. Community pledges are even more important than traditional offerings.

Exercise 8. Love Ritual

You can use this as the basis of your love magick rituals. It calls upon four Greek deities in the four quarters, along with the element and a spirit animal. Although very similar to the regular Magick Circle Ritual, the focus and flavor of this ritual is for love, self-love, romantic love, healing love, and sexual love. If you prefer another pantheon, make changes to suit your own needs.

- Stand before the altar. Do steps 1 through 4 in Exercise 1 (page 60) to get into a meditative state.
- With your wand, cast a circle in the usual manner, saying:
    I cast this circle to protect me from all harm. I cast this circle and invite in only the most perfect spirits of love and harmony. I cast this circle and create a temple of Perfect Love and Perfect Trust between the worlds. So mote it be!

- Call the quarters:

  To the north, I invite the element of earth, the great Bear, and the goddess Artemis to join me. Please bring your power to my work of love tonight. Hail and welcome.

  To the east, I invite the element of fire, the strong Lion, and the god Apollo to join me. Please bring your light to my work of love tonight. Hail and welcome.

  To the south, I invite the element of air, the winged Dove, and the god Hermes to join me. Please bring your wisdom and skill to this magick. Hail and welcome.

  To the west, I invite the element of water, the loving Dolphin, and the goddess Aphrodite to join me. Please bring your powers of love and attraction. Hail and welcome.

- Face the altar and say:

  I invite the Great Goddess, mother of all. I invite the Great God, seed of creation.

- Light the black and white candles.
- Light a love incense, such as rose, patchouli, or vanilla. You can make your own incense, using other herbs of Venus.
- Anoint your wrists and third eye with protection potions, saying:

  Blessed be.

- Perform the Great Rite, saying:

  As the blade is to the God, the chalice is to the Goddess. Tonight I evoke the powers of love and creation. I call on the Perfect Love and Perfect Trust of the Goddess and God. I drink in the power of this love, so I may feel this love and create the love that is for my highest good. Blessed be.

- Recite any of the charges on pages 122–24 to raise energy and increase your connection, if you desire.
- Do your spell work, raise the cone of power in the Goddess position, then reflect in the God position, and finally ground the remaining energy as needed.
- Close with a circle of healing if you desire, saying:

  All those in this circle receive the love and healing they need, for the highest good, harming none. So mote it be!

- Release the quarters, starting in the north and moving counterclockwise:

  To the north, I thank and release the element of earth, the great Bear, and the goddess Artemis. Thank you for your aid and power. Hail and farewell.

To the west, I thank and release the element of water, the loving Dolphin, and the goddess Aphrodite. Thank you for your aid and love. Hail and farewell.

To the south, I thank and release the element of air, the winged Dove, and the god Hermes. Thank you for your aid and wisdom. Hail and farewell.

To the east, I thank and release the element of fire, the strong Lion, and the god Apollo. Thank you for your aid and light. Hail and farewell.

- To the center, facing the altar, say:

   I thank the Goddess, God, and all spirits who have joined in Perfect Love and Perfect Trust. Stay if you will, go if you must. Hail and farewell.

- Release the circle, saying:

   I release this circle. The circle is undone, but not broken. So mote it be.

❋   ❋   ❋

The following are spells, potions, and charms that I have made over the years for myself and others. They can be made inside the circle created by the Love Ritual above. Use them as part of your own magical inspiration and create the spells that work best for you.

Love Potion

When you make this potion and charge the ingredients, you must specify what kind of love—romantic, self-love, or a general love—for whatever is correct and good. The lemon verbena is used to improve communication in love, and the patchouli is for physical love.

2–4 c. spring water
2–4 tbs. sea salt
½–1 tsp. yarrow
½–1 tsp. orris root
½–1 tsp. rose buds or petals
½–1 tsp. patchouli leaves
½–1 tsp. lemon verbena
3 drops hyacinth oil
2 drops rose oil
1 drop patchouli oil

Copper wire or cleansed penny
Rose quartz

Mix the potions in a ritual circle as you would normally, but add the drops of essential oil to improve the scent. Then wear a few drops on each wrist. Do not consume it internally. The potion will bring love, lasting for three to four days, to change the vibration of your aura. Anoint green, pink, or red candles with this love potion if you want to do a candle love spell.

Love Charm

I made this charm to attract a lover who is correct and good. This particular formula I designed for myself, to attract a gay man. If you're doing a lesbian love spell, you'll want to reverse the proportions of hyacinth and patchouli. Use 21 drops of patchouli and 5 drops of hyacinth.

2 tsp. rose buds or petals
½ tsp. yarrow
½ tsp. raspberry leaves
1 tsp. damiana
1 tsp. dragon's blood
1 tsp. mandrake
½ tsp. lavender
½ tsp. orris root
½ tsp. cinnamon
21 drops hyacinth oil
9 drops rose oil (or substitute rosewood oil)
5 drops patchouli oil
3 drops jasmine oil (or substitute lemon oil)
Rose quartz

Mix the herbs together with the oils, and charge a rose quartz to be the heart of it. Place it into a red or green bag and keep it with you until you find and enter a relationship with your new love. If you choose not to put it in a charm bag with the crystal, you can simply burn it as an incense on self-igniting charcoal to release its attractive powers.

Healing with Love

As the ancient wise ones were the spiritual leaders and physical healers in their tribe, part and parcel of the witch's craft was counseling, often on matters of the heart. When we experience a loss, we often call it a heartbreak, because that can literally be what it feels like. As relationships can bring people to the heights of passion, love, and spirituality, they can also bring us to the depths of our soul, forcing us to look into the mirror.

If all acts of magick are love, then all acts of healing are love as well. Having friends or a professional counselor to talk to when you're going through difficult times is very important. You must build a support system to help you work through your feelings. Denial of feelings cures nothing, it simply postpones the heartache. I've helped a few people release things they have carried around with them, psychologically and energetically. If we hold on to something that no longer serves us, it prevents us from completely healing and being completely alive.

An important part of magical practice is taking responsibility for our own healing and happiness. Many witches rush to magick when they want something, but forget it is there when times are tough. Magick is, first and foremost, a healing art. Even though you are down and depressed, you can still cast a circle or meditate. It will elevate you, and through your training, reconnect you to the source of Perfect Love and Perfect Trust, because, in truth, you were never disconnected; you just forgot in your pain. If you can't do it for yourself, seek out friends, covenmates, healers, counselors, or support groups that can help you, in both magical healing, and on every level.

Love Thyself

Self-love is the first place we should start with love magick. Without self-esteem, we cannot truly do magick as a form of spiritual practice. Because I'm publicly known as a witch, people ask me all the time to do spells for beauty. I've been asked to reveal the secret spells that will increase the size of your penis, grow larger breasts, get an instant muscular or curvaceous body, become taller, shorter, younger, blonder. Although I believe magick can do many things, and perhaps most of those, they really have no benefit in the long term without self-esteem. If you are looking for emotional security outside of yourself you will never find it because everything changes. The only thing you can count on is the relationship you build with yourself. I am sure you have noticed that depressed people often look less attractive. When they snap out of the depression, an inner light shines out of them, increasing their attractiveness, regardless of the body type. The most powerful beauty spells are those that bring out the inner strengths and beauty for all to see.

Spell for Self-Love

To do this spell for increased self-esteem and self-love, you'll need 5 pink candles and a cleansed copper coin.

- Light the five pink candles in a magick circle, all blessed with the intention of self-love. Feel their light bathe you with love.
- Infuse the copper coin with the intention of self-love. Say:
  I charge this coin to attract to me an abundance of self-love and self-respect. So mote it be.
- Release the circle and let the candles burn.
- Carry the coin with you, separate from your regular money. Keep it in a special pouch or pocket on your left side. The left side is the emotional side of the body. You can even carry it in your left shoe.

You can adapt this spell for making changes to your physical look, as well. If you're working on weight loss, do the spell on the waning Moon. If you're building muscle or creating a new image, do it on the waxing Moon. Remember, magick is powerful, but follow it up with real-world action. Spells to lose weight don't work if you don't change your habits.

After you have been carrying the coin around for a while and feel you no longer need it, bury it with a blessing of thanks.

Healing the Heart Bath

Unlike the other love spells, this one does not need to be done on a waxing Moon, but if you do this healing spell on a waxing Moon, phrase your intention to bring healing and self-love. If the Moon is waning, ask for your heartache to be banished, and let the water drain out of the tub before you get out. Be sure to cleanse the rose quartz before you do the spell.

3 tsp. lavender
2 tsp. rose petals
2 tsp. rosemary

1 tsp. catnip
1 tsp. chamomile
1 pinch of pansy flowers, if available
4 tbs. sea salt (optional)
1 rose quartz

Charge the herbs for healing a broken heart and soothing the end of a relationship. Place them in a muslin or cheesecloth bag and let it soak in warm bathwater. You can charge the sea salt separately, and add it loosely to the bath, to dissolve it. Salt absorbs all harmful energy, even sadness, anger, and pain. The other herbs aid in the purification process. Bless the rose quartz for self-love and place it in the water.

Soul Mates

People, gay and straight, talk a lot about finding their soul mate, but don't take the time to think about what that really means. "Soul mate" can have different connotations for different people, and the way you define it can indicate your healthy and unhealthy expectations in a romantic relationship.

Too often, people define a "soul mate" as "my other half. The person that contains the other half of my soul, like we were split before we were born, and spend the rest of our lives trying to find each other in the world. We are spiritually drawn to each other, and meant to be together." Sounds very romantic, but not very real. One of the first spiritual lessons to learn is that you are complete, just as you are. You need not do anything or be anybody. As a spirit with a body, you are prefect just as you are. Experiences can make things more or less enjoyable and satisfying on a personal level, but spiritually, you are complete. Trauma, abuse, illness, and emotional or mental difficulties may cause parts of you to feel less connected, rejected, and scattered and the healing journey asks you to recover your fragments and unify yourself—but no one contains half your soul.

A partner may complement your soul. A lover can resonate with you, but you shouldn't look to someone to complete you, for that places a lot of unreal expectations on your partner, even if they believe they are half of your soul. Subscribers to this system think the challenge is in the meeting, as if all life leads up to this dramatic, whirlwind romance. Events may fit together like a blockbuster movie, and once the lovers meet, problems disappear, like two pieces of a two-piece puzzle coming together. The pieces fit, puzzle solved, no more problems. Life doesn't work that way. Relationships are about partnership, balance, compromise, and these things need to be worked out through good-old-fashioned communication and expression. Magick doesn't whisk away the need to talk. Just because someone is intuitive or psychic, that doesn't mean he or she always knows what you are thinking and know when you are hurt and upset. Relationship is a journey together, side by side, not a puzzle. If you spend your walk looking to solve the puzzle and win the game, you miss the journey itself, which is the true reward.

Another definition of a soul mate is one who was your partner from a past life. Yes, those who we knew in other Earthwalks seem intimate and familiar to us, almost immediately, but you may have had many different mates from many different lives. And you can meet up with more than one in this life, or find a brand-new one in this life. All of them are not your "one and only" soul mate. We will explore past lives in chapter 13, but if you do any work in this area, you may find that someone who is your parent now may have been your child in lives past. Siblings become lovers and vice versa. You may feel an intimate, soulful link to someone in this life, but that doesn't mean they are going to be your romantic partner here and now. I feel a definite bond to my mother, and we feel we are soul mates, traveling many lifetimes together and changing roles. We have always felt this way, even when we were Catholic. But I knew that in this life I had a partner waiting for me with whom I also felt an intimate past-life connection. There is not just one intimate connection in every life. Explore the possibilities.

The problem with these views of soul mates is that they paint very unrealistic portraits of love, romance, and a spiritual relationship. We feel that because we have a soul mate, that they know us so intimately, no problems should arise. They know what our souls want. Perhaps our souls do, but our personalities, and our egos, do not. We are all having a human experience, and the quest for this perfect, divine, and often dramatic love can blind us to the wonderful relationships all around us. Movies, books, and television paint this relationship not only as the ideal, but the expectation. When we don't have a romance like the ones we see on television, we feel somehow cheated. When we get the drama and things don't turn out happily ever after, we want to quit. No one tells us relationships are work. They are hard work. These media relationships are so great to us because we close the book, turn off the TV, or leave the theater at the end of the drama. We don't see the day-to-day life and problems.

True love can be an expected and desired part of your relationship, but you do not need the Hollywood dramatics and intrigue to follow it. Be real in your relationships.

I prefer the term "life mate," a partner for us in this lifetime, with no expectations or responsibilities from any other incarnation or role. Even if a life mate feels like we have known him or her forever, we must actively work to reestablish these connections and get to know each other all over again. It's like catching up with a friend you haven't seen in ages. It can be a wonderful, magical, and spiritual love, but not the fantasy people associate with the words "soul mate."

Think about your feeling on soul mates. Do you use the term? If so, what expectations do you bring with it? Have they helped or hindered your quest for love and romance? Knowing yourself is the key to magick.

Rose Life Mate Spell

This is a particularly powerful spell used to find your mate, your partner. Attempt it only when you are ready, and feel good about yourself.

1 red rose
1 vase
spring water
1 pinch of brown sugar
1 pinch of dragon's blood

- Cast a circle and perform up to the Great Rite. Take the water of the chalice, after taking a sip, and put it into the vase.
- Add a pinch of brown sugar, for love and sweetness.
- Then add a pinch of dragon's blood, for power and passion.
- Take a freshly cut, live rose, and meditate with it. Feel your connection to the spirit of the rose. Join with its still living spirit. Pour out your feelings and emotions. Match the pure energy of love.
- Ask the gods of love and the rose energy to immediately *"bring me the life mate that is correct and good for me, harming none. So mote it be!"*
- Put the rose in the water and let it stay on your altar for a day or so, then let it dry up and keep the petals or whole rose in a safe, dry place.

If you are ready, and your mate is ready, you should come together in three to four months. With your mate, plant your petals in the ground after you've been together for five months.

If you don't meet at this time, let it go and don't do another love spell for a year. Work on your relationship with yourself and enjoy life, then try again.

❋   ❋   ❋

This is a powerful spell. Use it wisely. I met my husband through it. In my meditation during the spell, I was "told" by the Goddess that I would know him because he would give me a rose long before I ever thought of giving him one. On our first date, meeting through a personal ad and going out for coffee, my partner, Steve, gave me a rose as I walked him to his car. He nearly had to catch me as I almost passed out from the shock. We've been together ever since.

Love magick can be an act of transformation. We often have to kiss many "frogs" to find our prince or princess, but the first frog we must really kiss is our own self. We must transform ourselves through self-love and acceptance before we can ever find that ideal mate.

Rekindling Passion

As a relationship develops, many people feel that the passion of the relationship, the intensity, wanes. I understand the sentiment, but energetically the relationship is transforming. Our expression of passion is transmuting as the relationship deepens. At first, we experience an almost animal magnetism, drawing us together romantically and sexually. When we meet someone new, we are attracted to him or her because he or she expresses our dormant energies. Opposites have a strong attraction. I'm not talking about gender. In fact, the genders aren't really opposites. They are complements. The attraction of opposites comes from wanting to learn from someone who seems different from us, who seems to hold some knowledge, power, or way of living we do not express. We want to learn from them, and through relationship and sexuality, we exchange this information on a subtle, energetic level. The longer a couple is together, the more they bring out each other's dormant characteristics. Both people grow from the experience, but they often become more similar. The animal, magnetic pull of sexual passion is not as strong, because the need for learning from your "opposite" is not as strong.

Now that more raw passion and desire is transformed to a deeper spiritual passion. Spiritual love is not necessarily less physical, sexual, or romantic, but it can appear to lack spontaneity and ease because the need is not as urgent and unconscious. The deeper the relationship goes, the more you must become conscious about it. It becomes more psychic, emotional, and spiritual. You have to make the time and effort to deepen the bonds further. Here, we come across our fears and blocks to intimacy, because someone is really getting to know us on the deepest, most secret levels, and may find out we are not who they have idealized us to be. This is the toughest aspect of relationship.

It's easy to use intense sexual passion as a yardstick for a good relationship. If you do, you will constantly be leaving people when a relationship is truly getting deep and intimate; you won't develop a mature loving relationship, moving beyond your limits and boundaries of security and you won't grow and create something deeply meaningful.

Although I call the following a "spell to rekindle passion," it's not meant to bring you back to where you began the relationship. It helps you recognize the transformation of passion you are experiencing, and to tap in to this new passion. This spell brings new intensity into the relationship from the emotional, spiritual, and psychic levels, to be brought into the physical and romantic relationship.

Spell to Rekindle Passion

If you can do this spell with your partner, it will work better. Doing magical acts together can deepen the relationship and bring a new spark along with the intent of the spell. Most times a relationship begins to wane because it is not expressed on all levels—on the physical, emotional, mental, and spiritual. This ritual connects you and your partner on all of these levels in a deeper way, to rekindle the energy of the relationship in all four arenas, as needed, using the power of the four elements.

1 tbs. lavender
1 tbs. yarrow
1 tbs. patchouli
1 tbs. orris root

Mix the herbs together on the Moon's first quarter. Bottle them in an airtight container. When mixing them, hold the intention of healing and transforming your relationship for the highest good. Choose three nights of the waxing Moon and end the spell on the full Moon.

• On the first night, burn the herbs in a small fire or on self-igniting charcoal. Ask the element of fire to bring you and your partner passion on all levels—from the spiritual to the sexual. Save the ashes.

- On the second night, take one-fourth of the ashes, and mix them with a few drops of either jasmine oil or flowers, or rose oil or flowers. Scatter the mix to the wind. Ask the element of air to bring you clarity of mind and word. May it bring you a strong mental attraction.
- On the third night, take the remaining ashes and put them in a clear bowl of water, under the moonlight. Add a pinch of sugar. Ask the water to bring you a strong emotional and psychic connection. Leave the bowl outside, if possible. If it rains between now and the full Moon, look at that as water filling you up, cleansing and healing you both.
- On the night of the full Moon, add an emerald or green aventurine, pour the water into the ground, asking the earth element to bring you a strong foundation, manifesting this passion on all levels.

When the spell is over, make a conscious effort to rekindle your relationship. Make plans to be alone together. Rekindle your connections through your actions, because after this spell, the spiritual energy will be present to support your actions for the highest good.

Love and Astrology

One of the important aspects of your spiritual growth in a romantic relationship is understanding how a partner expresses love. Each of us expresses our love differently, and it's easy to assume the way we view love is the way a partner views love. Being aware of others' needs and desires, and communicating our own, is pivotal in developing a relationship.

Astrology provides a great tool for understanding the expression of our soul and many witches and mystics use it in their counseling work. As an astrologer, I dislike basic cookie-cutter descriptions of the signs. Astrology is much more complicated than that. When someone says, "Hey, baby, what's your sign?" they're talking about your Sun sign, the zodiac sign the Sun occupied when you were born. Although it is important, it is only a part of astrology. Everyone has all 12 signs and all 10 "planets" in their chart. The different combinations and positions represent the strengths and challenges we have in this lifetime.

LOVE NATURES OF THE 12 SIGNS

The zodiac signs reveal 12 twelve basic modes of operating through which our love nature can be expressed. If you understand how a partner expresses their love, you will take notice and appreciate it more. You'll know how to express love in a powerful way to your partner. You will also be better able to explain how you desire love to be expressed to you. If you don't have this awareness, relationship signals can be misunderstood and missed.

Aries: Aries energy is brave and bold, and will express itself in relationships as the natural adventurer. Aries love will want to share the adventure with a partner, but may have a problem if not taking the lead. The Aries appetite for adventure includes the bedroom as well. If you're partnered with Aries energy, go with the adventure when you can, and explain your boundaries when you can't.

Taurus: Taurean energy expresses love through the material world. Gifts, particularly sensual gifts and luxuries, are signs of love; so are handcrafted, heartfelt items. Sharing the gift of art and music is important to Taureans. Since this energy is so involved in material possessions, those with lots of Taurus energy often express love through food and music, but may have a hard time saying it.

Gemini: Gemini is ruled by Mercury, the planet of communication. A Gemini love nature will express itself through words and poetry. Although the words "I love you" may be very important to say and hear for the Gemini person, they can often be hard to say or viewed by others as "just words." Words are the method of expression for this energy. Learn to appreciate them.

Cancer: Cancer is the energy of the nourisher, and those with a Cancer love nature will be caretakers and nurturers. The energy is very home oriented, and tends toward nesting and domestic bliss, but can be very emotionally sensitive and protective. Making food is a sign of affection. Some people experience this energy as overly mothering.

Leo: Leo is the sign of the entertainer, the showman. Leo energy likes to be the center of attention, regardless of profession, and will use jokes, stories, and the like to entertain a lover or partner. Leos are very romantic. They are looking for approval, so take notice. They have a sensitive ego and are easily hurt, particularly by loved ones, but they don't like to show their pain.

Virgo: Virgo energy is down-to-earth and practical. Virgo is the sign of service, and will often desire to help partners in practical ways, offering advice and assistance, although sometimes when they are not asked. Virgo's gift is analysis, which can be a great asset, but also a liability when applied to scrutinizing every word, thought, and action. Virgo love expression does well when it can share a pursuit or goal with a partner.

Libra: Libra expresses its love nature through sharing artistic pursuits and interests. Libras are often concerned with the intellectual communication behind art, music, decorating, and sculpture. Libra energy is also concerned with fairness. Libra is the sign of the scales, and the real challenge of Libra is to balance the relationship. Libra-influenced people must learn to balance their own needs with those of their partners.

Scorpio: Scorpio energy is powerful and sometimes dark and mysterious. Scorpio loves to solve mysteries and explore the unknown and things that are often considered taboo by traditional society. Sexuality plays a strong role in the expression of Scorpio, so the Scorpio will express his or her love nature through sex, though not always romance. Scorpio emotions often run deep, but such people often have a hard time sharing those emotions and revealing them to the light of day. Scorpio people are often very intuitive.

Sagittarius: Sagittarius energy is all about freedom. This force likes to explore and have different adventures. Passionate and jovial, this love nature likes to share different cultural experiences and topics such as language, philosophy, history, and spirituality. Sagittarius can be very physical and enjoy games and athletics. Sagittarius people want a relationship that will help them expand their awareness, and shy away from those with too many restrictions and limitations. They might take the role of teacher, mentor, or student.

Capricorn: A key word for Capricorn is "responsibility," which Capricorn takes seriously. Love expressed in this way may seem formal, but will often have an Old World politeness and charm. Capricorns will strive to climb the ladder to care for a partner, but must watch out to not take responsibility for that partner. Capricorn is about honor, though a somewhat stoic exterior can often hide a more passionate and fun streak, since Pan, the goat god, is a symbol of Capricorn, the mountain goat.

Aquarius: Aquarian energy is innovative. Aquarians express love in unorthodox and unusual ways. They can be modern thinkers and have strange ideas about relationships. Although a strong expression of this energy is equality and universal brotherhood/sisterhood, Aquarians often seem detached from their emotions and relationships. Aquarian energy does well when sharing a social cause or goal.

Pisces: Pisces energy is highly sensitive to emotions, but those with it sometimes don't realize that others are not as sensitive as they are. They need to learn to communicate with partners. Piscean love can express itself through a desire to share creativity, imagination, and spirituality. Challenges for Pisces energy are self-sacrifice, escapism, addictions, lack of boundaries, and depression.

❋　❋　❋

In addition to studying your Sun sign, you may also want to look at the placement of Venus, the planet of love, and Mercury, the planet of communication, in your natal chart. Often they are in the same sign as the Sun, or one of the adjacent signs. I suggest consulting a detailed astrology book or, better yet, a professional astrologer to understand your entire chart and the relationship of your chart to your partners. Through it, you can better understand your views of lovers, marriage and sexuality, and why you are attracted to certain partners. Through a greater awareness, you can communicate better to any partner you may have.

Lust Magick

Lust magick has different connotations than love magick, but also has as many ancient and modern magical practices, though polite and reserved manuals tend not to discuss it. It's likely, however, that ancient pagans had a very different view of sexuality. Earth-honoring traditions tend to also be more body honoring, not looking at sexuality as being dirty, sinful, or evil, nor childbirth pain a punishment from the divine instead of a biological function. Pleasure is seen simply as a part of life. The European witches, the wise ones, held knowledge on childbirth, contraception, and abortion. For these reasons, many of these cultures were more accepting of homosexuality and they showed great respect for a woman's rights and autonomy.

Morality aside, consent and desire are key in pursuing pleasure with another adult. If sex without a commitment and relationship is not what you desire, you should not pursue it in hopes of fulfilling a pagan or gay societal aesthetic. We are each responsible for our own code of action and what will bring us happiness and what will bring us misery. Know yourself.

Herbal books and folklore will mention in passing the spells and workings of lust magick, but the very fact that such associations still survive in folklore show that it was a part of pagan magick, and a valid part of its reconstruction into the new century.

While the planet Venus rules love and attraction, Mars is the planet of lust, as well as protection and willpower. Mars is the warrior, and mythologically, as the Greek Ares, he was the clandestine lover of Aphrodite. Ideally, a healthy relationship will have sparks of both love and lust. Many seekers believe all their relationships must be spiritually pure when they're on a spiritual path, but sacred sexuality is a strong theme in all pagan religions. Sexuality in all its forms can be spiritual, including gay sex, role-playing, and all other acts of pleasure, depending on the intentions of those involved. All acts of love and pleasure are forms of worship to the Goddess.

Herbs associated with lust magick include coriander, damiana, dill, galangal, garlic, ginseng, hibiscus, peppermint, nettle, parsley, patchouli, rosemary, vanilla, and violet. Lust magick stones include red minerals such as rubies, garnets, and red jasper.

Use these ideas to spice up your love magick and add a bit of lust, passion, and desire to more traditional charms, or work with lust magick exclusively, if that is where your desires and intentions are. Just be sure, with lust magick as with love magick, to pursue a path of introspection, awareness, and self-love. Do not use sexual pleasure as a distraction from your own inner healing or to fill a void. Do not use it as a substitute for genuine love in your life. But there is nothing wrong with doing a spell for a healthy, fun, sex partner.

Lust Charm

Ideally you do this on a waxing Moon. Tuesday is a good day to do it, as it's sacred to the planet Mars, and the spring months, known for their fertility rites, are also good.

2 tsp. damiana
2 tsp. patchouli
1 tsp. dill
1 tsp. hibiscus flower
1 vanilla bean, whole or crushed

Consecrate all these herbs, mix together, and carry in a red bag.

IMPROVING SEXUAL PERFORMANCE AND RELEASING GUILT

So many corporations sell products to improve and enhance sexual performance, sexual desire, and sexual functioning. Although many people do suffer from medical conditions that impede their full functioning and enjoyment, many of these products and companies are taking advantage of people's insecurities by using exaggerated stereotypes and role models, particularly for men.

Symbol to improve sexual performance

In my professional practice, I've found that the majority of my clients with sexual dysfunction were actually suffering from an energetic imbalance, which had an emotional, mental, or spiritual root that was preventing their body from responding in the way they wanted. Magick to heal and support energetic changes can be much more effective and longer lasting than chemical stimulants, though they often force one to confront any of the emotional/mental roots. Some people prefer the pills because they are easier, but true healing is more rewarding.

Spell to Improve Sexual Performance

- Draw the symbol shown on page 172 on a piece of paper, cardboard, or small piece of wood and bless it in a magick circle.
- If you feel you need to enhance your direct, active role in sex, draw it in red. Carry it in a small red or white bag filled with any combination of damiana, coriander, and dragon's blood.
- If you need to enhance your receptivity to sex, draw it in green and carry it in a small green or black bag. Use any combination of the herbs patchouli, rosemary, lavender, catnip, and myrrh.
- Red and green are the colors of Mars and Venus, respectively, used to invoke these active and receptive energies.

Spell to Release Guilt

You can do this simple spell in or out of a magick circle. It's for releasing feelings of guilt around sexuality. In Wicca, there is neither guilt nor sin in sexuality. We simply live and learn from our experiences. For this spell to be truly effective, you must evaluate any behavior that leads to the guilt and determine if you honestly feel as if you have done something wrong, or if social programming and others' expectations are causing the guilt.

2 tsp. lavender or 5 drops lavender oil
1 tsp. lemon balm
1 black stone, such as obsidian, onyx, or smoky quartz

- Consecrate and place all the ingredients in a glass bowl filled with water. If the Moon is waning, put it in the waning moonlight. If the Moon is waxing, place it in sunlight. Leave it for at least 3 hours.
- Anoint yourself with this water. Wash your hands in it. Feel all guilt and shame leave you and go into the water, into the stone.
- Pour the water into the earth and bury the stone, leaving your guilt behind you forever.
- Thank the spirit of the Goddess, stone, and water for this gift.

12

Sex Magick

O Great Goddess,
O Great God,
O Great Spirit.
Through the ecstasy of our bodies,
Through the ecstasy of our minds,
Through the ecstasy of our hearts,
And through the ecstasy of our souls,
May we know you better.
May we see you in all eyes,
Feel you in all touch,
And know you in all love.

As all magick is a form of love magick, starting with the vibration of love, one can also say all magick is sex magick. Sexuality is the power of creative energy. Sex is energy coming together in union, bliss, or ecstasy, as part of the creative process. The trance of the shaman is often called an ecstasy, as are the witches' sabbat rituals. The enlightenment of the yogi is similarly described, called the bliss of the thousand-petaled lotus. This is the enlightenment experience, sometimes called *satori*, or "touching nirvana." At this elevated consciousness, we open past the awareness of separateness, to join with and experience another, and ultimately achieve oneness with the universe. All magick and mysticism work to see past the illusion that we are separate, and understand the greater truth that we are all one. In our Earthwalk, we simply have different viewpoints for a time.

Sex is a physical action that can unite us with another person on profound levels. Like meditation, breath, music, and dance, physical pleasure and exhilaration are a gateway through the veil, to glimpse a greater reality by making an intimate connection with another. It is powerful. Why else do you think there are so many people and institutions, particularly religious, trying to control its use? Whenever something is considered both powerful and potentially empowering, others use propaganda, fear, and rules to inhibit the use of that power. During the Burning Times, the Catholic Church essentially wanted to control how anyone contacted God, and set itself up as the sole intermediary. If you could make your own connection to divinity, through sacred sexuality, through magick and personal ceremony, you wouldn't need a church, and its power structure would crumble. The Church fostered shame about sex and associated it with sin to prevent people from experiencing the ecstatic mystical power that sex can provide them. Witches were persecuted because they knew how to empower themselves and others, and sexuality was a means of empowerment.

Nature-based paths incorporate all aspects of life, so the divine was seen in the harvest and grain, the Sun and Moon, the animals, and the planet, itself. They are all a part of the cycles of life, and pagans paid great attention to them, not only religiously, but also as a matter of survival. Sex was also a matter of survival. Fertility rituals were for the bounty of all the tribe members as well as the crops. Sexuality, and the ability to continue as a people, was another aspect of life, like the propagation of plants and animals. These pagans also saw the divine in the self, so human sexuality was divine. Humans reflected the gods' natures. If one is naturally inclined to have same-sex unions, then there must be gods with that tendency, too. If gods can be homoerotic, then that is just as divine as heterosexuality.

Ancient cultures perceived deities as sexual beings, and their images of gods and goddesses were often portrayed with enlarged sexual characteristics. In Egypt and Africa, the fertility goddesses are portrayed as divine mothers. In Greek art, the gods were portrayed as perfect physical specimens, often nude or semi-nude. Nudity and the body were considered divine as well. There was no shame regarding the body. Male deities, such as Pan, are pictured with an erect penis. Many of the ancient myths involve sexuality and relationship between gods and between mortals. The myths also include relationships between deities and the humans, bridging the gap between the two. Zeus's exploits alone can fill volumes. In the men's mystery school of the Dorians, found in Ancient Greece, it is possible that part of the education and inspiration between male teachers and students occurred sexually. Semen was

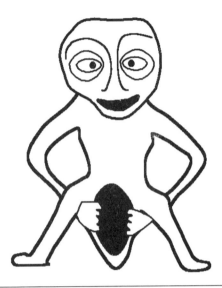

SheelaNaGig

considered a sacred substance, a vessel to exchange soul wisdom and power between the two men. Such acts were not just educational, but holy, spiritual rituals. Similar concepts and rites can be found in many tribal coming-of-age rites for young men. In Egypt, some statues were carved with erect phalluses as well, scandalizing the Victorian Egyptologists. In the Celtic lands, we have discovered the Cerne Abbas (see chapter 4) and the SheelaNaGig carvings.

Creation myths are also interspersed with homoerotic and transgendered elements. Bisexual and transgendered deities make love to themselves to create mates, partners, creatures, and humans. Sexuality is an act of creation, the ultimate act of magick. Magick is creation.

Ritual and ceremony usually incorporate symbolic, imitative actions to create change. When we make a change on a small, symbolic scale while in sacred space, we can make changes in the larger universe through our actions. Magicians call this sympathetic magick, and the best-known example is the voodoo doll. A doll is made in the image of the person. Symbolic actions of healing or harm to the doll, like sticking pins in it, create change in the person through the principles of sympathetic magick. If such symbolic acts are a fundamental part of magick, then it is no surprise magick workers would imitate the creative actions of the Great Spirit, as manifested in mythology through sexuality of the gods and goddesses.

The image of the priapus, or phallic pole, is often found in magick and worship. In Europe, reports of such sexual worship can be found well into the

13th century. Dances and processions would be led around it. We find the same imagery in a less overt form in the May Pole dance performed on May Day, or Beltane.

During the witch hunts, tales were told of men and women with demon lovers, called incubuses or succubuses, who would come in the night and steal vital life force through sex. These demonic tales were told by the Church, but they could point a finger of truth to sexual imagery in meditation and shamanic journey. Siberian shamans report in their ancient traditions that some spirit helpers and guides would help the shaman through spirit sex. They would be spirit lovers or spirit spouses. If you experienced such a thing today, most would chalk it up to a vivid fantasy, but perhaps these witches were having divine awakenings with the gods and spirits through the imagery and energy of sex. Perhaps it is part of a long-standing tradition once lost to the world, but now being reclaimed and explored.

One way modern witches symbolically tap in to this vast creative power is through the Great Rite. The Great Rite is a symbolic ritual act, using the athame or wand as the phallus and the chalice or cauldron as the vagina. It commemorates the creative union of the Goddess and God to manifest the universe. In a sense, in the sacred circle, a witch is creating, through symbolic enactment, a new mini-universe, gathering the elements needed for creation, and empowering it to manifest as a spell intention. The Great Rite generates that creative energy.

In the early days of traditional modern Wicca, the Great Rite was not always symbolic. The ritual was physically enacted between the high priestess and high priest of the ritual, who embodied the Goddess and God. The energy of their physical union was used in the making of magick. Although it's an unusual practice these days, when the Great Rite is physically enacted, it is often done between consenting individuals who understand the working. Most often it occurs between couples practicing the faith together, but it is not limited to long-term, monogamous relationships.

Many gay people turn off to Wicca because of the heterosexual imagery of the God and Goddess. As a gay practitioner of Wicca, it is vitality important that you realize creative energy is not limited to those of opposite genders. The concept of fertility in our understanding of the ancient foundations of paganism relates to the fact that we each comprise creative energy—male and female—in action. Some magical scholars actually believe that two men or two women cannot generate sufficient magical "current" in order to work together and that magick needs both genders to generate sufficient energy. If that fiction had any credence, solitary magick would not work at all—but we know it does.

In the modern world, the idea of fertility is not limited to the land and to bearing children. We know of fertility in ideas, writing, music, art, and performance, and fertility of compassion, talent, skill, and dedication. The concept of fertility can be applied to all areas of life. Much of the neo-pagan community is unaware of the hidden history of queer-positive deities, myths, and customs among the ancient civilizations, and has based their fertility ideas on heterosexuality. If our understanding of the ancient pagans is limited to strict physical fertility, perhaps as a community, we are again limiting our views and limiting the power of fertility. Both views are important.

Aleister Crowley proposed a very interesting concept upon which other gay magicians and pagans have expounded. Being bisexual himself, and versed in a variety of magical systems and mythologies, he experienced sex magick from both a heterosexual and homosexual viewpoint. Through his research, past-life memories, inspiration, and innovation, Crowley brings a unique perspective, although much of his work is not accessible to the average reader. Crowley and others theorize that the energies generated in heterosexual relations are used generally for the effort of procreation, and maintaining the life energies of the physical plane. Homosexual unions are free to focus energy on spiritual pursuits, enlightenment, magick, and healing. These energies help maintain life and flow on the spiritual plane. Perhaps heterosexuality is dominant because more energy is needed to maintain the physically dense plane, while less energy is needed to sustain the ethereal planes. If such beliefs are even partially true, it would explain the draw of gays, lesbians, bisexuals, and transgendered people to the clergy, and in particular, the ancient sects of such priests and priestesses. We are naturally attuned to it.

Exercise 9. Sex as Worship and Celebration

If you have a partner who is interested in this path, you can celebrate the ritual of the magick circle together, perhaps for the full Moon. Make sure you are both comfortable with the basic concepts and actions of the circle and feel relaxed and aware.

Enact the Great Rite physically, instead of ritually, making love with your partner. Use ritual sex as a form of worship, both as an act of love to your partner, but also as an act of love to the divine. Feel the divine in your partner. Feel the barriers break down and a feeling of Perfect Love and Perfect Trust flow between you. For now, take your time and do whatever feels right. "All acts of love and pleasure" are forms of worship to the Goddess.

Instead of doing a spell, simply raise the cone of power with the intention of sharing this love with the world. Later, you can add the techniques of formal sex magick and tantra in the sections below to your work, but for now, just do what comes naturally. Make every act, every pleasure an act of worship. See the gods and goddesses in your partner. As you bring pleasure to your partner, you bring love and pleasure to the universe. As you see the divine in your partner, you see the divine in everyone and everything. Your time together doesn't have to be preplanned.

When both of you are intimately familiar and comfortable with sex magick, you can work with the invocation techniques of Exercise 6 on page 120 to embody homoerotic deities and commune with Spirit in that direct manner. With invocation, you are both directly recognizing the divine. It becomes less of an attitude to maintain and more of an act of worship through your partner.

If you do not have a partner, don't feel you have to find a sex partner to complete this exercise. You don't even have to do this if it doesn't feel comfortable. I share it for those who are on the path together and would enjoy the experience. If you have a partner who is uninterested in Wicca, please do not force them to participate. This is not a part of everyone's life and doesn't have to be. Always do what is best for you and your relationship, and talk about things before rushing into them. Ideally, it should be done between those who understand the concepts and energy behind the actions, but the awareness of worship through pleasure can be added to any sexual experience you have, including masturbation. Many witches have found sacred sexuality as a powerful way to introduce the concepts of paganism and magick into the relationship. Your partner doesn't necessarily have to be an initiated witch to be initiated into the magick of sacred sex.

Tantra

The roots of our modern knowledge on sacred sexuality are in the East, in India and Asia. While such workings were not always common knowledge, it was preserved among adepts and initiates, unlike in the Western world, where the Church tried to stamp out this information. Much of our modern use of sex magick in the Western mystery traditions is borrowed and adapted from the East. Like all magick, they come from a similar inspiration.

Sacred sexuality is often called tantra, though *tantra* is a Sanskrit word literally meaning "text." The tantras are sacred texts with information on many subjects concerning life, including diet, society, relationships, and spiritual practice. One of the most famous of these sacred manuals is the *Kama Sutra*.

The *Kama Sutra* teaches us about sacred sexuality. Unfortunately, the text loses a bit in the translation and interpretation by most Westerners, not coming from a culture in which these basic concepts were ingrained. Most think of it as a somewhat kinky foreign sex book, but the text is really a spiritual manual. Although the *Kama Sutra* is a Hindu text, there are other sacred sexuality manuals, and the basic concepts have been practiced in Arabia, China, and Japan.

Most of this material has been oriented to the heterosexual couple, particularly the translations that made their way to the West. Now, you can find books and videos promising to increase the length and intensity of orgasm through the ancient secrets of tantra. Contrary to popular opinion, tantra's goal is not an amazing orgasm, but enlightenment. Increased pleasure is simply a by-product of the practice, and extending the orgasm is a technique.

Eastern practitioners feel that a man loses vital life force if he ejaculates too frequently, so they encourage techniques that allow prolonged or multiple orgasms without ejaculation. Contrary to Western society's common understanding of orgasm and ejaculation, the two are not synonymous, though that is difficult for a man to understand until he experiences it. The goal of tantra is no goal. Goal attainment is a Western concept; if you start something, you must find the end; if you have sex, the goal is orgasm. For those on the path of sacred sexuality, the journey, the exploration, the moment is everything, not the end. Your lovemaking could be so prolonged and intense that there is no need to orgasm or ejaculate. If there are goals, they are not so physical or measurable by success or failure, hopefully negating performance anxiety that many men suffer from. The true goals are appreciation and unconditional acceptance of one's self and lover, communication and spiritual expansion to touch the divine.

One of the few rules of these practices is to first give. Emphasis is not on your own pleasure, but your partner's. If both of you follow this rede, your own pleasure will be taken care of. The process is about learning and exploring. One-night stands might be physically enjoyable, but run contrary to the tantric texts. The experience grows over time and with personal intimacy. You cannot learn everything you need to know for a spiritual relationship over the course of one night.

Try these exploratory exercises to get a feel for the energies of sacred sexuality. They are not strictly traditional tantric exercises, but modern explorations of sacred sex.

Exercise 10. Sacred Sexuality Exploration Alone

The first step in sacred sexuality is self-acceptance and self-love, as with all magick. Stand naked in front of a mirror and look at yourself. Touch and caress yourself. Stroke and massage yourself. The goal is not orgasm, but feeling every inch of yourself. Touch places often forgotten, such as your little toes, behind your ears, below your eyes, and the back of your hands. Be one with your entire body. Tantra is not about physical perfection. You are a vessel of divine energy and perfect in every way, just as you are. You do not have to look like an underwear model or porn star to like the way you look and feel. This acceptance comes from within. You are your first and most important spiritual partner.

Next, focus your attention on the chakras, using massage. (Review chapter 7 to be more familiar with the chakras.) You might want to lie down for this part. Use a little warm massage oil if you like. Start at your root, between your anus and genitals, and move in gentle circles over the chakra. Most people prefer clockwise circles, but do what feels right for you. Visualize the color associated with each chakra as you massage: Root—red, belly—orange, solar plexus—yellow, heart—green, throat—blue, brow—indigo, and crown—violet. Feel the chakra open with a slight tingle or warmth and then move on to the next. Feel each one open like a flower, or the drawstring of a pouch. Feel yourself energized and free flowing.

If you would like, masturbate, while exploring your body. Treat yourself like your partner, like your greatest lover. Many focus on the goal of masturbation, the release, and do not take time to enjoy every part of the body. As you pleasure yourself, be aware of all the sensations in your body, particularly the flow of energy through your chakras.

Exercise 11. Locking Technique for Men

This next technique is for men only, to work on prolonging the orgasm, and ultimately feeling orgasm without ejaculation. It builds the energy and redirects it into the higher centers of your body. Once you have "opened" all of your chakras, masturbate. When you feel you are very close to orgasm, stop and pull in your lower abdomen and stomach, rectum, and the muscles around your penis and testicles. This is called "locking." You can also take your first and second fingers and apply pressure to your perineum, or root chakra, between your anus and scrotum. Apply pressure, but do not cause pain. This should prevent you from ejaculation and after a few minutes of rest you can continue to build up this energy through more stimulation.

One technique might work better for you than the other, but both are effective, alone or together. Find your own pace and rhythm and don't be surprised if you ejaculate the first time you try it. There is a "point of no return." You get better at anticipating orgasm with practice. As your timing improves, you can feel the orgasm without ejaculating, allowing you to have multiple orgasms during one session. Don't feel that you need to use these techniques every time you masturbate or have sex. Slowly work them into your life.

Exercise 12. Soul Baring

This exploration takes the foundation of the solo experiences and brings it into a partnership situation. Do Exercise 10 at least once alone to become comfortable with the techniques before doing this exercise with a partner.

First, decide which partner will be receiving the attention. He or she simply lies back for now, while the active partner massages the chakras, starting at the root, and moving up the spine, at the corresponding place for each chakra. The active partner then rolls the receptive partner over and, continuing the chakra massage, moving back down from the crown to the root. You can use oil; most texts recommend something with jasmine because it lightens the vibration of the physical energies, raising them through the higher spiritual chakras. Other herbs associated with sex magick and tantra, or used as aphrodisiacs, are Solomon's seal, mandrake, male fern, damiana, mistletoe, and satyricon powder (dried orchid root). These herbs are not to be taken internally or topically, since most of them are poisonous. Instead, use them in charms and consult a good medical herbal when taking herbs internally or topically.

This exercise can be expanded to kissing and licking the chakras and moving up the chakra path. Instead of solely concentrating on the pelvic area and genitals, as it's tempting to do, work with the entire body. Nipple play activates the heart. Kissing the neck opens the throat. Kissing and stroking the face works with the brow chakra. Touch and massage the scalp to open the crown.

Once the chakras have been opened, the receptive partner should masturbate, while the active partner continues to massage and play, touching everything but the genitals. When the receptive partner indicates he or she is ready to orgasm, look deeply into each other eyes. Do not close your eyes. Don't look away. Lock your gaze deeply into each other, baring your soul and creating an intimate link. Then reverse roles.

Exercise 13. Shower of Light

During intercourse, partners exchange energy. The type of person you are attracted to, including gender, indicates the type of energy you are most comfortable with, that harmonizes your system best. In your next session of sacred sexual play, try to feel the energy move through you.

While making love to your partner, be it masturbation, oral, or anal, feel the energy rise through the chakras. You can both do this simultaneously if you are both being stimulated. Usually it starts at the root and can be felt there or at the belly chakra. Anal sex particularly activates the root of the receiver. The energy exchanged with your partner at this base chakra helps "pump" the energy up your spine.

As you are stimulated, visualize the energy moving up the chakras until you feel a warmth or a tingle. As it reaches each energy center, you can feel different emotions, sensations, and perceptions activate. It can bring up feelings to share and issues to talk about in your relationship work. Sometimes they are joyful and blissful, other times we recall things we have shut out of our consciousness. We remember them in an effort to heal. They come back into our awareness to be resolved.

Don't get discouraged; it takes practice to raise the energy through the chakras. You may feel it only a little, or be unsure you are feeling it. This is normal. When you feel the energy reach the crown chakra, it will flow out like a fountain of light, showering you both with love and healing.

Experiment and play with this exercise until you find your own pace. If you're a man, you can use the techniques in Exercise 11 to prolong the movement of energy, to balance, cleanse, and heal you and your partner on all levels. Sacred sexuality is healing on all levels, as well as spiritual and fun. For some, this is the best way to heal old wounds and trauma regarding sexuality. If it brings up issues you and your partner cannot handle on your own, then seek out professional help as needed. Once you clear the blocks and baggage in the chakras, you are both open to a deeper and truly heartfelt sense of love and commitment.

Combining Sex with Spell Work

Just as a lone priest or priestess can embody both God and Goddess for a solitary Great Rite, a same-sex couple can embody all the energies they need for the making of sexual magick. One does not necessarily take the feminine, receptive role while the partner takes the strictly masculine projective one, unless they choose to as a couple in life, or in a particular ritual. The balance of energy is fluid and changing, moment to moment, because both need to be expressed in each individual. One can even perform sex magick alone.

You can use masturbation, intercourse, or any sexual pleasure that builds up in intensity and then releases in the making of magick. The act itself is like the ritual circle. As you enact the ritual, you build intention with the intense energy, and release it through the cone of power into the universe to fulfill the spell.

Having to rush over to the altar and read a petition spell can dampen the excitement of sex magick, and you might have trouble visualizing a complex set of images during the height of orgasm. One very effective technique, which is not limited to sex magick, but can be applied in any type of spell, is the use of sigils.

A sigil is a symbol you have built by deconstructing your intentions to their most basic components—simple letters. You start with a simple intention, and cross out all the repeated letters. Say you are feeling a bit sick, the start of a cold, and you want to do a healing spell. You might word your intention as:

I am completely healthy.

Now cross out all the repeated letters:

I a̶m̶ c o m̶ p l̶e̶t̶e̶l̶y̶ h̶e̶a̶l̶t̶h̶y̶

Leaving you with the letters:

I C O P

You have reduced your first statement to its barest components, I, C, O, P. Some types of sigil magick have somewhat complex systems of converting letters to numbers and plotting them on geometric patterns, but the easiest technique is to take the letters and graphically create a pleasing symbol from them, as in the figure below.

Can you see the four letters in this symbol? You can use lower case or capitals, and double or triple letters as needed. You can even retrieve one of the crossed out letters if you need to. The only rule is that it must satisfy you.

Now you can draw the symbol on a good piece of paper. You can do such sigil sex spells in a magick circle, or outside, but I prefer within the circle. As you masturbate, hold it in front of you, or hang it on the wall. Focus on the symbol as you are aroused. Do not focus on the goal, just the symbol. The symbol has now become your link to the goal. Feel the energy rise in your chakras, from root up to the crown. The closer you are to orgasm, the higher it gets. When the energy reaches your third eye, visualize the sigil in your mind's eye, with your physical eyes closed. At the moment of orgasm, feel the energy rising up like the cone of power through your crown, taking the symbol with it, out into the universe. You can then burn the paper (or later bury it) and ground yourself as needed before releasing the magick circle.

Couples can use the same technique. You can hang the sigil up in an easy-to-spot point in the room, so no matter where you move you can see it. You don't need to orgasm simultaneously. Think of it like doing two identical spells in the ritual. You could both even be doing two different spells, with different sigils, though you should always share your intention with your part-

ner before doing sigil magick, just as you should always share your spell intentions with all members of a working magick group.

If you don't like the sigil technique, you can simply visualize your intended result instead. In the above example, you can simply visualize yourself completely healthy. Visualizations can be more complex and distracting, so that is why the technique of sigils was created, but do what works best for you.

Health sigil

Healing Sexuality

Although there is no guilt around sexual conduct in Wicca, we can create experiences in our life through our relationships where we feel hurt, used, abused, or otherwise lose our sense of self and personal power. Sometimes these feelings are from legitimate experiences, and other times they are biased opinions. But in either case, they are real to us, and need to be addressed. Whenever you have sexual contact with someone, you make an energetic connection. That connection can last years after the relationship ends. That is why letting go of a past sexual relationship can be harder than any other type of relationship. It holds an intense energetic intimacy, along with the emotional and physical intimacy. We open ourselves to the energetic intimacy. The results can be beautiful, but sometimes come with unexpected additions.

Regardless of the type of sex you are having, from romantic to wild, magical to fantasy role-playing, you are merging your energy bodies. Even if you don't realize it, and think it is strictly physical, you are still merging energy and making an energetic connection. There is no casual sex. There can be casual attitudes about sex, but energetically, it is always something more.

Many spiritual teachings say you should not have sex with anyone whom you are not committed to. Most religions frame it in terms of the institution of marriage. What has been misunderstood in the teachings is the reasons why. Marriage and even a domestic commitment is not the issue. Love is the issue. I would rephrase it as you should not have sex with anyone whom you do not love. Now I'm sure to get a lot of criticism for that, but love has many different meanings. I do not necessarily mean a committed relationship, although that is wonderful if that is your desire. I don't mean "in love," that bubbly feeling you may have at the start of a relationship. When I say love, I mean the vibration of unconditional love. When you make a connection to someone through this love, that is the only bond you create. That is the nature of the connection. There is no unhealthy attachment. The energy will not push and pull you off center. Unconditional love is an unattached love. You can still hold a commitment and partnership with the person, and live up to the obligations of such a commitment, but you don't have to have that type of relationship to have a healthy sexual experience. When you merge your energy with a partner through the energy of unattached love, you do not make the same unhealthy energetic connections that you may when not in this state.

Unfortunately, in practical terms, this is much easier said than done. It's hard to hold a state of unconditional love all the time, in every sexual encounter. We feel very attached about our emotions, desires, and sexuality. It is a great gift and teacher because it helps us work though these things. Practically, it can be easier to work through these issues, mentally, emotionally, and energetically, with one committed partner than many casual partners. There is nothing wrong with many partners as long as you understand the energetic dynamic and take responsibility for it. This is not a conservative call to monogamy if that is not your path. I think of the sacred prostitutes of the Goddess in ancient times, male and female, having many sexual partners and using that experience to heal and transform. You must find the path that is right to you. Simply be aware.

When addressing HIV education, people often say that when you have sex with your current partner, you are also having sex with everyone your lover has had sex with up until that point. That is at least a biological truth in terms of physical infection. When you merge your energy with another, you are potentially merging with everyone they have ever sexually merged with and, taking the concept of energy exchange to its logical connection, all their future lovers. If you are not in a state of clarity, or understand energetic health and cleansing, you may feel muddled by the psychic imprint of many people and have difficulty sorting your own "stuff" out from others. Energetically, you can have a sexual exchange with someone without even touching.

Many people go into sex with fear, shame, and a need to be completed by another. This is not the vibration of unconditional love. When you move energy with such emotions, that is the nature of your bond. You may feel these feelings when reflecting on the relationship. It is particularly tough for gay lovers, because society imprints us with so much fear, shame, and guilt about our sexuality. Even though we might not originally create this energy, if we carry those feelings and self-judgments, then we must take responsibility for it. The more unhealthy or abusive the relationship and your view of it— whether a long-term situation or a one-time encounter—the more the energy connection adversely affects you. You may feel you have given away a part of your personal power and soul to one who has not respected and cherished you in love. Time can heal such wounds, but magick can make the process both quicker, by moving energy, and more conscious, by helping us to take responsibility for our actions and the feelings around them. The only fulfillment and healing we have comes from within.

Try the following ritual to reclaim any lost sexual, personal, and spiritual power from difficult relationships.

Exercise 14. Reclaiming Lost Power

1. First, reflect on all your lovers. Make a list, literally or mentally. Do not
   judge how long or how short it may be. Simply reflect on it and how you
   feel about all these past partners. Do any stick out as particularly bad
   encounters that still need to be healed? Be honest with yourself.

2. Do steps 1 through 4 in Exercise 1 (page 60) to get into a meditative state.
   You can do this meditation in a magick circle, or without. I like to ritualize it and do it in the circle, myself.

3. Send yourself to your place of power and call upon your animal guides
   and the Goddess and God. Ask for their help in this ritual and follow any
   messages they give you. They may have specific instructions for you as
   you proceed, or be present simply as your loving support.

4. Create a doorway before you. It can be solid, like a real door, a cave opening, or a gateway of light. Call out to the first name on your list of past
   lovers. Ask their higher self to be present. If you have any unfinished
   words to say or questions to ask, do so now. When you feel closure, say
   this or something similar:

   > *I thank you for our time together and the gifts you have given me.*
   > *I now release any parts of you that I should release for the high-*
   > *est good.*
   > Exhale and release.
   > *I now reclaim any parts of myself that should be with me for my*
   > *highest good. So mote it be!*

   Inhale deeply, and feel your power move toward you. It passes through
   a rainbow mist to be cleansed and healed before entering your body with
   the breath, restoring itself to your spirit. Imagine the Goddess or God
   holding a sword, severing any unhealthy cords of energy between the two
   of you. Thank and release that lover's higher self, sending him or her
   through the gateway. If you can, send the past lover a blessing of unconditional love and forgiveness to transmute any remaining energies
   between you.

5. Repeat the process with all your past lovers, as much as you can do this
   time. Know you can come back to complete the ritual later if it is long.
   Some will return a tremendous power. Others return little to none,
   because they don't have any. Some will keep energy that was freely given
   and not in your best interest to have returned anyway. If you feel a particular lover is resisting, withholding energy you know belongs to you,

ask the guides to help you. Send that lover a ball of healing, loving light that will dissolve all resistance and restore balance to both of you.

6. Thank the animal guides, and the Goddess and the God. Say farewell to all and return from your sacred place of power to your physical body. Ground yourself as needed. When done with the entire list, burn it if you have written it out.

❋   ❋   ❋

In the future, be aware of the energy dynamic in your sexual relationships. Our society is largely ignorant about the nature of energy, let alone the nature of energy and sex. Reflect and be aware. See how your sexual encounter affects you both during and afterward. Learn more about energetic health (see chapter 13) to maintain your own health and balance. As you educate yourself on physical health and protection, educate yourself also on psychic health and protection.

In the end, all sex is a spiritual exchange, from a romantic kiss and long-term marriage to a whips-and-chains orgy. Every time you express your sexuality, you are expressing spiritual, psychic, and magical energy, even if you are not conscious of it. A good witch becomes conscious of it and uses each experience to bring a greater state of healing and balance.

Exploring the Taboo

Even in the realms of magick and the gay culture, there are realms that are considered off limits, taboo to most people. Certain things go beyond most people's boundaries. Strangely enough, things like magick, psychic development, personal religions, hallucinogenic substances, gender variance, and homosexuality have all been considered taboo topics among more traditional society.

Many magicians explore the taboo, because often such restrictions were placed in society in an effort to control a group. Sexual freedom, sexual energy, and personal mysticism can help bring about a greater awareness and personal enlightenment, diminishing the need for an institution. One wonders why other subjects are considered off limits or distasteful. What secrets could they be hiding? Often they hide none. But sometimes you come across something that can completely change your point of view of the world and of yourself. Exploring the unknown with care and common sense can be a powerful agent of transformation.

In traditional Wicca, you can find items that would be more common in a BDSM context. Because of this, and the mainstreaming of many practices, you won't find them all that often in books and classes on Wicca. Many consider them distasteful relics of the past, remnants of witchcraft's patriarchal ideology absorbed during the Christian dominance of Europe. Some covens would use a scourge for light ritual whipping as an initiation—like fraternity paddlings— or more intense flogging. The flogging draws blood to that part of the body, helping to induce a trance state. Other traditions may use cords to bind parts of the body and control the flow of blood to induce trance. Many practitioners ritually use plant substances to help induce trance and journeying while other traditions consider that "cheating" or dangerous. The use of psychedelics runs throughout the history of indigenous magical cultures.

For me, the magical potential of exploring taboo subjects is not to yield a new and more powerful technique. My experiences have been much more personal. They come from creating intense experiences that force me to examine my beliefs, ego, personal hang-ups, and ultimately, my self. Witches, magicians, and mystics are pioneers in consciousness, and must understand their own consciousness to effectively work magick and develop spiritually. It is difficult to tell if our self-images and personal notions are really ours, or are adopted from others, such as our families, societies, and religions. Do we fear or dislike something because someone told us to, or do we really understand it or have experience with it? Are we really who we think we are? All these issues are even more difficult around sexuality and personal power, including claiming magical power.

Placing yourself in such situations, times that test your beliefs, self-image, and boundaries, are considered the act of "undoing" yourself. They can appear completely mundane, but can be very magical, even without traditional ritual trappings. By exploring something that seems to be out of your comfort zone, you are forced to deal with situations that you have never prepared for. You often step out of your ego awareness of individuality, and see yourself in a larger context. If you are not your self-image, and that false self-image is challenged, you realize the "true" you, your "soul," for lack of a better word, is the real you, beyond shape and form and image. It owns your self-image, like a tool, just as it owns your mind, emotions, and body. They are not you. They are just tools.

This is the true experience of spiritual initiation, waking up to the greater sense of self and greater sense of connection in the universe. That is the experience of the shaman, and the result of those who have a near-death experience. Acts of undoing yourself may not be exactly the same, but they have a similar initiation quality. To paraphrase Friedrich Nietzsche, if it doesn't kill you, it will make your stronger. Exploration of taboo topics, personal or magical, done in a way that challenges your ego, more than your health and safety, can be very beneficial to the spiritual path.

Taboo images and topics fill ancient paganism. Terrence McKenna, author of *Food of the Gods* and an accompanying tape series, *The Search for the Original Tree of Knowledge,* envisions an ancient Stone Age Goddess tribe celebrating the cycles through ritualistic community orgies while on magic mushrooms. To him, such taboos were the secret to their success as a community. Other pagan traditions are filled with sexual ecstasy and indulgence. The rites of the Saturnalia and Bacchanalia are reminiscent of our Mardi Gras and Carnival. Although massive parties reminiscent of gay club circuits, they were not necessarily lifestyles maintained all year long, but seasonal celebrations. During the trials of the Burning Times, those accused of witchcraft were accused of homosexuality and having sexual orgies with the devil. Perhaps the persecutors witnessed some ancient sacred sexuality rites and misunderstood what they saw. The taboo is part and parcel of witchcraft. In fact, to most people, witchcraft itself is still considered taboo.

As a gay male witch with a Roman Catholic background, I challenged my previous beliefs, particularly around sexuality. I explored topics I felt were taboo, including role-playing and bondage, forbidden language, pornography, and adult entertainment. Rather than being the fantasy that many suspect, they were real challenges to the ego and my sense of being a "good" or "nice" person as I realized those things do not conflict with being a "good" person. I understood better what were my experiences and what was a preprogrammed belief. Through witchcraft, I continue to challenge my notion of my self, the universe, and the purpose of life. I highly recommend challenging your self, as well. Only then will you truly know who you are.

Safe Sex and Magick

Whenever doing sex magick, tantra, or sacred sexuality of any kind, use common sense. Practice safe sex. Several texts talk about the power in consuming your partner's bodily fluids. Some say to drink from the divine chalice of woman (or man) after spreading your seed is the attainment of the Holy Grail, the ultimate Great Rite. Others feel that semen can transfer spiritual energy and wisdom and such transmissions were the basis of the sexual relationship between older male teachers and younger male students in the Greek mystery schools. These ideas and original teachings were also written long before the advent of HIV and AIDS, and before the understanding of sexually transmitted diseases. Don't think because it is sex "magick" that you are magically protected from a lack of common sense! The magick is in the perception and the change you create, but you are still open to physical dangers present in the biological world. Don't do anything you normally wouldn't do with a sexual partner, just because it's magick. Energy can be transferred without sperm. I've done it and I'm sure you can, too. You can experiment all you want with your own bodily fluids. If you choose to experiment within the bounds of a long-term, safe, and monogamous relationship, then that is your choice. Just don't throw away your common sense when practicing magick. A witch must walk and function in both worlds, the material and spiritual.

Goal vs. Experience

Now that you have a concept of sacred sexuality, from the Eastern tantric view and the Western magical system, and an understanding of the underlying concepts beneath the two and how they pertain to the gay practitioner, explore on your own. Explore with a partner. Work in the Eastern view of experience and enlightenment, or the manifestation and magick of the Western mysteries. Some use the terms "inner alchemy" for inner world spiritual transformation and "outer alchemy" for outer world change and magick. Learn to fuse the two into your own practice, and omit the parts that don't work for you. Don't be caught in the polarity of putting the experience before a measurable goal, or the goal before enjoying the experience. They are not mutually exclusive. Both are a part of life. Both are needed for balance, and a witch is one who seeks balance in the forces. Sex magick, and in particular gay sex magick, is one of the most exciting frontiers in the modern New Age movement. So little has been written and put into practice. Embrace your sexuality. It is one of your greatest strengths.

13

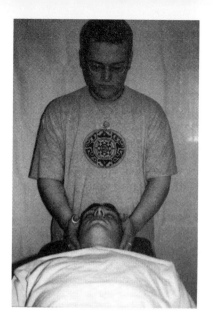

Magick for Healing

The highest art of witchcraft is the craft of healing.
We are healers of the body, healers of the heart,
and healers of the soul. But the first step is healing yourself.
You cannot heal others unless you walk the road yourself.

As heir to the European shamanistic practices, a witch's primary role in the community is that of healing. A healer must be well versed in all areas to effectively treat the ills of an individual and the society. The wise ones of old Europe were not doctors, but they held the foundations of medical lore and medicines in basic first-aid techniques and in-depth knowledge of herbs and minerals. Most important, they were well versed in the practices of healing the spirit.

In the modern world, we find a host of specialized disciplines practiced by traditional physicians, psychologists, psychotherapists, ministers, and holistic practitioners. In such a sea of healing professionals, where does the witch fit in? Although witches learn many of these modalities as a modern foundation of healing, the witch is ultimately a spiritual healer.

Our understanding of the word "healer" is often misguided. We think of a healer as one who heals us. We go to our healer—spiritual or medical—with a problem and we get it fixed. This view makes us into cars and appliances that simply need a good mechanic. In reality, no one heals us. Others act as healing facilitators, helping our process along, but really, our own body does the healing. Medicines, surgeries, or supplements can provide a healing environment, but they do not do the actual work. In psychological terms, most

practitioners guide you to find your own answers by being an impartial lis-
tener, and pointing you in a direction of more awareness. But they must let
you come to the conclusions yourself. That's why they ask so many questions
about what you think and feel. They are asking you to be introspective,
because only you can heal it. If they give you all the answers, you will not
integrate the necessary changes in your life to improve.

When we go to a healer expecting them to fix us, we give away our power
and responsibility in the process. We are responsible for our own healing. Our
body is involved in the process of healing, obviously, but so are our mind,
will, intention, and emotions. Modern science continues to validate the age-
old belief in the mind-body connection. Healers are actually healing facilitators, aiding and coaching you on the process of self-healing.

Witches are healing facilitators as well, working with a holistic paradigm.
Witches know that all work must be balanced through the four elements, all of
which are involved in the dynamic process of healing. We are constantly challenged to remain balanced through these elements, earth, air, water, and fire,
and any imbalance can change the shift of health within our being. Our healing must take place on the physical, mental, emotional, and spiritual worlds in
order to be effective.

Like other spiritual and holistic healers, witches look to the root of disease for the effective cure. To do this, we must look at the actual root of the
word "disease." Break it apart and you find "dis-ease." Disease is a lack of ease,
a tension or block causing an imbalance. Witches view the body as energetic.
The emotions, mind, and spirit make energetic bodies around and through the
physical body. When you block the natural flow of energy in your emotional
or mental body, you eventually create a corresponding block in the physical
body, causing illness. Psychics can sometimes see "thoughtforms," masses of
unhealthy thoughts and programs in the energy bodies. They represent our
stuck thought energy, our harmful affirmations that get endlessly repeated
back into our consciousness. If you think "I am unhappy" often enough, you
etch the thought into your mental landscape, and endlessly visit it. The same
is true with healthy affirmations. That is why they work to improve life.
Healers often describe the old emotional patterns needing to be removed as
"muck" or "slime." As water relates to emotions, such images indicate water
that is stuck in the emotional body. Emotional clearing and re-patterning
clears away the muck, and often, it feels just like this image. We clear our own
personal sewers and closets of all the refuse we hide away.

Disease is the last-ditch method our higher consciousness has of pointing
out an imbalance. We can ignore our mind at times, seeing things the way we

desire. We can repress memories, rewrite our personal view on a situation, and justify our actions. We can ignore our feelings and shut down unpleasant emotions before we process them. But we have more difficulty ignoring pain in our body. We can shut out a certain amount of discomfort and pain, through our force of will, but as the body deteriorates, we are forced to look at what is happening and deal with it. We attract injury and illness to show there is a weakness in our sense of wholeness and balance.

When we direct our efforts to heal only on the physical level, disease will usually reoccur, unless we treat the underlying cause of the illness. The energy blocks will manifest in other ways. When we get to the root, we restore balance to the energetic pattern, and true healing can occur on all levels. Sometimes "miracles" occur during spiritual healings, and illnesses simply go away without a scientific explanation. To the spiritual healer, the energetic template of the illness, the block, was removed. Without it, the illness could no longer thrive.

The variety of illnesses and body parts corresponds to various emotional, mental, and spiritual issues. By looking at the body symbolism of the disease, we can decode the message our body is trying to give us. Various systems of body symbolism exist, from the chakras, astrology, Chinese medicine, and Ayurveda. Each has a system of correspondence between the physical body and the energies it represents. When you understand the root of the illness, your body gives you instructions to heal it. Only through balance of the body, emotions, mind, and soul can we find true health.

Chakras and the Roots of Disease

One of my favorite systems to use is the chakra system. It is simple and direct, and most witches are familiar with it. Chakras also relate to the elements and astrology, which is helpful. With any imbalance or illness, determine what chakra relates to it. You might find more than one is out of balance. If dealing with a physical disease or injury, look to the chakra closest to the problem. In general, problems on the right side of the body indicate issues with masculine energy, leadership, logic, and aggression. Issues on the left side indicate feminine imbalance, regarding emotion, intuition, and being receptive to input from others. Left also deals with the past and right the future. Issues in the lower body involve physical and material concerns. Issues in the upper body indicate mental and spiritual imbalances. Let's look at the chakras individually.

The root, or first, chakra drives the reproductive and excretory systems. The sexual glands—gonads in men and ovaries in women— physically manifest the energy of this base chakra. It relates to the elements earth and fire. Earth is the foundation to remain in the physical world, while fire here is the life force that animates us. The reproductive system biologically urges us to continue, as a species, while elimination clears out poisons. Here we manifest in the world, and choose to live or die on the physical level. Physical urges, basic principles of pleasure and pain, are linked to the root. The root chakra also involves those we trust for immediate survival. Although first-chakra physical problems indicate root issues, problems such as suicidal tendencies and impotence are also signs of dysfunction. Mars and Saturn are the planets associated with the root, respectively representing will and manifestation of karma in the physical plane. Pluto, the planet of sexuality, is a recent association. Those who are ungrounded, or "spacy" are lacking root grounding energy. Caroline Myss, author of *Anatomy of the Spirit*, says that the tribe relates through the root. Those with root difficulties often feel betrayed or unsupported by their tribe, or extended family/society. HIV/AIDS is connected to the root, both because it can be sexually transmitted, via the blood, as the root is the red chakra associated with blood, but also because many of the groups affected by it feel disenfranchised from the whole of society.

The belly chakra involves our ability to relate to another individual. It works in the area of physical contact and trust. Moving beyond the simple need to survive, the second chakra deals with primitive emotions, longings, and instinct. When we trust or distrust someone, we say we feel it in our gut. We actually feel it in the belly chakra. You may describe this as the social communication chakra or sexuality chakra as well. Water is the element of the belly, and the Moon and Mercury are its planets. It relates to the lower body, the intestines, kidneys, spleen, and pancreas. When we move from one extreme to the other, as in mood swings, addictions, tension, ulcers, or even promiscuous behavior that leaves us unfulfilled, we are having belly chakra concerns.

The solar plexus chakra is our place of power. At this level, we move beyond simple trust into power. We can claim our own power, try to claim power over another, or give our power away to another. When we claim power over another, we are usually afraid of their power. Fear is at the solar plexus. We also try to control when we get upset if something doesn't happen the way we want it to. We get frustrated and angry. The stomach, gallbladder, adrenal glands, liver, and musculature system are linked with the solar plexus. Chinese medicine calls the liver the throne of anger. The liver filters and stores toxins. Emotionally, anger is a toxin. The fight/flight stimulation of adrenalin, from the adrenal glands, also works through this chakra. Metabolism, from hyperactivity to chronic fatigue, is ruled by the solar plexus. Our muscles give us the ability to move, our ultimate sense of power. Fire is the obvious element, and both the Sun and Mars have been named the planet of the solar plexus. Here we also have our self-image, healthy or unhealthy. Here we relate to our own power and feelings about it. Power used responsibly is not bad. Like any tool, it depends on how one wields it.

The heart chakra is the bridge between the upper and lower chakras, and it can be a difficult bridge to cross. At this center, we first realize empathy. We take care of the lower issues of survival, contact, and power, and now see others for the first time as independent beings, not what they can do for us. We empathize with their feelings and situations and start to understand love. Heart chakra love encompasses family, friends, romance, and spiritual love. Inability to love, show emotion, be compassionate, or remain emotionally balanced indicates heart issues, as do fear, guilt, shame, and the inability to touch others in an emotional way. Venus, the planet of love, and Neptune are the heart chakra's astrological associations, and the elements of earth, air, and water are all associated with the heart. The obvious body system is the heart and circulation, along with the thymus and immune systems. Heart conditions, high blood pressure, chronic illnesses, and immune deficiencies are physical manifestations of imbalance. Skin is also part of the immune system and elimination. Rashes and infection can indicate a heart or heart/root imbalance.

The throat chakra is the first of the upper centers, relating to the concept of communication and expression, and the bodily systems of the throat, larynx, voice mechanism, tonsils, respiratory system, and thyroid. Illnesses in those areas usually indicate something is not being expressed fully. The block in the throat chakra means the truth is not being spoken, and needs to be. Silence is not the only block. Sarcasm and verbal abuse are other symptoms of a dysfunction in the throat chakra. You are not saying what you really want to say, so you express it in a hurtful way. All relationship communication issues fall under the domain of the throat, as do psychic abilities involving hearing and speaking with spirits. Speaking is not the only function of the throat. Here we must listen and receive information as well. Air is the element, and the planet of communication, Mercury, is related to the energy of the throat.

At the brow is the third eye chakra, linked physically with the eyes, pineal gland, nervous system, and lower brain and energetically with the ability to perceive, visualize, manifest, and receive information in an intuitive or psychic manner. It relates to the sixth sense, as the psychic eye gives us our inner vision. Those who have physical ailments in these areas, inability to follow intuition, or a difficulty in manifesting their dreams can have issues in the third eye area. Water, air, and fire are associated with the brow, as well as Jupiter and the Moon. Blocks or intense energy through the area are often called "third eye headaches" and can occur before deep cleansing of the third eye. Migraine headaches are also associated with the third eye and crown chakras.

The crown chakra, the last of the major seven, relates to the pituitary gland. The crown is the master chakra, and the pituitary is the master gland. At this point we find our connection to the divine. Those lacking a purpose, direction, or sense of spirituality and connection to the universe have crown issues. Physically, all diseases may have something to do with the crown, since all diseases ultimately can be healed through our divine connection and renewal. The physical systems are the upper brain and higher aspects of the nervous system. Body-wide illnesses—immune system breakdowns, skin problems, and environmental sensitivities—have been associated with the crown. The element is pure spirit, and the planets are the Sun, Jupiter, Saturn, or Uranus. At this chakra, we claim our spiritual power.

Healing Others

Once you have an understanding of the metaphysical energies involved in creating and maintaining a dynamic equilibrium for health, you can determine which modalities, or forms of healing, are most appropriate in a given situation. Witches who feel their calling is to work in the healing world usually train in several modalities. Some are strictly magical, falling naturally under the training of Wicca. Other modalities focus on more mainstream traditions, with which someone from a traditional spiritual background, or with no real spiritual background, would feel comfortable, such as herbalism or aromatherapy.

As a practitioner of several modalities, the most important thing I've found is the person being healed must resonate with the technique. If you use ritual magick with someone who is afraid of the concepts of magick and witchcraft, it will not work. If they are open to it or, better yet, pagan themselves, it could be very powerful. If they are not, you might go another route if qualified to do so, or refer them to a healer who is more appropriate. Certain people will be drawn to witchcraft, Reiki, shamanism, flower essences, or hypnotherapy because that technique resonates with them. It doesn't hurt to discuss possibilities and use what you feel is needed intuitively, but always take time to talk with the person with whom you are working, and understand their needs.

Most witches get involved in healing by accident, and do not plan on setting up a sign on their door. That's fine. People will be drawn to you if the time is right, and if they are not, perhaps healing is not your calling. There are many ways to heal. Some focus on the environment or community. Many witches simply model a healthy way of living on all levels, and lead by example.

We usually start our healing magick by working with friends and family. It can be a double-edged sword. Though they can trust us, and feel comfortable, we as healers often take on a "responsibility" to heal them, feeling it is our duty to maintain the health of our loved ones. You must always remember you are a healing facilitator and your only job is to aid and empower them. If your ego and attachment to the result is getting in the way, help them find a less involved healer. Often, the ones we are the least attached to emotionally and socially are our greatest success stories.

Psychic Healing

Psychic healing is the province of the witch and many others who use their intuitive gifts. In reality, all healing is psychic healing, using the powers of our mind, soul, and will to create change in the body, consciously and unconsciously. Psychic healing is a catchall phrase for those actively using their abilities to induce health in themselves and others.

Psychic healing uses the power of intention, often through the medium of sight and visualization. The third eye rules our psychic ability and inner sight. You don't necessarily need great visualization skills to be a psychic healer, but you do need clear intention.

The first healing technique I learned to use is the power of healing light. I still use it, and it is one of the most powerful tools I have in my healing "toolbox." Each color is a vibration, and our visualization of a color activates that vibration on a "higher," or metaphysical, level, creating changes in our subtle bodies and chakras. Each of the chakras is a color of the rainbow, indicating states of health. By visualizing a colored light around a person, you fill them with that vibration and can effect change and healing. You can do this in person. Some like to make physical contact. Or you can visualize the person in your mind's eye, regardless of where they are physically, and "send" them the light by "painting" their image with it.

In either case, you start by getting into a meditative state, relaxing, and centering yourself. Second, ask permission. If someone is physically with you, explain to him or her what you are going to do, and usually there is no problem. When doing distance work, you should try to get verbal permission.

Sometimes this is not possible, or you would like to send healing light, but if you tell the person, let's say a conservative family member, that it involves witchcraft, they might want nothing to do with it. You can explain this is your tradition's way of praying for healing. Or you can get into a meditative state and ask permission of their "higher self." Then, with an open heart, listen to your intuition and you will know if you have permission. You can't go around healing everyone without permission. Many people don't want to be healed; they might not want to take responsibility for the healing, or maybe the illness is serving a higher purpose for their soul to grow and expand their awareness.

Once you have permission, you can then start the healing. Think of the person, and let their image appear on the screen of your mind. If you're with them physically, focus on the energy around their body. Hold the intention of the "highest healing good." Imagine you are picking up an imaginary paint brush and painting the light all around them, you can imagine colored fog surrounding them, rainbow-colored "stars" absorbing them, showers of colored water or colored films laid on top of their image, like a stage lighting gel. By holding the image in your mind for a few moments, you build the energy and intent. When you release the image, you are "sending" it back to the person, wherever they are. You are not draining your own energy doing this, but calling upon the natural vibrations of the universe.

The technique is very simple. The most complicated aspect is deciding what color to use. First, meditate on the person. Think about what is wrong, if you know. Let the images and ideas come to you without judgment. Sometimes it is suddenly clear as to what light will work. Other times, you have no idea. In general, I use green for minor ailments and injuries, for general growth and healing. Shades of red and orange are used for more major healing, critical situations to bolster life force. Blue is used for bringing peace and spiritual healing, and purple for guidance. White can work in any case. If you know the area of the body affected, or chakra involved, you can use the color of the chakra. Imagine bright, vibrant, jewel tones. You can even do the rainbow, starting at red, and using all seven chakra colors to balance and harmonize. Refer back to the colors in the candle magick section in chapter 10 for more ideas.

Other forms of psychic healing can be more involved. When creating a physical change, you can visualize the effect you want in your mind's eye as you send healing light. Each case is different, but you create an image—literal or figurative—that gets your intent across to the body. For example, if you're working with a cancer patient, you can visualize the sluggish and weak cancer cells getting devoured by healthy and strong white blood cells. You can see the tumors dissipating, breaking down little by little, and being replaced by new, healthy tissues. Or you can visualize the white blood cells as the hounds of the Goddess, running wild through the body, devouring all the cancer monsters, and leaving the body clean. One image is more literal and medical, and the other more symbolic and mystical, but both get the job done.

Psychic healing can be done for anything, not just critical healing. Although I don't often go out drinking socially anymore, when I do, I end the evening with a short visualization of drawing the alcohol molecules out through the pores in my skin. I bless a glass of water to heal and cleanse before I drink it and go to bed. By using this technique, I made it through my rock-n-roll college days without ever getting a hangover.

This visualization technique is the principle that hypnotherapy works under, along with creative visualization. Through suggested affirmations and visualizations, the one under hypnosis undergoes a fundamental programming of the mind, affecting the body-mind connection. What makes this psychic is the fact that it works not only when the patient is the one affirming and visualizing, but also when a healer is directing those visualizations and intentions at the one in need of healing. If you are working with someone, help him or her take an active role in the process. Guide them in a meditation, to get down into a deeper state of relaxation and awareness. Guided meditation is simply a form of self-hypnosis. Guide them through affirmations and healing visualizations, to make them an active part of the process.

Exercise 15. Sending Light

1. Pick someone to whom you would like to distantly send light for healing and do so. First, ask their permission, or do so when in a meditative state by calling on the person's higher self.
2. Call their image to your mind's eye. The visualization may be clear or fuzzy, full body or just the face. Go with whatever comes.
3. Decide what color(s) you are using. If you are not sure, use a multicolored rainbow light, like the blaze of an opal. Keep a clear intention of the highest healing good.
4. Vibrantly visualize the color surrounding your target. Hold the image and intention for as long as you can. Then imagine sending both to your target, "erasing" the image from the screen of your mind.

❈ ❈ ❈

This last aspect of psychic healing crosses over to our next topic—energy healing. Psychic healing naturally crosses these borders. More in-depth healing techniques in this vein are called psychic surgery, or shamanic surgery, and involve psychically removing the energy and patterns of illness.

Energy Healing

Energy healing is a process of using vital life force to stimulate a person's natural healing abilities on all levels of being. Energy work is a process of supplying extra life force, used to increase vitality and to gently flush the system of any harmful energy blocks. Think of yourself and energy as a glass of water. There is some mud at the bottom of the glass. Most of the water is clear. When you have a trauma or illness, you stir the water up, and feel like things are murky, dark, and depressed. You cannot "see" where you are going spiritually. Energy work is like adding fresh, clean water to the glass. You fill up and overflow. The new water may kick up more mud, until the mud is eventually flushed from the glass, leaving you with only clear, clean water. Most of us have many layers of mud in need of cleansing. Traditional forms of psychotherapy, counseling, and medicine can do the same thing, but energy workers feel this process both quickens and eases the transition back into balance.

Vital life force is called by many different names, depending on the culture and time period. I've heard it called *chi, ki, prana, mana, numen, sekhem, ruauch, od, odic force,* or *orgone.* Each has a slightly different definition, but they essentially mean the same thing. I usually call it prana. This vital force is in all beings. It is a universal life force, animating all life, on every level, from humans and animals, to plants and minerals. The energy is the foundation of our energy bodies, the patterns for our physical body.

We absorb this life energy through the air we breathe, our food, if it is nutritious, through the water we drink, and the elements around us—wind, moisture, sunlight, and walking on the earth. Most people don't recognize the energy is present in everything, and tend to ignore it. Sometimes the energy gets dense and stuck, preventing the flow of new revitalizing energy to a place in our body. Other times our reserves get low, and we feel rundown and susceptible to outside illness and injury. When the flow is strong, balanced, and dynamic, we are healthy.

Use the Energy around You—Not Your Own

The biggest mistakes many healers make are to use their own personal life force energy as the source of healing, or to absorb the illnesses and blocks into their own bodies. The first example expends the healer's energy, making him or her susceptible to illness and low vitality. No matter how energetic you are, you can only contain a finite amount of energy. If your client needs more than you have to give, you will become overwhelmed. Only through connecting with a more infinite source are you safe from this danger.

In the second example, the healer takes on the pain of the client, feeling the healer has greater mastery of his or her own body, and by absorbing the problem, it can then be more easily banished. This is not an effective long-term technique, since it puts the burden on the healer's already-taxed body. Illness and pain can linger and remain, even after the healer feels they were banished. I don't suggest either of these techniques.

Like many other witches, I use the power of the Earth and sky. They represent a balanced polarity of Goddess and God energy, and through them, we connect to the infinite Goddess and God, directly to infinite Spirit. This connection is our supply of healing energy as well as our protection.

Exercise 16. Energy Healing Method

To use this method, sit or stand in a comfortable position, and have your client into a comfortable position. I usually stand with someone lying down on a massage table. As in Exercise 1 on page 60, count yourself down into a meditative state, yet remain aware.

1. State your intention of healing for the highest healing good, harming none. Call upon the Earth goddess and sky god, and your favorite gods and spirit guides.
2. Visualize roots growing out of your legs and feet, as if you are a great tree. Imagine the roots going deep into the earth, connecting with the center of the Earth.
3. Imagine the center of the Earth glowing brightly, like a green star. With each breath, imagine your roots are drawing up the green energy, through the layers of the Earth, and into your feet. The energy flows up your feet and into your body.
4. Visualize branches reaching up from your crown, high into the sky, reaching to the Sun, Moon, and stars. With each breath, you draw down their energy through your branches, down into your crown and into your body. Bring the Earth and sky energy to your heart, and think about Perfect Love and Perfect Trust.
5. As you exhale, imagine exhaling the energy out through your shoulders and arms and through your hands. Place your hands on the client's body, particularly over the areas in need of healing. Feel the energy flow into them, bringing healing.

6. Follow your intuition and guidance to know when to change hand posi-
    tions and when to stop. You can even do this on your own body, direct-
    ing the energy through your own hands, or through intention, from your
    heart to any internal area.

✳ ✳ ✳

Energy healing can quite effectively be combined with the examples of
psychic healing above and other techniques. Follow your intuition, while
holding an intention for the highest good.

Other formal systems of hands-on energy healing include Therapeutic
Touch and Reiki. Both are powerful and fairly easy to learn with a good
teacher. It is important to realize that just because you may do hands-on healing or other energy work, you are not necessarily using these well-known systems of healing. The idea is the same, but the educational structure and technique are different.

Crystal Healing

Crystal healing is the use of minerals, and their vibrations, to effect healing in the body. Each stone has a different energy, or vibration, and can be
used in magick and healing. Just like herbs, stones carry a spirit with them,
corresponding to the elements, planets, and chakras. They can be used in
charms, potions, and other spells. By connecting with such energies, you
bring balance into the energy body. My friend Jessica describes vibrational
healing as "shaking out all the bad vibes," and that is as good a definition as
any. Vibrational healing is like cleaning out the glass of water again. Crystals
are another form of energy healing, but instead of channeling it through the
healer's body, the energy is transferred through the stones. Crystals, quartz in
particular, are said to amplify energy and intent. Energy healers will often
hold a quartz "wand" to direct and amplify energy to individual body parts
and chakras. Although often viewed skeptically by the modern medical community as a "New Age" practice, crystal healing has a long history among
Native peoples. The foundation of crystal magick is how we've obtained the
modern birthstone association. The twelve stones for the twelve months of
the year are actually based on the twelve signs of the zodiac, which don't
match exactly with the month. For example, some people think that because
Aquarius goes into the month of February that amethyst is the Aquarian stone,
but it's really Piscean.

Some Stones and Their Healing Properties

Here are some popular crystals and their associations, along with lore concerning gay myth and mystery.

Agate: Agate is a sacred stone of Hermes/Mercury and Artemis/Diana from the Greco-Roman period. It is a form of chalcedony, and comes in a variety of patterns and colors, influencing its properties. In general, agate can be used for balancing extremes—yin/yang, masculine/feminine, logic/intuition—to promote healing. It fosters the ability to go within to discover the source of the imbalance, and creates a greater, balanced awareness of yourself and the world around you.

Amethyst: The stone is named after Artemis's beloved nymph, who was killed by the tigers of Dionysus. Artemis could not restore her to life, but transformed her into a beautiful stone, much like the story of Apollo and Hyacinth. *Amethyst* means "not drunk," as Dionysus poured his wine as an offering to the spirit of Amethyst, for forgiveness, giving it a purple hue. Later it was used to prevent drunkenness, and associated with the worship of Artemis, as well as gender-variant people. Amethyst is a form of quartz, and aids in spiritual pursuits, third eye development, meditation, and a sense of peace and tranquillity. It is also used in cases of addictions, disenchantment, or when spiritual pursuits become an unhealthy escape from real-world responsibilities.

Aventurine: Aventurine's most common color is green, and it resonates with the energy of the heart and unconditional love. It helps cleanse, open, heal, and protect the heart chakra, attunes one to loving spirits and guides, and in general balances both masculine and feminine and the upper and lower chakras.

Carnelian: A form of agate that usually comes in the shades of red and orange, carnelian is used for aligning your mind and your instincts, aiding the ability to trust yourself and others, and igniting your passion or spark. Carnelian can be used by public performers and actors. It protects you from the more "negative" emotions such as fear, envy, anger, or sorrow.

Citrine: Citrine is a form of yellow, gold, or brown quartz, used for manifestation of wealth, prosperity, and transmuting blocks. It also heals the solar plexus, helping us with problems of self-image, esteem, and fear. Citrine shines the light of truth in all areas, clears the mind, and uplifts attitudes, particularly of people who are in a place of darkness or depression.

Emerald: Emerald, a green form of beryl, is powerful both in love and prosperity. It opens the heart chakra to self-love, loving relationships, and a feeling of worthiness. You will then receive what you desire. It balances and harmonizes the emotions. Emerald helps connect you to spiritual guidance through the heart chakra. It also eases stress and tension, particularly in the heart and eyes.

Jade: In Chinese mysticism and alchemy, jade symbolizes the balance between yin and yang, male and female in perfection, and is often used in reference to genitals and sexual fluid. Jade is used in dream work, to heal, learn, or spiritually solve problems while sleeping, or to remember dreams and interpret their meaning. It aids in meditation and shamanism. Jade brings wisdom through the heart, and promotes fidelity in romantic relationships.

Jasper, Red: Red jasper is very grounding, but it does not give a sense of heaviness like other stones—only stability. Red jasper reminds one of responsibilities and how best to serve those responsible. It holds the vibration of the Earth Mother.

Lapis Lazuli: This blue, speckled stone is used to open the throat chakra, helping you speak your truth and express yourself. A stone of power and prosperity, lapis aids all expression and manifestation. Ruled by the planet Jupiter, it can bring good luck in business and the home, or turn inward to bring you greater spiritual awareness. Lapis can facilitate dream work.

Malachite: Malachite cleanses, clears, and grounds all chakras, but particularly works through the heart chakra as a balancer. Malachite grounds wisdom in practical terms, helping to illuminate the path of what you should or shouldn't do for your highest good.

Moonstone: Moonstone contains a healing and soothing form of feminine energy, like the Moon. It allows greater access to emotional memories, to process, heal, and release them. Moonstone also stimulates your intuition and awareness, helping you to be more sensitive to your own feelings and to others'. Moonstone is a favorite choice of modern witches.

Pyrite: Pyrite is also called fool's gold because of its goldlike appearance. This mineral is used for protection and health on all levels. It also clears away illusion, particularly those of your ego.

Quartz, Clear: Clear quartz, sometimes cloudy or milky white, is a great all-purpose stone, used to heal on all levels. It can be used on any chakra. Crystal points direct and amplify energy, so be careful what intent you place into them. They will simply amplify it, like a loudspeaker. Quartz can be used with any intention and magick.

Quartz, Rose: Rose quartz is a stone of unconditional love. It brings a feeling of warmth, reconnecting you to the Goddess and God as divine parents.

It helps support and stimulate all your creative talents and repressed feelings, allowing you to express yourself fully and freely in love.

Quartz, Smoky: Smoky quartz is a powerful grounding stone, to help bring you back into the physical and feel centered and present. It also is used to slowly move through blocks in all chakras. The energy is gentle and feminine, connecting us to Mother Earth.

Quicksilver: Quicksilver, or mercury, is obviously associated with Hermes/Mercury and androgyny, but because of its toxicity and fluid form, it is not used in modern crystal healing. Aluminum is often used as a substitute for quicksilver in charms and ritual tools. Some use the planetary symbol of Mercury for rituals involving the balance of gender energies.

Ruby: Ruby is a high-energy stone, bringing fire and intensity to all healing sessions. It stimulates you to follow your passion and bliss. It asks you to find your fire. Ruby can be used with both the lower chakras and the heart chakra. It heals the blood and circulatory system and helps remove toxins.

Turquoise: Turquoise is another great all-purpose stone, used by many American Southwestern tribes. It can be used much like quartz, for almost any intention. It brings protection, peace, and spiritual insight and aids in communication.

How to Work with Crystals

To use a crystal in healing, cleanse it like you would any other ritual tool. The geometric pattern of the crystal's structure is said to record and retain energy, like magnetic tape. It is important to clear it before use. Although many books recommend soaking a crystal in salt water, I feel such methods are too harsh, and prefer incense, pure water, visualized light, or strong intent.

Consecrate it like you would your other tools, but use the intention for healing. I usually say, "This crystal will be used for the highest healing good, harming none. So mote it be!" Then, carry the stone with you or lay it on the body. Follow your intuition. If you are attracted to or strongly repelled by a stone, it may have an important energy for you. The ones we are attracted to are easy, but sometimes we don't want healing, and the ones that we don't like can have just as valuable a lesson for us.

When working with a client, lay the stones on his or her body. The vibration can easily pass through clothing, but some prefer skin contact. The simplest layouts are of seven stones, following the chakras. Use a stone with the same color as the chakra, or simply use quartz. You can apply ruby, red jasper, garnet, or smoky quartz to the root. Carnelian or moonstone works for the

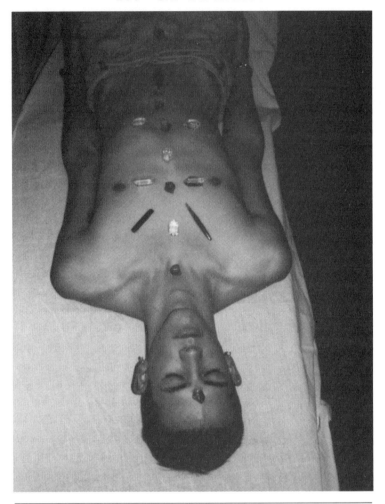

Crystal layout

belly. You can use citrine or pyrite on the solar plexus. For the heart, any green or pink stone such as emerald, aventurine, jade, malachite, or rose quartz will work. The throat can be healed with blue lace agate, lapis lazuli, or turquoise. Use amethyst for the third eye. Clear quartz is great for the crown. If you have a specific issue, and the stone is noted for healing that issue, use it whenever you feel called to.

Witches and healers will often wear jewelry with the seven chakra rainbow stones, creating their own magical pride necklaces and bracelets.

Start slow and simple, keeping the stone on for only a few minutes at a time. When you and your client are more comfortable, leave the stones on longer, and if you choose, use more complicated layout patterns. As you develop as a healer, follow your intuition. You can then feel more comfortable varying stone/charka color combinations. Sometimes the heart needs a blue stone. Sometimes the root needs green. Ask your spiritual guides to help you.

When you remove the stones, imagine a string is still connecting it to the body. With your hand, pretend to cut or break the string as you remove the stone, releasing the energetic connection. Cleanse all stones when you are done.

Ritual Healing

Ritual healing is often seen as far more religious than the psychic and energy healing above, though it need not be. Many equate it with faith healings found in several religious traditions, but ritual healing, from a witch's point of view, requires no faith on the part of the client. They don't always need to be present. I think ritual healing is much like prayer, except the form our prayer takes is a healing spell.

Healing spells are like any other spells. The Magick Circle Ritual is at the heart of this technique. You can use the waxing Moon to bring health, and the waning Moon to banish illness. Use the magick circle and write out your intention.

I, [state your name], ask in the name of the Goddess and God to immediately grant complete and total health to [state the name of your recipient] for the highest good, harming none. I thank you for all favors. So mote it be!

or

I, [state your name], ask in the name of the Goddess and God to immediately banish all illness from [state the name of your recipient] for the highest good, harming none. I thank you for all favors. So mote it be!

The intentions can involve more specific information, such as naming the illness itself, or naming where you want the healing to occur. The recipient can be in the circle with you, or not actively involved. It doesn't matter, unless they want to be present and are open to the idea of ritual healing. I prefer that the recipient be present, but it is not required. You can add the following invocation to your healing ritual.

To Hermes who walks between the worlds,
We call upon you.
To Hermes who carries the healing staff,
We ask for your presence.

To Hermes who guides all journeyers,
We ask for your aid.

Thrice Great Hermes
Bring healing complete and whole,
In body, mind, and spirit to (recipient's name).
Guide him/her on the journey and ward off all future harm.

So Mote It Be.

To Hermes, who walks between the worlds,
We thank you.
To Hermes who carries the healing staff,
We thank you.
To Hermes who guides all journeyers,
We thank you.

Hail and Farewell.

You can augment this magick by using candles that have specific healing colors, as you would with psychic healing. The healing power of herbs, in potion magick, is also quite effective.

Healing Potion

2–4 c. spring water
2–4 tbs. sea salt
1–2 tsp. ginger
1–2 tsp. ginseng
1/2–1 tsp. frankincense
1/2–1 tsp. myrrh
1/2–1 tsp. vervain
1/2 tsp. apple blossom, seed, or peel

Prepare the potion as described on pages 144–45, charging each ingredient as you add it to the mix. You can anoint the ill person, a candle, or a representation, such as a photo or poppet, with the healing potion.

How to Make and Use a Healing Poppet

A poppet is a doll made to represent the ill person, and the healing is done through the doll's image to reach the actual person. Cut out two duplicate human-shaped pieces of black, white, green, or red cloth. The doll doesn't have to be large. The size of your hand will do nicely. Sew it all together, but leave a hole to fill the doll. Charge and mix the following herbs:

2 tsp. vervain
2 tsp. lavender
2 tsp. sage
1 tsp. ginseng
white cotton balls
copal, quartz crystal, or a white pebble

Stuff the doll with these herbs and some white cotton. If you have a piece of copal, place it in the center for the heart. You can also use a quartz crystal or even a white pebble instead of the copal. Sew it up. If you have a photo of your recipient, paste his or her face onto the doll.

While in the circle, name the doll after your recipient. Feel the two become connected. You can then use psychic or energy healing on the doll, as if the person was with you. You can use your wand, or even a needle, to point and direct energy to a chakra or organ. Poking or piercing the doll with a healing intent will not cause pain or injury in the recipient.

When the doll has outlived its usefulness, cast another circle on the waning Moon, and intend to banish the connection between the doll and recipient. Take your athame and pass it all around the doll, breaking the connection. Dismantle the doll, and bury the herbs and cloth, allowing the earth to reabsorb any magical energies within the doll.

Spell to Cleanse the Spiritual Bodies

Not only do we maintain the health and cleanliness of the physical body, but we must maintain the good energetic health of our spiritual, or subtle, bodies. Try this spell when feeling tired and overwhelmed by other forces. It will help cleanse your aura.

1 tbs. lemon balm
1 tbs. chamomile

1 tbs. lavender

½ tbs. myrrh

4 tsp. sea salt

1 beer (bottle or can)

1 fluorite crystal

Mix together the herbs and salt, charging all for cleansing, healing, and peace. Draw a bath and soak the herbs in the bathwater, letting the salt dissolve. Add the beer to the bathwater. Yes, beer. Sounds strange, but the folk remedy probably comes from the idea of barley water, and barley is a sacred grain of the Goddess. In fact, all grains are. The use of beer is our modern equivalent. Bathing in it, rather than drinking it, can cleanse the energy field of harmful energies, judgments, and ill will from others. Charge the fluorite for cleansing and protection and keep it near you but out of the water. High temperatures can cause it to crack. Fluorite is an energy cleanser, purifying your aura and strengthening your protection shields to increase your natural defenses to energy pollutants.

Think about your unwanted aches and pains, emotions, mental stresses, and other drains. Inhale deeply, and as you exhale, imagine releasing them into the water. Do this until you feel you have let go of everything to evaporate away in the warm water. Stay in the bath as the water drains out, taking with it all unwanted forces. Then shower off lightly and carry the fluorite with you as needed.

Healing Addictions

Addictions are tough obstacles to unlock and overcome. Each can share a beautiful lesson with us, if we let it. We all have addictive behavior, but in my work, I've noticed a great deal of these issues run strongly in the gay community, both out and closeted. Perhaps it is because many gays feel they have no culture beyond simply being gay. We use addictions—from the obvious cigarettes, intoxicants, and sex to the more subtle food, computer, television, and even relationship addictions—to cope with our illusions about our community, the world, and our self. These behaviors represent mechanisms to cope with our illusions.

The spiritual energy of addiction is tied very strongly to the planet Neptune. In astrology, Neptune is the energy going deep within us, named after the sea god of the Romans. Symbolically, going deep within the oceans of the self means self-exploration. Because of this spiritual exploration into unknown depths of the self, Neptune's highest form is unconditional love. Unfortunately diving to the bottom to retrieve this sense of love is a difficult thing. Many people get lost along the way and don't want to face what lies in their personal depths. Because of this, Neptune is also associated with disillusionment. We become disillusioned and disenchanted when we find a love that turns out to be conditional. We become bitter, or even lose ourselves in our own escapist behaviors and illusions of how we want things to be, never facing the reality.

Those who deal with these feelings in a healthy manner often express it through art, music, dance, writing, and other forms of creativity. Creativity is a form of exploring unconditional love. Some become mystics, having difficult inner experiences but eventually emerging from the oceans triumphant and sharing knowledge with the community. Still others do not cope well. They find coping mechanisms that distract them from the journey, but can have a similar feeling of depth as the oceans of the soul. These mechanisms often become our addictions if we let them become more than temporary tools. Things like substance abuse help cloud our vision, distracting us from our true emotions, our true selves, because they can be too difficult to bear. We attract the addictions that suit our personality and fears the most.

No one spell will take care of an addiction instantly. Spells can be part of calling upon a higher power for guidance and help, as found in many twelve-step programs. This spell is the first step in a longer road of healing and self-awareness. You have chosen to express this addiction on some spiritual level to teach you. As you learn and integrate the lesson, you are freed. Magick will not take that gift away from you, but it can give the process more ease, grace, and gentleness.

Spell to Heal Addictions

For this spell, you'll need grapes—one for every addiction you wish to heal and release—and two bowls. Place the grapes in one bowl, and leave the second empty.

- Gather your grapes on a waning Moon, preferably on a Monday or Friday. If you can pick them from a living vine somewhere, that's great, but the supermarket is just fine.
- Cast a circle in the traditional way, but call upon the god Dionysus along with any other patrons and spirits. Dionysus is a Neptunian figure, patron of ecstasy, grapes, wine, and the arts.

- After the Great Rite, focus on the addiction or addictions you are healing. Even if you are focusing on one addiction, there can be many aspects to it, so make sure you have enough grapes.
- Pick a single grape, and focus on releasing your addiction into it. When you feel it is "full," squish it and place it into the second bowl. You are breaking its hold over you. Say:

  I ask in the name of the Goddess and God, in the name of Dionysus, to be free of this addiction, to heal it completely and immediately, with ease, grace, and gentleness. I release myself into your highest guidance and draw from you my strength. So mote it be.

  For every thought regarding the addiction, or aspect of it, pick a grape and repeat the squishing and affirmation. For example, you may be focusing on alcoholism, but there may be many issues related, such as drinking for acceptance by others, drinking to relax, self-esteem issues with a parent, drinking to forget past relationships, and so forth.
- When done, release the circle. Take the bowl of punctured grapes and release it in a place that will go to moving water. It can be a river, stream, ocean, or even down the sink, garbage disposal, or toilet. Release the old addictions into the water.

Healing Homophobia

Homophobia is one of the biggest problems facing the gay community, but it unfortunately sneaks in where we least expect it, in the gay community itself. Internalized homophobia is one of the worst detriments to living a life in Perfect Love and Perfect Trust. Sometimes we think we have hang-ups about how other gays live and act, but often really have the problem with ourselves on some level. Others just act as a mirror for things we fear about ourselves. If we truly are living "do what thou will and let it harm none," we wouldn't have a problem with people acting in any way that pleases them.

Spell to Heal Homophobia

Use this spell to acknowledge and heal any internalized homophobia you may be holding, so you can live in peace and freedom. It can be done on either the waxing or waning Moon. You'll need a gazing surface such as a crystal ball, crystal point, black witch's mirror, silver mirror, or bowl of water that you have consecrated for this purpose.

- Make a list of all the people you feel you have a problem with in the gay community. It can be friends, enemies, fictional characters—anyone. Reflect on each name and determine whether a personal event between you has soured your feelings or if there is something in their personality or behavior that you don't like. Some of us feel others act "too gay," meaning too effeminate, too masculine, or otherwise too stereotypical.
- Write down all the behaviors, actions, and mannerisms that bother you and people you associate with them. Think of all the behaviors and mannerism, you have that you might not like either. Reflect on why you don't like these things.
- Then, with your list on hand, cast a magick circle, creating your sacred space.
- Gaze into the reflective surface you have blessed and think about the items on your list. Project your mind's eye into the reflective surface, and imagine yourself doing those behaviors, even if they are alien to you. Watch yourself in new roles and identities. Watch yourself with compassion. You may laugh or get upset, or think the whole ritual is silly. Simply continue until you work your way through the entire list.
- Understand that all these behaviors, and all these people, are reflections of yourself, reflections of the divine mind. We are all one, and all have a right to our own behavior and identity. One way is not the right way for everybody. Diversity is truly the key.
- Surround yourself with pink light for self-esteem and self-love. Then imagine all the people who were on your list are in the circle with you. Fill the circle with pink light, sending them all Perfect Love and Perfect Trust. You don't have to like everyone. You don't have to be friends with them. But you can accept them and love them on a spiritual level. You can feel a connection to them and not feel anger or fear.
- When done, imagine the pink light reaching out to these people, like weaving a cosmic web. Release the circle as you normally would.

Freedom from Past Abuse

Many of our tribe have faced not only prejudice for being gay, but outright abuse—verbal and physical. From schoolyard bullies shouting "faggot" or "dyke," subtle slurs from family and friends, to actual gay-bashing violence, we endue the potential for danger. Most of us have been on the receiving end of some form of abuse at some point in our lives, and perhaps we have even given it out to others. There is a natural tendency to want to hurt someone who has hurt you, or hurt someone else to feel your sense of power and control return. Even if we don't ever carry it out on the physical plane, we harbor secret fantasies of getting even. As we study magick, we learn that not all action takes place physically, and our thoughts and feelings have power. Those very thoughts and feelings, those secret grudges and long-held fantasies, could be holding us back and preventing us from being in the present, fully healed and realized. A part of us is stuck in the past, and stuck in the pain. We need to acknowledge it and move through it to move on.

Ritual to Release Past Abuse

To let go and forgive these past abuses, try this ritual. If possible, do it on the waning Moon. Sit down and meditate on your past, and write down all the people or situations by which you feel abused or maligned. Reflect on each one. Does it stir any emotion? If so, even if it is a tiny emotion, keep it on the list. Make the list as long and as specific as possible. Write down every hateful name you have called someone or called yourself.

Then go out and find a round rock roughly the size of your fist. It can be any type of rock, from a polished crystal to a beach or river stone. Meditate with the rock. Ask yourself if the rock feels like it is a healing stone. Ask the rock itself if it wants to help you heal.

Once you find an appropriate rock, take your list and wrap it around the rock. Bind the paper to the rock, wrapping thread or yarn around it, as many times as needed until the paper is secured to the rock. Put all your feelings of trauma and abuse into the stone and paper. Thank the stone for its aid, and say:

By the spirit of this stone, and the spirit of the Earth Mother, I ask for healing. I ask to release all pain, abuse, and trauma I have ever suffered. I ask to release it to the Earth for transmutation. I ask the Goddess for her support and stability in this time of healing. So mote it be.

Take the stone and either throw it in a body of water, such as a lake, ocean or river, or bury it somewhere no one will dig it up. The water and earth will eventually dissolve away the paper and, more importantly, heal the energy. Then reciprocate. An opportunity to help someone else heal will present itself for you. It could be volunteering for a social center or organization, or simply listening to a friend in a time of crisis. Be there when called and you, too, will have the help you need to heal.

✳   ✳   ✳

And as usual, follow up this ritual with real-world action. If you need to see a counselor to help move through these pains, please do so. Magick can help the process along, and you can repeat this spell as many times as you need, but take action in the world.

Past-Life Healing

Sometimes an issue in our healing journey becomes so stubborn we cannot understand or remove it. We work through all the experiences, traumas, and abuses we have in this life, yet certain issues, making no logical sense, persist. Once we have exhausted all the practical possibilities, we may look for the roots of the imbalance in our past lives.

The belief in past lives is not exclusive to nor did it originate in witchcraft. Much of our modern understanding comes from the East, India and Asia, but tribal people all over the world have always felt a deep connection with their ancestors, feeling the children of the tribe are a rebirth of the ancestors. Julius Caesar, in his account of the Celts, gives us some evidence that the Celts believed in some form of reincarnation. Through this report, many modern witches adopt the belief in past lives, but then explore it through direct experience.

The basic concept of past lives is that our soul is immortal and goes through various incarnations into physical life. In each life, we go through experiences that act as lessons for our soul's own growth. Personally, I feel we know everything on a higher level and our "lessons" are simply new ways to remember our divinity.

Through these lessons, we create karma, a relationship with ourselves and other souls, giving us duties, obligations, and benefits. *Karma* simply means "action," but also refers to the results of our actions. Some look at karma as a bank account. Good karma is a credit, while bad karma is a debt that must be paid. Another view is karma as a contract made between souls when on the "other side" beyond our subjective, polarized view of good/bad, right/wrong, and happy/sad. We agree to be parents, lovers, children, friends, teachers, healers, employers, and enemies to other souls to create situations of growth and spiritual awareness. Eastern philosophies believe your duty is to clear all karma, good and bad, and free yourself from the wheel of rebirth. Upon that freedom, you come into your spiritual mastery.

Issues that have no root in this life and experience, or unexplained illnesses, are often attributed to a past-life memory. As we go from life to life, shedding the physical body, we take with us aspects of our spiritual bodies. They retain our "lessons" and past incarnation memories. If someone fears water, but has had no "bad" experience with water, why is this person so vehemently fearful? Perhaps they experienced drowning in a past life.

By exploring past-life experiences, you can understand, acknowledge and release the root of the fear. The therapy consists of undergoing a regression, through hypnosis, self-induced, or with a practitioner specializing in accessing past-life memories. Though it can be attempted individually, I don't suggest that. Past-life memories can be traumatic and you need an experienced person to help you through the process, guide you back, and counsel you afterward. If you're interested in this type of healing, I suggest going to a healer, clinical or metaphysical, with experience in this field.

Other Healing Modalities

This is by no means a complete list of metaphysical healing modalities. Some require training, certification, or a state license. Others are more intuitive and mystical. This just touches the surface of the healing worlds, and most topics go beyond the scope of this book, since they require a certain amount of training before application. Witches can be involved in herbal medicine, aromatherapy, nutrition, flower and gem essence consultation, psychotherapy, hypnotherapy, breath work, Reiki, acupuncture, acupressure, Rolfing, and massage therapy. If you desire to follow this path, check all the opportunities available to you.

14

Turning the Wheel of the Year

We are a part of the Earth. As the Earth dances with the Sun, as the seasons change, we too change. In Perfect Love and Perfect Trust, may we walk together with the Mother and the Father, turning the wheel of the year together, and welcome the changes of our lives.

Another religious practice in Wicca is celebrating the turning the wheel of the year. This eight-spoked wheel turns with the cycles and seasons of the planet, and witches feel a desire and responsibility as caretakers to participate in the turning of the seasons, and honoring our partnership with nature.

Because of houses, indoor heating, plumbing, air-conditioning, supermarkets, and electric lights, the modern person is not as observant of the changing patterns of nature. They do not directly affect us if we choose not to be a part of them. Night is not longer as frightening. Day is no longer dramatic. We do not observe the planting, growing, and harvesting as our ancestors did. They had a direct partnership with nature and the gods and goddesses who embody nature because survival and well-being directly depended on them.

Modern witches know our direct survival may not be affected by observing the holidays, but our ultimate survival, as a species and a planet, does. We observe the wheel of the year by directly participating with these energies, to bring ourselves in harmony with the planet and to maintain the balance and awareness. Those with a greater understanding and respect for nature can then bring that awareness into day-to-day living.

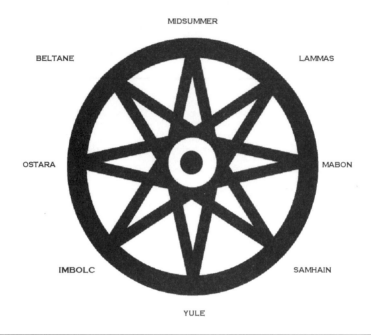

Wheel of the Year

By actively celebrating the wheel, a witch gets to know and understand the changing faces of the God and Goddess, as represented through the various myths associated with the holidays. The direct experience that can come through ritual and meditative celebration is more important than intellectual understanding.

By itself, the wheel consists of four solar festivals—the two equinoxes and two solstices—and four fire festivals, celebrations between those solar holidays, marking shifts in humanity's relationship with the land through agriculture. Fire is used in such celebrations for light, cleansing, and energy, hence the name fire festival. Collectively the wheel of the year is the story of the Goddess and God and their relationship.

On the winter solstice, called *Yule*, the Sun has reached its darkest point. Here we have the longest night of the year. From this point forward, until the next solstice, the light and day will grow stronger and longer. The Sun represents the God, as it has in cultures across the world. So, symbolically, we say the Great Goddess gives birth to the Sun, as a child of light. With each day, he grows stronger. The Goddess enters a winter slumber.

Imbolc, celebrated on February 2, is next. The name is often translated as "yew's milk" and was originally a Celtic celebration in honor of the goddess

Brid or Bridgit. The Christians turned her into St. Bridgit, and renamed the holiday "Candlemas." Candles and lights are burned to cleanse and bless a home at the end of winter. Protective charms for children are made. The light symbolizes the light used to awaken the Goddess from her slumber.

On the vernal equinox, the day and night are equal. The Goddess rises from her slumber, rejuvenated as the maiden. Some pagans call it *Ostara*, after the Teutonic goddess Ostre. Eggs and seeds are blessed. The God takes his place in the sky to bring warmth to the lands of the Goddess, helping to resurrect the growing world. Persephone is also associated with this time of year, rising to meet her mother, Demeter, to bring the growing season.

At *Beltane*, May 1, we celebrate the first union of the Goddess and the God. He rises as her son, but soon to become her lover. Sexuality, fertility, and passion are celebrated, often with the May Pole dance, a fertility symbol of the God, as the pole, entering the Goddess, as the land. The God takes on less solar aspects, and becomes one with the living vegetation, sometimes appearing as the Green Man. In ancient times, cattle were herded through two sacred fires, to banish the last illnesses of winter. Modern pagans still walk or dance between fires to celebrate Beltane.

On the summer solstice, or Midsummer, as it is called, we undergo another fundamental shift. The Goddess and God take their place as King and Queen of the Land. She is exemplified as Mother, giving birth to the fruits and grains of the land. She is pregnant with the seed of the God, to give birth to him again at Yule. The God is the solar king and grain lord. Part of this holiday is celebration, with revelry and enjoyment. Midsummer is also associated with faeries and opening the door between worlds to their realm. Today is the longest day, with the longest twilight, a time between worlds. But here, the God must face his shadow, his dark half. The dark aspect of the God defeats the light, and from this point on, the dark will grow stronger.

On *Lammas*, or *Lughnassadh* (pronounced Loonassa) in the Irish traditions, celebrated on August 1, we have the first harvest. The solar and grain god of the light is sacrificed by the god of the dark. We take the first grain harvest, and offer it to the gods. This is a funeral celebration, thanking the god of grain for his sacrifice, so that we may live. The Celtic god Lugh is associated with this harvest, being both a grain and solar figure.

Mabon, the autumn equinox, is named after the Celtic god who, as a child, got lost in the underworld. On this day, the veils between worlds begin to part, and the God's light aspect, sacrificed on Lammas, descends into the underworld. The Goddess begins her mourning, as the trees turn and plants wither. Mabon is the second harvest, the fruit or wine harvest, and wine is often used in rituals on Mabon. Dionysus is also associated with this time of year.

The last of the eight festivals is called *Samhain* (pronounced "Sow-wen"). This is the celebration of the dead. The Goddess travels to the underworld in her mourning, opening the gates of life and death. Samhain is also known as the meat harvest, because livestock was killed and salted or smoked to preserve through the coming winter. On Samhain, we honor the ancestors and spirits, making meals for the dead, and lighting candles to guide them. Spiritual work and divination are powerful this time of year. We consider this the Celtic New Year, because it is an ending, and a beginning.

Same-Sex Imagery in the Wheel

As you can tell from the story of the God and Goddess, a great emphasis is placed on the union of man and woman and physical fertility as embodied by the land. Some conservative pagans have used this as an excuse to be homophobic and are closed to other interpretations. The heterosexual symbolism has a certain universal power and truth to it. Even as gays and lesbians live a life of same-sex orientation, most of the world does not. We come from a variety of family structures, but biologically we each contain the union of male and female in some form.

As we look to the ancient truths and lessons, we know homosexuals played a part in the religious world and the interpretation of life. As modern witches, we know the story of the Goddess and God, and the wheel of the year is one way to describe vast and powerful energies. Although these descriptions are an amalgamation of European myths, they are neither the only applicable myths nor the only relevant interpretations.

As we discover the divine masculine and feminine within ourselves, we are free to find the divine in many forms, and use the images and myths more appropriate to our own spiritual practice and well-being. We can see the story of the wheel of the year taking place in our own individual selves.

By using some same-sex mythology, we are not denying the power of one aspect, God or Goddess, any more than we are denying heterosexuality exists by having same-sex partners. We are simply focusing our energies on an aspect of life that we can relate to best.

THE GODDESSES OF GREECE

In ancient Greece, the story of the seasons only peripherally involved the gods. The goddesses were the focus of the wheel and changing seasons. They held the power of the Earth. The Greek traditions divide the provinces of nature and man among twelve deities, called the Olympians. The great grain mother, Demeter, known as Ceres to the Romans, is in charge of the growing season. She traveled the world with her daughter, Kore, and wherever they walked, the earth would sprout and bloom, giving flowers, fruits, and grains. They maintained a veritable paradise on Earth with a never-ending growing season. The weather remained temperate to keep the fruit on the vine. The land continuously replenished itself. Humanity wanted for nothing. All was provided by the mother and her maiden daughter.

Then, tragedy struck. Kore was wandering off in a meadow, picking narcissus. The king of the underworld, Hades, looked up from his kingdom and saw Kore. Some say he wanted to possess her beauty, others say that he fell in love. He rose up out of the ground and snatched her down into the underworld. The older, Orphic versions of this myth say he seduced her with music to come willingly to the underworld. To all, she had disappeared without a trace.

Demeter searched the world for her daughter. The Sun could not see her. The other gods could not help. Because she embodied the land, she withdrew into herself, and so did the land, bringing the first autumn. She mourned for the loss of Kore and the world mourned with her.

Eventually, she found herself at Eleusis. She pretended to be mortal and was hired by Queen Metanira to nursemaid her son Triptolemos. Demeter decided to give Triptolemos the gift of immortality, and while she was burning away his mortal side by smoking him in the fireplace, Metanira interrupted the process. He was unharmed, but Demeter had to reveal her divinity. She mourned by the well at Eleusis, and eventually a temple was built in her honor that would later house the famous Eleusinian Mysteries and initiations. The queen's daughter Baubo kept the goddess company and some say she revealed Kore's whereabouts to Demeter. Baubo and her friends had seen Kore's abduction in the meadow.

Meanwhile, Kore remained in the underworld. In the gentle versions of the story, Kore fell in love with Hades; whereas in the violent versions, he raped her. In either case, she ate six pomegranate seeds, the fruit of the dead. Hades fed them to her because once she ate of the fruit of the dead she could never leave.

The dark goddess Hecate, Queen of Witches, lived in the underworld, but did not rule it. She noticed the newest addition to the land of the dead, and expressed her concerns to Zeus and Demeter. Zeus wanted to support his brother Hades, but feared what would happen if humanity perished with no food. Demeter refused to make the earth grow without her daughter. Zeus declared Kore would be returned to Demeter, but only if she did not eat the food of the dead. Hades forced her to confess that she did. Demeter would not budge. Finally, they struck a compromise to have Kore spend half of the year with her mother, Demeter, and half with Hades. When she is walking upon the Earth with her mother, her mother would allow life to grow. As she rises from the underworld, she brings spring. When she goes to the underworld, Demeter mourns again, and the world withers to bring fall. Modern practitioners usually focus on the equinoxes as the time of this shift. The story of Demeter and Kore is recounted in many Ostara and Mabon circles.

Kore, assuming responsibility as queen of the underworld, was renamed Persephone, and became a powerful and dark goddess in her own right. She controlled life and death, using the power of the living season and the dying season by her passage. Her movements affected and controlled two of the most powerful deities in the Olympic pantheon, Demeter and Hades. She is the power of change, cycle, and season. Although not specifically a lesbian myth of the seasons, it details the powerful feminine energy apparent on all cycles.

THE KINGS OF THE CELTS

To look for a male-oriented seasonal shift, we can look to the Celtic traditions. Though very Goddess focused in their modern reconstruction, the Celtic traditions have a twofold God, one of light and one of darkness, embodied in the Oak King and the Holly King. The Oak King is the lord of light, life, and vegetation, sometimes depicted as the Green Knight, Green Man, or Jack of the Green. He rules the year from the winter to the summer solstice, growing from a babe and taking his place as king and champion.

The Holly King is the lord of darkness, death, animals, and withering. He is pictured as a Red Knight, or horned god, resembling Cernunnos. He is the avenger. The Holly King is older, and rules the land from the summer solstice to winter. He rises from the underworld, like the green god's shadow, and in the twilight, they battle, but the outcome is never in any doubt. During this waning time of the year, he ushers in autumn and winter, and his wild hunt runs free to protect and avenge. On the winter solstice, the forces of light and dark battle again and the Oak King rules that day. The light of his birth banishes all shadows and darkness back to the underworld.

Unlike the well-documented Greek myths, there is no specific story to the Oak and Holly King myths, just fragments and themes. They survive in our modern understanding of the mysteries. The most important of these understandings is the fact that this light and dark battle is not one of good and evil. Both are necessary, and as divine personas, both are loved by their people. Though no modern person wants winter, withering, and death, to the Celtic worldview, it is a necessary part of life, a time for the land and spirits to renew.

The most amazing part of this mythology, for my personal practice, came from a posting on an old America Online message board. Unfortunately, I lost the direct information, but I incorporated it into my own practice with my partner. This person suggested the Wiccan Great Rite can be expressed by two male partners during the wheel of the year celebrations through the imagery of the Oak and Holly King. One partner plays the role of the Oak King, and the other the Holly, in the roles of the Great Rite. It's an excellent, gay-positive symbol system for lovers who practice and celebrate together.

Usually the younger partner plays the role of the Oak King, while the older is the Holly King. Or the choice can be made through astrological Sun signs, to fit energetically with the seasons. Those with the Sun in Capricorn, Aquarius, Pisces, Aries, Taurus, or Gemini, being born between the winter and summer solstice, would take the Oak King role. Those born between the summer and winter solstice, or the signs Cancer, Leo, Virgo, Libra, Scorpio, or Sagittarius, would take the Holly King role. Use whatever system works best for you, or simply choose the roles that fit your personality best. Who is the darker or lighter of the couple?

During the waxing year, when the Oak King rules, he carries the blade and will be more "responsible" for leading the circle, most likely casting the boundary himself. For the Great Rite, he will take the role of the "ruling" god and act as high priest. If you incorporate sexuality into your practice, and would like to enact the Great Rite through intercourse as a part of your spiritual expression, then the Oak King is active, while the Holly King is receptive. At the summer solstice, a ritual drama of "passing the power" represented by the blade, wand, or staff can be done. You can even do a ritual battle, or wrestle for "control," but the outcome is never in doubt. The Holly King rules this half of the year, and the ritual roles are reversed for the next four holidays.

The benefit of practicing with your partner is a shared spiritual experience, role reversal, and opening the lines of play and communication. This is an intimate, special, and sacred experience, but it can also be fun and playful. For me, it has been powerful to unite my sexuality and spirituality with my partner's.

Transgenderism and Magick

Queer couples and covens do not have to look exclusively to same-sex imagery in their spirituality. In fact, if our premise is to find both genders in

Horned God

each of us, then we must be willing to explore such roles. Ritual dress for magick and celebration can be very important. Many who cross-dress—gay or straight—view the process of transformation as a ceremony. When we look to the masks, wigs, and costumes of age-old shamans, the process is much the same. There is an element of theater to it, but the transformation is much deeper than surface makeup and preparations. In fact, the very act of walking between the gender worlds is the process of shamanism and ritual. Makeup, potentially with magical symbols and designs, body painting, costume, jewelry, wigs, masks, and crowns are a part of ritual drama and magick. They are particularly powerful for rituals of invocation. You do not have to identify with the opposite gender in everyday life to express yourself in ritual and ceremony. Such magical times should be a time of exploration and create a safe boundary to do things you would not do in your everyday life. Ritual is a place where things that are often considered taboo in the outer world become sacred to the inner, spirit world.

The transformation does not necessarily need cosmetic alterations. It can be completely internal and energetic. Although I love the concept of the Oak and Holly King in sex magick and celebration, when a man is in the receptive role, identifying with the power of the Goddess is powerful magick. In our past patriarchal society, we look to women and receptive men as being submissive and subservient. In a Goddess-honoring path, receptivity is magick and power, the power of love and creation. The formerly dominant, active partner becomes the servant of the powers of love and creation. Remember that role reversal in your life and in your rituals. Be bound only by the powers of your imagination and your highest guidance when performing creation rituals and sacred drama.

Rituals of Celebration

There is no right or wrong way to celebrate the holidays. Celebrations can be as simple as a prayer or meditation. They can be intimate gatherings of one, two, or three people. They can be as elaborate as a large gathering with singing, dancing, and complex ritual, but the most important aspect of the holidays is to *celebrate*. The rituals are a focus for harmonizing yourself with the energies of the year, to flow with the tides and recognize how you interact with the world and all of nature.

Here is a sample of a summer solstice ritual. Use it. Be inspired by it. Take it apart and make it your own. Following it are several ideas for each of the holidays, suggesting myths to study and other ritual correspondences. Experiment, play, and have fun. Use song and dance in your rituals. All arts are sacred to the Goddess and God. If there are public circles in your area, attend them to see how others celebrate. No book can give you the feeling of a good group ritual. For more holiday celebration ideas, I suggest *Wicca: A Guide for the Solitary Practitioner* by Scott Cunningham, *The Spiral Dance* by Starhawk, *Celebrate the Earth* by Laurie Cabot, and *The Witches' Bible* by Janet and Stewart Farrar.

Summer Solstice Ritual

You will need a quartz crystal for everyone who attends the ritual. The crystal can be substituted with a piece of metal jewelry. You will also need some ritual cakes, a red candle, a green candle, a bowl of milk, a bowl of honey, and the standard altar setup.

- Ritually cleanse yourself and put on your ritual clothes.
- Cleanse the space and attend to all your necessary tools.
- Stand before the altar. Guide yourself and anyone else attending into a meditative state.
- Cast the circle:

  We cast this circle to protect us from all harm. We cast this circle and invite in only the most perfect spirits. We cast this circle and create a temple between the worlds. So mote it be!
- Call the quarters, turning to each one as you say:

  To the north, we invite the element of earth, the Great Stag, and the Holly King to join us. We welcome the changes you bring, for without death, there can be no life. Hail and welcome.

  To the east, we invite the element of air, the Dark Crow, and the Crow Mother to join us. Please protect us with your feathery cloak and guide us through the coming dark. Hail and welcome.

  To the south, we invite the element of fire, the Red Fox, and the Oak King to join us. We wish you well in your passing and will welcome you again. Hail and welcome.

  To the west, we invite the element of water, the Loving Dolphin, and the Mistress of the Ninth Wave to join us. Please bring the waters of clarity and creation. Hail and welcome.
- Invite the Deities into the space. Light the black and white candles, saying:

  We invite the Goddess and God into this circle, the King and Queen of the Land, to guide and guard us.
- Light green and red candles and your incense. The incense should be a solar one, such as frankincense or copal. Say:

  We invite those from the realm of the Fey who come in Perfect Love and Perfect Trust to join our celebration.
- Anoint wrists and third eye with protection potions.

  Blessed be.
- Perform the Great Rite. As you raise the athame, draw in the last rays of sunlight rather than moon. Fill the chalice with the power of the solar fire. Say:

  We draw in the power of the Sun god, while he is at his peak of power. We take in this energy and bring it to the Earth, to the Goddess, for our health and prosperity, guidance and protection, for the coming winter. So mote it be.

• If there is more than one participant, pass the chalice around and let those who desire to, drink from it.

• Bless the cakes, saying:

With the light of the God, we bless the grains of his body on Earth, and thank him for the sustenance provided. We thank the Goddess and God for all their bounty on this summer day.

Set the cakes aside to be passed around at the end of the ritual.

• Bless the honey and milk as offerings for the faery folk. Offer a libation (pour them out onto the ground, if outside):

We ask for the blessings of the Fey, for the good of all, harming none.

• Guide yourself or the group through this meditation:

Feel the Sun above you, today, the longest of days. Feel the golden rays rain down upon you like a beam of light. Feel the light descend down into your crown, energizing and healing your body. Feel the light descend down into the brow, clearing your sight and perceptions. Feel it move into your throat, healing your communication. Feel it in your heart, opening the heart to love, feel it move through your arms, surrounding this circle with the love you have for all those here. Feel it in your solar plexus, granting you personal power. Feel it move into your belly, giving you trust. Let it move into your root, clearing your foundation. It moves down your legs, connecting you, with love and trust, to Mother Earth. Feel the solar energy rush into Mother Earth for her healing as well. As you heal yourself, you heal the world. Feel the energy fill this circle, swirling around in golden light.

Pass the chalice around a second time, and let all present dip their crystal or jewelry into the water, to absorb the solar power and carry it with them. Pour the remaining water onto the ground if you are outside. If not, wait until the ritual is over and then go outside and pour out the water.

• Close with a circle of healing:

All those in this circle receive the healing they need, for the highest good, harming none. So mote it be!

• Raise the cone of power.

• Ground the remaining energy. Make sure everyone releases any excess energy from the solar meditation. Holding on to it will not bring more health or power. Too much makes you light-headed and unbalanced.

- Release the quarters:

  To the north, we thank and release the element of earth, the Great Stag, and the Holly King. Thank you for your gifts and blessings. Hail and farewell.

  To the west, we thank and release the element of water, the Loving Dolphin, and the Mistress of the Ninth Wave. Thank you for your gifts and blessings. Hail and farewell.

  To the south, we thank and release the element of fire, the Red Fox, and the Oak King. Thank you for your gifts and blessings. Hail and farewell.

  To the east, we thank and release the element of air, the Dark Crow, and the Crow Mother. Thank you for your gifts and blessings. Hail and farewell.

- To the center, facing the altar:

  I thank the Goddess, God, the Fey and all spirits who have joined in Perfect Love and Perfect Trust. Stay if you will, go if you must. Hail and farewell.

- Release the circle:

  We release this circle. The circle is undone, but not broken. So mote it be.

- Pass the cakes!

Ideas for Celebrating the Seasons

Yule: All our modern holiday traditions—the use of evergreens, Yule logs, mistletoe, and holly—come from European pagans. Pagans, too, celebrate the birth of the God. Create magical ornaments and bless them in ritual. Learn about child gods, like Mabon and Pryderi. Meditate upon welcoming the Sun back into life.

Imbolc: Imbolc is a time for pre–spring cleaning. Clean your home of physical and energy dirt and clutter. Use incense or sage to purify it. Light a ring of candles for guidance and ask the goddess Brid to bless your home and family. Charge the candles for health in the last winter months. Meditate on the growing light of the Sun. Traditionally, corn dollies (see "Lammas") were made and laid in a crib to represent the growing God. Corn stalks and wheat were also braided into Brid's cross, a protective charm for children and home.

Ostara: Ostara is the egg and seed celebration. Color eggs and paint them with magical symbols and mythic themes. Charge them as part of your spells for protection and prosperity for the season. Bless seeds for your garden or window box. Reenact the return of Persephone from the underworld, or the resurrection of Dionysus. Learn about the true roots of the Christian celebration of Easter.

Beltane: Learn about the Celtic fire god Bel. It is in his name that you celebrate Beltane. If you have enough participants, dance around a May Pole. Light two fires and dance through them to purify yourself of all lingering ills. Wash your body with clean spring water to purify yourself. Sexuality, in or out of a ritual, is an appropriate celebration on Beltane.

Litha: Litha, Midsummer, and the summer solstice all denote the same holiday. Learn about the faery folk from Celtic myth. Study Shakespeare's *Midsummer's Night Dream* for inspiration. Litha is often playful and mischievous. Instead of drawing down the Moon, draw down the Sun, and ritually absorb the energy for healing and health over the winter. Charge crystals, charms, and potions with the power of the Sun.

Lammas: Lammas is the first harvest when effigies of the God, made from grains and cornhusks were sacrificed. Make your own by gathering hay, cornhusks, dried grass, or dried flowers. Bundle them with string to form the figure of a man. In ritual, burn the corn dolly in your cauldron or if you have a fire. Burn offerings of cornmeal or wheat. Bake and share bread as a part of the Great Rite. You are consuming the grains of the God. Although this is a funeral, think of it as a celebration. Games are often played on Lammas. Learn about the myths of the Celtic god Lugh.

Mabon: Learn the myths of the Celtic god Mabon and his mother, Modron. Also study the Greek god Dionysus. Mabon is the time of the wine feast. Wine is often used in the ritual chalice to "open the gates." Pomegranate seeds can also be blessed and used in ritual. Meditation and shamanic journey into the dark, into the underworld to face your fears and shadow self, are important.

Samhain: Study the myths of the Celtic Morgan and the Dagda to prepare for this ritual. Learn about the true origins of Halloween. On Samhain, make an altar to your ancestors. Put out pictures of loved ones, friends, and family who have passed on. You can even use pictures of spiritual ancestors—historic, political, and entertainment figures—who have inspired and guided you, or whom you seek to emulate. Light many white candles in their honor, and prepare any of their favorite meals or sweets. You can then leave the food outside as an offering, to be consumed by the earth and any critters that may come along. Scrying, gazing into a crystal ball or black mirror, is a popular activity for this time. In ritual, stare into the crystal and ask any questions you have for the New Year. Look for symbolic images you must interpret, like dreams, to appear as you gaze into the crystal or mirror. Make New Year resolutions.

Honoring the Ancestors

Part of many Samhain celebrations involves honoring the ancestors. Acknowledgment and relationship with the ancestors played an important part in most tribal societies. As queer people, we often feel a disconnection from our family and society. When we look to history, we don't see our ancestors reflecting our path. Although some feel that the traits of homosexuality is genetic, I know I can't conclusively see it in my family tree. So who do we honor as the ancestors? We honor the gay tribes, those brave men and women who have come before us.

Samhain Celebration

As part of your next Samhain celebration, make an ancestor altar. Use images of actual relatives you honor, as well as passed loved ones who have been like family to you. Use images of artists, writers, and performers with whom you have felt a kinship. Research gay history and find your ancestors, your own patron saints and guides.

You should change and adapt the following evocation to suit you and perform it as a part of your celebration. All the people I mention are often cited as a part of gay history, and although many of them might not align themselves with modern gay identity, it is upon their dreams and work we continue to build our own. It is upon the shoulders of the ancestors we climb.

To Sappho and Socrates, Aristotle and Alexander, we call to the ancient ancestors of our tribe.

To Caesar and Hadrian, we thank you for your power.

To Michelangelo and Leonardo, we thank you for your visions.

To Byron and Whitman, Wilde and Stein, we thank you for your words.

To Uncle Aleister and the Faeries past, we thank you for your magick.

To Those With the Triangles who died in the Concentration Camps.

To Harvey Milk, Mathew Shepard, and all those who gave their lives in the struggle for awareness, equality, and healing.

We honor all the ancestors, known and unknown, loved and unloved, near and far.

We reach through the strands of the Goddess's web, all the way back to the first ancestors.

We thank you for paving the way for us and all our children to come.

Blessed may you be, in this world and all others.

15

Rites of Passage

Birth, Adulthood, Initiation, Partnering, Elderhood, and Death.
These are all sacred times to honor and acknowledge,
to mark and to celebrate, for they are the unique milestones of this life.

Tribal societies all over the world, from ancient to modern pagans, celebrate significant passages in life. As we celebrate the seasonal cycles yearly, we realize that each life has its own rhythm, cycle, and seasons to be celebrated. We pass through certain marks of life, and they should be prepared for and celebrated with our loved ones.

Mainstream society marks some of these rights of passage, drawing from traditional religious sacraments and ceremonies. Such practices grew out of the tribal rites and, unfortunately, most have lost a lot of their spiritual significance and simply become the expected or polite thing to do in our modern society. Much of the ritual has been stripped from acts such as birth, becoming an adult, marriage, or death, and the ritual that remains is often misunderstood.

Pagans celebrate several rites of passage. First is a welcoming ritual for a newborn child. The act of birth itself was performed ritualistically in ancient days, as the priestesses and witches were the midwives. Modern blessings are now called Welcoming ceremonies, or for those specifically involved with Wicca, a Wiccaning. Others include coming of age, spiritual initiations into the craft, handfasting or partnering, elderhood, and crossing over/funerary rites.

Those who live on the edges of society, such as gays and lesbians, need these rituals just as much, if not more, than others. They bring not only a sense of belonging but a sense of celebration to lives that are not typically celebrated in the world. I've always been struck by the particular word "family" we use to refer to our gay brothers and sisters. There is a sense that all queer people have a common bond. We often "make" our families out of our friends and loved ones. They are not necessarily our blood family, but they become a part of our tribe.

The following life passages may have already taken place in your life. That is no reason to not ritually recognize them if you are just now adding ritual to your life. You can also use this material if you are called upon to minister and guide others. If the ceremony calls for a minister or high priest/priestess, then I use the abbreviation HP/HPS. Otherwise, you can adapt the rituals for your-self or with a minister. Feel free to add all your own personal touches, includ-ing music, song, chant, and dance, to make it more yours.

Coming of Age and Coming Out: The Ritual of Rebirth

We are sorely missing the ritual of becoming an adult in our modern world. We grant adult rights at a certain age, but there is no real ritual to cel-ebrate and recognize it, other than drinking, driving, or voting. No process leads up to it. All rites of passages are initiations of a sort, processes that change us. In times past, sometimes an initiate received a physical mark to signify the change, such as a piercing, to represent a deeper, internal change of worldview.

For women, the passage into adulthood comes physically, with the onset of menstruation. Though something to be celebrated, many girls enter this process with fear because they were not prepared for it. Menstruation signals the transformation into womanhood, but today the role of women can seem very confused. Although we are opening to an age of opportunities for women, the experience is still markedly different from the ancient Goddess cultures. Then, there was no doubt. Woman was life. Woman was wisdom and healing. Woman was the embodiment of the Goddess.

For men, the process is now even more nebulous. Boys have no first hunt, no vision quest, and no initiations into the secrets of being a man. We have great expectations and place responsibilities as to what it "means to be a man" but give no instruction, counsel, or wisdom.

For gay people, one of the most important coming-of-age rites is the process of coming out. Coming out is a combined spiritual initiation and coming-of-age ceremony, although it is not as respected or welcomed as a formal cer-emony. Coming out is an initiation, a potentially traumatic situation that tests your resources. It tests your inner spiritual and emotional resources, your courage, and your relationships Afterward, you will never see life the same way. Like any initiation, you step through a door, and once you walk into the new world, you can never really go back to the old one with the same comfort. You can try, but you will fail. You have changed too much. Through the process, you come into your own truth, a very adult truth, and hopefully become the man or woman you wish to be, one who can be happy and well adjusted, living in the truth.

Although the coming-out process may become less difficult as we see a decrease of homophobia, the process itself is still initiatory. No matter how loving and supportive a family or society feels, it is extremely difficult to come to the internal realization, and then admission, that you are different from the majority of your peers. This occurs in the initiation of the shaman. The tribal healer would often experience something, such as a vision or fevered illness inducing vision. This experience would threaten to kill or drive the potential shaman mad. Not only must he or she seek out the truth and overcome the potential for disaster internally, the healer must heal and then return and offer the truth to the tribe.

The wise ones often lived on the outskirts of the village—in the world, but not of it, always slightly separated from the rest. The witches of Europe would gather together with their own kind for the major holidays, and form tight-knit groups, extended families of witches that have become known as covens. To me, it sounds strikingly similar to tight-knit gay communities, forming their own extended families outside conventional society, where comfort and then empowerment can be generated, by finding others who share your difference.

Gay practitioners of the art of magick, and witchcraft in particular, feel they have already had an initiation prior to their involvement in magick. Coming out was the experience that changed their worldview long before they understood spells and rituals. The study of magick simply added to it or acted as a secondary initiation, no less powerful, but still striking a similar chord. When hearing about the witches and shamans, and in fact, all mystics called to the path of initiation, they feel a certain kinship. I came to Wicca before I came out, so for me personally, the experience was a bit reversed. Both were initiations, filled with fear and doubt, but once they were completed, each in their own way helped me shed an old identity that no longer served, like the snake shedding its skin, and become a new person. Each process helped me get to the center of who I am and what is right for me.

I came to terms with my homosexuality, at least internally, at the end of high school. On my eighteenth birthday, I marked the time by piercing my ear. Although I didn't tell anyone at the time, it symbolized that from this point forward, I could do what I wanted, and be who I wanted to be. I graduated from an all-boys Catholic school that had a dress code. I immediately wanted to do something to break myself from that, so the piercing, along with

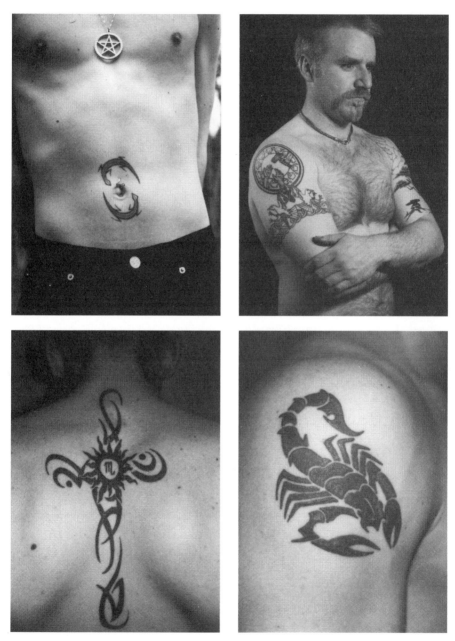

Piercings & tattoos

growing out my hair, helped me redefine my self-image in college. Later, through my mystical studies, I learned that piercing was often part of a coming-of-age ritual in tribal societies.

Tribalism in general has become a strong influence in contemporary society. Starting in fashion trends, tattoos, and body piercing, I hope some of the more spiritual and societal aspects of tribalism enter our consciousness. As we swing into the modern world, with our cities and technology, it's ironic that we're creating a kind of urban tribalism and urban shamanism to assist us in these challenging times.

My friend Jessica has taught me a great deal about merging magick and body modification as parts of rites of passage. She pierced her tongue to remind her to think before she speaks, since in the past she has tended to do the opposite. She has had many of her animal totems tattooed on her to remind herself of the lessons she has learned, and the medicine she carries in this world. To her, they are not just trendy fashion statements, but magical rituals. As I write this, I've experienced a year of lessons in regarding the body and physical health. I am contemplating piercing my navel to remind me of my relationship with food and exercise!

You may want to make body modification a part of your ritual celebration of coming out. It can signify acceptance of queerness, acceptance of being outside the mainstream, or empowerment of finding your true self. Although tattoos and piercings are permanent modifications, you can use less permanent modifications. Temporary henna tattoos, face painting, and other forms of temporary body art are wonderful tools to make this ritual special for you.

Although coming out is not often celebrated by family and friends, it should be. No traditions that I know of have formal rites for coming out. I suggest using these simple rituals to inspire your own. Even if you came out years ago, the ritual acknowledgment and celebration of your own gayness can be a very powerful experience. It brings your sexuality into the sacred when so many others would leave it in the realm of taboo. In many ways, coming-out rituals are like traditional baptisms or welcoming ceremonies. They welcome you into your new life and new community. It doesn't mean you necessarily leave the old. You simply gain a new sense of belonging from this baptism. Coming out is a rebirth.

Coming-Out Ritual

If you can gather your friends and "family" with you, or even have them participate in the ritual, so much the better. Or you can do it alone, reminiscent of the lone shaman's initiation. The choice is up to you.

- You'll need a mirror that you have consecrated for this ritual.
- Prepare for the ritual celebration by cleansing yourself on all levels. Start with a magical bath or shower. Honor and accept your body. Let all stress and tension wash away. If possible, do some simple breathing exercises and meditation before you do the ritual, either prior to gathering with others, or doing it on your own.
- Cast the circle and call the quarters in the traditional way.
- Invite any particular gods, goddesses, spirit guides, and power animals into the circle.
- Light any incense or candles you have. Use protection potion. (Optional)
- Perform the Great Rite. (Optional)
- If you have something that symbolizes your time in the closet—an article of clothing, jewelry, book, magazine, or even an old nickname written on a piece of paper, hold it up. Think about what this symbolizes, and what you are leaving behind. Once you walk out, there really is no going back. You can ritually offer up the item. If it is something small and flammable, you can burn it. Or you can simply cast in on the floor now, and bury it after the ritual. If you don't have a physical symbol, simply visualize a "shedding of your skin," of your past identity and self-image, to enter a new freedom to redefine yourself in any way you choose.
- Hold up your ritual mirror, or have a friend or family member hold it up to you. Gaze deeply into the mirror. Gaze into your eyes. Look at who you are and love yourself wholly and unconditionally. While looking in the mirror, say this or something similar:

    I thank the Goddess and God for my unique blessings. I thank them for all the gifts and talents they have bestowed upon me. I accept my magical heritage fully and completely. I accept myself as a [use whatever word you may identify with—gay man, lesbian, bisexual, or perhaps gayness or queerness; use whatever you like]. I love myself unconditionally. Blessed Be.

- If gathered with others, pass a pink, purple, or rainbow candle around the circle. Let each person say a blessing, words of encouragement, or anything else that spirit moves him or her to say while holding the candle. If you are alone, say a word of encouragement and blessing to yourself. When you start to pass it around, light it. Let its magical light shine on you.

• Complete the circle, thanking all present, release the quarters, and release the circle.

Spiritual Initiation and Dedication: The Awakening

Spiritual initiation is a rite that not many people undergo. Mainstream religions often have ceremonies, such as confirmation, to welcome an adult member into the religion, but the rites of spiritual initiation are more like taking the vows of a priest or minister. Witches are priestesses, priests, and ministers by their very definition. Even if they choose not to be community leaders, they are their own priests and priestesses in solitary and group practice.

Various traditions of witchcraft and magick have very different systems of initiations. Some are hierarchical, based on degrees and titles. They have typically at least three levels and some have as many as ten or twelve. My own tradition has five, based on the five elements. Others are nonstructured, and are not based on formal rituals or degrees, but on a simple dedication ritual. Many solitary witches opt for the dedication ritual, for which an aspiring witch will study for a period of time, usually a year and day, and decide if this is the path or not. If it is the right path, the student will perform a ritual of dedication to the path and to the Goddess and God. Although the word "vow" is rarely used, it is a decision, or pledge, to live a magical life and assume its powers and responsibilities. We all live magical lives. Witches, pagans, and magicians are simply the ones who know it consciously and act from a place of magick. Spiritual initiation and dedication rituals are an acknowledgment and awakening to that fact. Unlike in other priestly orders, there are no vows of poverty, chastity, or obedience to another. Witches seek direct contact with the divine rather than a place in an institution.

If you aspire to be a witch, have studied and practiced the material in this book, along with some self-study from other books and resources, and feel this is truly the path for you, do a dedication ritual to mark your "coming out" into witchcraft or paganism. Just like sexuality, this is a personal matter, so you do not have to announce that you are a witch to everyone unless you want to. Personally, I'm out of the gay closet and out of the broom closet and can't imagine it any other way, but different lives require different decisions. Choose wisely and let this ritual be your inspiration.

Initiation Ritual

For this ritual, write out a pledge, in your own words, to the path of the witch and to the Goddess, God, and Great Spirit, however you view them. Make it heartfelt and sincere. Also, make sure you have a special oil or potion for ritual anointment. If you don't, use a mix of sea salt and water. You can do this by yourself, or another witch can do it with you.

- Ritually cleanse yourself, energetically, or take the time to have a ritual bath and cleanse on all levels. You are entering a new phase of life and, in essence, are breaking with the old.
- Cast a circle.
- Call the quarters.
- Call the Goddess and God—call those deities you feel most connected to for the process of dedication.
- Read your pledge as if it were a spell, and burn it, releasing the energy to you and the universe. Raise the cone of power, assume the Goddess position and then the God position, and ground yourself.
- After taking the pledge, be anointed with these blessings:

    Anoint your feet: *Blessed be my feet, growing roots deep and strong.*

    Anoint your root: *Blessed be my root, so that I may survive and prosper in this world. May I give and receive pleasure.*

    Anoint your belly: *Blessed be my belly, so that I may nourish myself and others. May I always listen to my instincts.*

    Anoint your solar plexus: *Blessed be my power, so that I may find it and use it when needed, and have the self-esteem to truly embrace it.*

    Anoint your heart: *Blessed be my heart, so that I may always walk in Perfect Love and Perfect Trust with the Goddess and God.*

    Anoint your throat: *Blessed be my throat, so that I may speak clearly, and understand others.*

    Anoint your brow: *Blessed be my brow, so that I may see clearly in all worlds.*

    Anoint your crown: *Blessed be my crown, may I always know my connection to the universe.*

- Complete the circle, thanking all present, release the quarters, and release the circle.

Formal initiations in more traditional covens often use the five-fold kiss ritual, from the high priest or high priestess to initiate, either kissing five points up the body with blessings, or kissing the five points of the pentagram found in the human body—the two feet/ankles, two wrist/hands, and the brow—creating a star. Other initiation rituals have coven members wash the initiate before entering the circle, or have them vow to enter the circle only in Perfect Love and Perfect Trust, at the threat of a ritual sword or athame.

First Love, Commitment, and Partnering:
The Handfasting

Our first love and, in particular, our first gay love is definitely a rite of passage. All relationships bring us something from which to experience, share, and grow, regardless of the outcome. Our first experience is one of the most important, be it first kiss, first sexual experience, or first actual relationship. Each is a milestone that transforms us significantly. Recognizing the personal and spiritual significance of each event is important.

If we desire a life partner, and find one, that relationship can be the most transforming of them all. A long-term commitment places us in situations that force us to grow, expand our awareness, and move beyond our sole needs, to create a home for the relationship. Although not always easy, the rewards can justify the difficulty. In most societies, the act of partnering is celebrated by the community through what is now called a marriage. Unlike simple lovers, a marriage asks the community to recognize and support the public relationship. Many in the gay community refer to their partners as "lover." Although very true, I always found that funny. Having an astrology background prior to a deeper experience in the gay community, I noticed how astrology always divided the two, having a separate space, or "house," in the chart for partners and another for lovers.

Astrologically, and personally, the two have very different energies. When two people make their commitment public, it transforms the experience, although for those who have been together for a while the transformation is subtle. My partner, Steve, and I lived together for a few years, and had been together for many years before we had a public ceremony. Nothing seemed to change, but looking back on it many months later, I realized the dynamic of the relationship changed slightly, presenting new challenges, as well as new growth.

In witchcraft, the marriage rite is traditionally called a "handfasting," referring to the binding of hands together that is an important aspect of the ritual. Although some extreme Wiccan ministers view it as a binding of souls together for this life and all others, most moderates, myself included, feel the loose binding of the hands symbolizes the conscious choice of two to walk together on the road of life. Most witches believe in reincarnation of some sort, and feel we are not wise enough now to know what we will need in all lifetimes. Decisions made in this lifetime should only be for this lifetime. If you are "meant" to partner with a soul throughout eternity, you can renew your vows in each lifetime.

Part of the tradition from the Celtic background is a year-and-a-day trial period for the partnership. In this time, a couple really discovers life as married partners. The trial period is much like the time of study for an aspiring witch, before truly committing to the path. The process starts with an initial handfasting ceremony, usually done in private. After the year-and-a-day period, the couple renews the handfasting as a more permanent commitment, typically through a more public ceremony and celebration. If the couple chooses not to continue after the year and a day, there is no guilt in the dissolution. It is considered wise to own up to your feelings and make life more pleasant for all concerned rather than stick to a decision because everybody expects it.

Another beautiful part of the ceremony is the jumping of the broom. Jumping the broom can be found in many traditions. The broom symbolizes the threshold. Witches often put their ritual brooms, used for cleansing a space, on the edge of the circle. When a couple jumps the broom, they are "jumping" into their new life together as a couple. Many brooms are made with an ash or oak handle, with the plant broom, itself, as the bristles, which are tied together with willow. They can be decorated with magical keepsakes and are put over the couple's hearth. Other popular plants used in the ceremony are rosemary, for remembering your love in times of difficulty, and rose, for love. Some make the handfasting cord from a garland of rosehips, for passion and desire in a marriage.

The most wonderful thing about handfastings is that most Wiccan ministers will perform handfastings for gay couples. Some are ordained ministers, for couples who can legally marry. I hope that someday all gay couples will have the legal right to marry, but at the moment, we do not. Many Wiccan priestesses and priests will also perform ceremonies for those who are not on the pagan paths. I feel the rites of handfasting and commitment are very important to the gay community, but many couples feel they cannot have it, and others say they don't want it, and don't need what the straight world needs. Perhaps they really don't, but some say it out of spite. But rituals and ceremonies are part of our rich history as queer people and it's time to reclaim them, on our own terms, with our own definitions. If you don't want to define your partnership in traditional marriage roles, then don't. Your partnership is between you and your partner and can be whatever you make it. Ceremonies are ways to acknowledge the importance of the commitment between you, celebrate it, and ask for the support of the family you have gathered around you. They can be simple and short ceremonies, or elaborate with formal receptions. Through commitment, we work on our relationship development, and thereby develop and mature our soul.

The Handfasting Ritual

Use this ritual, very close to my own handfasting, to inspire your own handfasting rituals. In my own ritual, we involved many people, including parents, covenmates, and good friends, to act as our "bridal party," call the quarters, bring up ritual tools, and recite blessings.

- Couple enters the circle from the east, for new beginnings.
- The HP/HPS casts the circle.
- The HP/HPS calls the quarters. You can call particular deities or animals to bring their blessing to the handfasted couple. You could use a call such as:

  To the north, I invite the element of earth and the great Bear to join me. Please bring strength and stability to this couple. Hail and welcome.

  To the east, I invite the element of fire and the great Lion to join me. Please bring courage and light to this couple. Hail and welcome.

  To the south, I invite the element of air and the great Crow to join me. Please bring wisdom and clarity to this couple. Hail and welcome.

  To the west, I invite the element of water and the great Dolphin to join me. Please bring love and healing to this couple. Hail and welcome.

- If outside, scatter a clockwise ring of flower petals around the circle, for the blessings of life and the element of spirit.
- The HP/HPS calls the divine:

  I invite the Goddess, God, and Great Spirit to this sacred rite. May you guide and witness this ceremony, and this couple through their life journey together. We invite all spirits of Perfect Love and Perfect Trust into this space.

- Burn a love incense of some kind, such as rose. (Optional)
- The HP/HPS says:

  [Names of couple], you are about to step into the destiny you chose before entering this life; to make a promise of commitment, the fruits of which you will carry throughout this lifetime and others to come. Knowing this, are you prepared to continue?

  Couple responds with

  I am.

- Lighting the Family candles: If each partner has a family member present, such as a parent, or a loved one who is like blood family, the family representative comes up to the altar, and lights a candle for that family. Colors of the candle should match the clothing/theme of each partner. The HP/HPS says:

  May we have the families come together, to light the sacred candles to represent these two sacred families.

- Exchange of vows: To each partner, the HP/HPS says:

  Do you [partner's name], take this man/woman to be your husband/wife, your partner for life? Will you remain at his/her side when life is good, when it is filled with challenge and fear? Will you laugh and dance with him/her in joy? Will you share his/her burdens, dry his/her tears, and hold him/her to your heart when he/she doubts himself/herself? Will you share his/her dreams, support his/her ideals while holding fast to your own? If you can promise these things, without reservation or hesitation, please answer by saying, "I do."

- Personal words of commitment: The couple says their own words or vows to each other if desired. The HP/HPS says:

  At this time I ask you to offer your own words of love and commitment.

- Great Rite: The couple can perform the Great Rite together if they wish. They can drink from the chalice together, and share it with the group if they choose. I prefer to keep the chalice between the couple only.

- Exchange of rings: You can have family members or "best men/brides-maids" bring up the rings. To each partner in turn, the HP/HPS says:

  [Name], place the ring on [Name]'s left hand and repeat after me: "I, [name], pledge to you my troth, with total and unconditional

love. I will love and honor you from the depth of my heart, in this life and all others. Please accept this ring as a sign of my love."

- Binding of cords: The HP/HPS wraps cords around the couple's held hands and says:

    The binding of hands is a powerful ceremony uniting two hearts together as one, yet retaining their individuality. The cords are wrapped loosely around the hands demonstrating the free choice of each to walk hand in hand, in sacred union to the journey's end.

- Lighting the Unity Candle: The couple lights the main unity candle from the flames of the two family candles. The unity candle can be any color the couple wishes. HP/HPS:

    The couple will now light the candle symbolizing the unity of their two families.

- Jumping the Broom: The couple, still handfasted, jumps the broom together, jumping into the west, the land of love. HP/HPS:

    It is now my honor to invite you into the most magical transition, as you jump the broom from solitary life into the union of partnership.

- Rosemary Blessing: The HP/HPS gives each partner a sprig of rosemary. HP/HPS:

    I offer each the gift of Rosemary, the herb of remembrance. Keep these sprigs in a place where you will be reminded of your love. Call on Rosemary if ever you feel doubt, and be reminded of your love.

- Pronouncement: The HP/HPS says:

    With the sacred power invested in me, I pronounce you life partners. You may seal your vows with a kiss.

- Complete the circle, thanking all present, release the quarters, and release the circle.
- Couple exits the circle from the west, for happy endings.

Ending a Relationship: Rites of Dissolution

Just as starting or committing to a relationship is an important rite of passage, ending relationships are very important. From the first breakup to the ending of a long-term commitment, proper endings are critical to our emotional health. Now we call it "getting closure." Ancients didn't use these words, but they had rites of closure. Traditional marriages have divorce, a civil remedy to a relationship that is ideally more than just a legal arrangement. Even the straight world doesn't have many spiritual rites around dissolving a relationship.

In other lands and other times, divorce had no social stigma to it, as it does today. There were rites of dissolutions as there were rites of marriage. Goods were divided up, the parting was recognized, and the couple was free to pursue other destinies. The social stigma of divorce didn't come until the officially sanctified institution of marriage and the role of the wife as subservient to the male, at least in many early religious communities. While many gay couples do not bear the same rights as legally married couples, they still get to carry the same shame and stigma, at least personally. However, they need to see the split as it really is—an ending—not as a source of shame or indication of failure.

Endings are symbolized by the Death card in the tarot. Although it seems like the end, Death represents a new beginning, a rebirth into another space. Have you noticed how, in many ways, all rites are about recognizing rebirth? It is the thread between them all. But telling someone to look at it as a new beginning is easier said than done. That is why we need ritual.

I once heard a wise woman say that those who do not ritualize the events of their life are forced to live the rituals as drama. I agree. Look at how much of the world has become a living soap opera. Notice how much energy we put to the drama of our relationships, particularly when they are breaking up. Drama is not exclusive to the gay community, but we do more than our share. We draw others into the drama, to hear our story, and we play the part over and over again. We don't know how to escape the cycle. At least I didn't. The key is ritual. Ritual allows us to focus our energy, and release it, so we are not forced to live the drama.

We are naturally drawn toward drama, remembering the original urge to create sacred drama, to create art. Unfortunately, we don't often see the sacred in our art and we don't understand its magical aspects. As a musician myself, a singer, I had a hard time reconciling my magick and my art. Magick teachers would tell me that my thoughts and words create my reality and here I was singing song after song of tragedy, heartbreak, and misfortune. Although writing about my past experiences was cathartic, I wondered if singing them over and over again was preventing me from healing and releasing them. It wasn't until I understood more about shamanism and sacred drama that I knew the secret to magical performance. A sacred performer can invoke the spirit of the story or song for the others, yet remain detached from the story when it is all done. The story flows through the performer. The performer is not forced to remain trapped in the story through retelling. Those who do not see the sacred in their art, and let it flow through them, often become trapped in it. I think that is why we have such tragic histories with our performers, artists, and rock stars. These rituals of art are about wearing and removing masks, but not getting stuck in the identity or time in life. Sacred art is about change and flow. Ritual and art honors the experience of the change.

If you can get your former lover or partner to take part in this private ritual of dissolution and healing, it can have more meaning for you. If they are unwilling, then you can do it on your own.

Dissolution Ritual

- Cast the circle and call the quarters in the usual way.
- Call upon the god and goddess, and any spirit guides or totem animals you work with. In particular, call upon any goddesses and gods of love, such as Aphrodite or Eros.
- Use the protection potion. If you are both present, anoint each other. If not, simply anoint yourself. If your partner is not with you, make sure you place a photo or object symbolic of them in the circle.
- Burn a healing or cleansing incense, such as sage or lavender. Say:

    We ask in the name of the Goddess and God, for your healing and guidance at this time. We ask you to recognize the end of our time together and to support each of us as we walk our separate paths.

- If you have anything to return or exchange, such as giving back rings or necklaces, do so now. Say any last words you need to say to bring closure to the situation.
- If you are both present, each of you should hold a thread in one hand, between you both. If you are alone, hold one end of the thread and tie the other to object or picture of your past partner. If you had a formal handfasting ceremony, you can use the garland that bound your hands. Take a pair of scissors or a ritual blade and cut the thread. (Note: some traditions believe an athame ritual blade should not be used to cut anything, not even in ritual. In those traditions, a pair of scissors, a sickle, or a boline should be used.) Say:

    We end this relationship, with Perfect Love and Perfect Trust. May we each find love, happiness, health, and prosperity on our separate roads. So mote it be.

- Bury or burn the thread/garland.

- Complete the circle, thanking all present, release the quarters, and release the circle. If you are outdoors, each of you should exit in a different direction.

Rituals of Exploration: Heterosexuality

One subject that is often the most taboo in gay culture is exploring heterosexuality. Many times we feel threatened when others open a door we have closed. No one is asking us to open the door for ourselves. Rites of heterosexuality may be left behind after the coming-out process, if explored at all. They are not a mandatory ritual for all of us, but many people benefit from exploring all aspects of sexuality. They are not necessarily going through a phase, but an honest exploration where their self-image is more fluid than others.

Sexual identity as gay, straight, bisexual, or transgendered was probably not as crystallized as it is now in the postmodern Judeo-Christian Western world where one is forced to choose sides and labels. Our surviving tribal societies lead many to believe sexual orientation was probably much more fluid in the ancient Western world. Gay communities as social and political engines have evolved out of a need for camaraderie, solidarity, protection, and identity in a hostile world.

Bisexuals often have a very difficult time because they perceive themselves as having to "choose sides" in the gay/straight clash. If there is no clash, no war, then there is no need to choose any side. There is no need to define your sexuality in rigid roles, gay/straight, top/bottom, or butch/fem. I use the word "gay" throughout this manual, but it is for the ease of communication. I don't define it in a rigid way. Many spiritual teachers and traditions believe we are all moving toward a sense of androgyny and bisexuality as we balance ourselves and our polarities.

When someone defines themselves as gay and then has an experience or meets someone that prompts them to redefine themselves, it can be an unnerving experience, much like the undoing process discussed in chapter 12. To a gay pagan, there can be no guilt or trauma associated with it unless you let it. To the Goddess, all acts of love and pleasure are her rituals, including straight ones. Sometimes a ritual will help us not live the drama of confronting such a possibility, but give permission to ourselves to explore this new area, with the blessing of the ancient and shining ones.

Ritual for Exploring Heterosexuality

- Cast the circle, call the quarters, and create a sacred space in the usual way.
- Pick a particular patron from the pantheons of gods, goddesses, animals, and angels that you feel will be able to guide you through this process. It may be one you already encounter in your meditation, or a power being new to you, to symbolize the newness of the experience. Invite that patron into the circle:

  I call you, [state name of patron], to this sacred circle, to guide and guard me in this time of transition and exploration. Hail and welcome.

- Light any sacred incense you use.
- Anoint yourself with protection potion.
- Perform the Great Rite, but in particular, pay attention in your mind as to how the physical act of your sexuality will be different in the next part of your life.
- Meditate on your patron. Go to your inner sacred space, and ask to speak with your new patron. Ask any questions you have. Your patron will offer advice and blessings through words, visions, or feelings. Your patron will guide you through this whole process.
- Complete the circle, thanking all present, release the quarters, and release the circle.

Call on your patron as needed in upcoming situations, simply for guidance and reassurance. If you feel this experience was a phase or an exploration that has ended, do a similar ritual to thank and release this patron, or ask to take your spiritual work together in another direction.

Becoming a Wise One: Elderhood

In much of the world, getting old is scorned. We want to remain young and beautiful forever, unchanging. That is not the way of the world or the Goddess, who changes from Maiden to Mother and finally Crone, to be reborn again. The only thing constant is change, as my mother wisely tells me.

Elderhood is something to be celebrated. When you reach a certain age, hopefully you have gathered some wisdom, some secrets about going beyond survival to prosper and love in the world. Wicca often refers to the wise, so we must honor the wise. Both paths, witchcraft and homosexuality, are often seen as inborn, but we choose how we live. Living on these paths in the modern world can be a difficult road. Only by discovering the wisdom of our elders do we understand how to function, grow, and guide the next generation.

In the gay and pagan communities elders are extremely important, but not always well respected. We look to the young as role models. We look to rock stars and actors. They don't know any more than anyone else does. They are simply famous, not wise. Only by knowing where we come from can we know where we are going. Our gay and pagan elders faced many challenges for us, and we enjoy the freedoms they have won for us through their own blood and sacrifice. Because of the brave activists in both communities, I don't have to be afraid to live with my husband, walk hand-in-hand down a street, openly declare myself a witch, and write material on witchcraft. My coming-out process, as a witch and gay man, was far easier than my elders', who may not have been able to safely come out at all.

Instead of dreading the passage into elderhood, embrace it because it is your time of wisdom and power. The physiological changes that result from this shift, from hormone imbalances to the end of menstruation indicate that your true power is being put into your consciousness, into your spirit. Use this ritual to celebrate your newfound awareness. For those truly celebrating elderhood in the craft, and not simply elderhood in life, use this ritual to really demonstrate the skills you have learned in the craft. Make your own incense, ritual drink for the chalice, and design your own meditation and blessing. Perhaps the use of elder tree flowers or berries could be a part of the ritual. At first, this might seem to be a dark ritual for some, but witches never shy away from the cycles of change. We reflect on them. Use this ritual as a means of empowerment, reflection, and thanks. Use it to synchronize yourself with your new adventure into wisdom.

Ritual to Celebrate Elderhood

- Cast the circle and call the quarters in the usual way.
- Call upon the god and goddess, and any spirit guides or totem animals you work with. Especially call upon any goddesses and gods you associate with maturity, wisdom, or elderhood. I would choose a crone/underworld goddess such as Hecate, queen of witches.
- Light any incense you use.
- Anoint yourself with protection potion.
- Perform the Great Rite and drink from the chalice.

- Say whatever words you are moved to say at this time. Let them come from your heart.
- While in the circle, go to your inner temple, and ask to meet with the Goddess and God, to ask their counsel and blessing for entering your elderhood. They will have messages and blessings for you, and may tell you what to do to complete the ritual. They will welcome you into the council of wise grandmothers and grandfathers, the spiritual elders of the tradition. Reflect on the fact that someday, you will be walking with them in the spirit lands.
- When you return from the meditation, anoint yourself with a special oil or potion. Anoint the various parts of your body with "blessed be" as in the initiation ritual. This time, really look at your body, and accept the changes that have come with elderhood. Thank your body for its service to you. You have been its guardian, and it will continue to serve you well in the many years ahead. Reflect on the gift the body has been in your life.
- Complete the circle, thanking all present, release the quarters, and release the circle.

Crossing and Funerals: The Rites of Death

The last rituals of this life are the rituals of death. Death, like the end of any situation or relationship, is not the end, but another beginning. Death is the end of your current relationship with the physical world, and most important with your physical body. To the witch, death is a natural part of the order. We seek neither to speed our journey there nor to prolong our lives. We take care of ourselves, live in a balanced way, and when we are done with our work here, we move on to the next phase of existence.

Most people fear death because they fear it is the end, possibly stemming from a lack of belief in spirit, in something beyond this world. Many religions foster a belief in the nonphysical worlds. Some religions lead people to fear a "final" judgment and that one afterlife is a reward and the other a place of punishment. Before I became a witch, that was my view of the afterlife and I often assumed, because I was gay and that was against my former religion, that I was bound for hell. But as I later learned, witches don't believe in hell. The underworlds are places of rest and regeneration. The only hell is of your own making. In fact, in many ways, witches don't believe in anything regarding the afterlife. We have experiences. When you speak with Spirit, travel out of your body, visit spirit worlds, and have direct contact with the divine, you don't need to believe. Belief sustains you when you lack experience. When you have experience, you don't need to believe another's words or views. You have your own and it can change and adapt as your experiences change.

Gay people may be called as ministers, priestesses, and priests to administer to the dying and the family of the dying. Andrew Ramer, author of *Two Flutes Playing*, says that in ancient times, gay men were the midwives of the dying, as the priestesses were the midwives to the living. He believes this association is why we are feared. On some primal, cellular level, much of the world remembers that our presence often comes with death. Although this is more a poetic truth than a provable archaeological fact, I must say his words struck a chord with me. Perhaps that is why so many gay people are involved in the healing arts, particularly nursing. It is most often the nurses, not the doctors, who administer to the dying. Even the HIV/AIDS crisis in our community may have been a spiritual call to reconnect to this role and take care of our own healing.

HELPING PEOPLE CROSS OVER

If called upon to work with the dying, you can use my suggestions for ritual to guide you. Remember that every situation is different, and work within the framework of the person you are helping. Not all who come to you will be pagans. If you are working with a Christian, calling upon Jesus rather than the Goddess may be more comfortable for that client. In such times, it is important to adapt to the given situation if you can be comfortable with those terms. I can do so in private with individuals, for their personal ease, but in public rituals, it is not my calling.

Crossing rituals are the acts of leading another to the next life. The shaman or witch often acts as psychopomp to guide souls crossing between worlds. We fulfill this function to help those crossing have the most gentle experience as possible, truly acting as midwives to the dying. One does not need a guide in this process, but it can help, even simply to be there to hold a hand and say a few words. Sometimes the psychopomp cannot moderate the pain, fear, regret, and loneliness the person is feeling, but can be part of the transition experience the soul has chosen on the highest level. All you can do as a guide is your best.

Magically, I call upon my spirit guides and deities with whom I feel the strongest connection. I will do it silently if the dying person is not of my faith. If they have their own faith, or own personal guides and deities, I will petition them as well. You don't need to have ritual tools and candles. In hospital settings, these things are usually difficult to use. You may want to have some blessing oil, either a magical oil or potion, you've created. Protection potion works nicely because it has many spiritual herbs to help the crossing. You can even use simple olive oil or salt and water. I will anoint the dying on the wrists, and then, if possible, move up the chakras starting at the root area, belly, solar plexus, heart, throat, brow, and crown. As I anoint, the intent is to open these centers and allow the spirit to flow up and through them. Most traditions view the most gentle transition as through the crown chakra. The lower chakras close down one by one, until the soul energy releases from the crown.

Holding the dying's hand, I close my eyes and visualize myself and my guides and gods guiding their soul into the next world. Call upon their guides, ancestors, and even deceased pets to help them. Some witches insist it is up a staircase, to a ball of light. Others down a staircase, to the land of the ancestors. Shamanic practitioners will move through the world tree. The direction or image doesn't matter. Where they are going is beyond direction or image. The symbols help you interact with the experience.

Even though you may have the image of them crossing over, the connection and release may not be complete. Some people end their physical life abruptly, while others linger. You will know when your part is done and the divine spirits are guiding the dying's soul. Thank all spirits involved, and imagine yourself returning to your body.

Although funeral rites are to honor those who have recently departed, in practical terms, they are really for those left behind. The rituals are a way to openly grieve, say good-bye, relate to others who have experienced loss, and bring closure to a difficult time. Most witches believe that just because someone dies, that doesn't mean your relationship is over. We believe loved ones and ancestors still work with us, but our relationship does change, and the funerary rite helps us transform the relationship and accept the death as a new beginning.

Funerary Ritual

Unfortunately, Wiccan funeral rites are not that common. Often, the deceased is the lone witch in the family, and others opt for a more traditional or even nonreligious burial because family members won't understand. In the case of a witch's funeral, a traditional circle would be cast in celebration and farewell, and the witch may be buried or cremated with particular special magical tools and garments.

- Cast the circle, call the quarters, and create a sacred space in the usual way.

- When invoking deities, consider calling on gods and goddesses of death and the underworld, such as Osiris, Hades, Persephone, Hecate, Ereshkigal, Hel, Morgan, Cernunnos, Kali, Sedna, and Tlazoteotl, or deities who act as guides for souls such as Hermes.
- HP/HPS:

   We have gathered together to celebrate the life and passing of [deceased's name]. As family, friends, and fellow practitioners, we know that all things return to where they have come, and all cycles end to begin again. This is not an ending, but a transformation.
- If possible, with the group gathered, anoint all with protection potion.
- Light incense. My favorite funerary incenses are myrrh and orris root. Other herbs and flowers associated with funeral rites can be used as decorations in the ceremony. They include apple, bluebell, elder, marshmallow, narcissus, willow, and vinca.
- HP/HPS:

   We ask in the name of the Goddess, God, and Great Spirit, all powers gathered here today, to guide the spirit of [name] to their next life, be it here in the world, or in the next realm. Guide him/her, guard him/her, and let him/her know we honor him/her still.
- The HP/HPS then speaks on the nature of souls in the pagan viewpoint, and the deceased's own beliefs on the matter. The talk can be followed by the Great Rite and/or a traditional eulogy. In the style of group consciousness, the eulogy doesn't have to be a lone speaker. Everyone in the circle can have a chance to speak if that is feasible. The HP/HPS could do a gentle guided meditation to connect with the deceased and say farewells. For some, a song or chant could be more appropriate. Each will depend on the group gathered, the guidance of the HP/HPS, and the desires of the deceased.
- For the Final Blessing, the HP/HPS says:

   As the body returns to the earth, the heart pours back to the waters of life, the mind returns to the clear sky, we know the soul returns to the light of the Goddess, God, and Great Spirit. We know this is not an end, but a beginning, and wish you well on your journey. Blessed Be.
- Complete the circle, thanking all present, release the quarters, and release the circle.

16

The Beginning

All beginnings contain their own endings. And all endings contain a new beginning. That is the cycle of life. That is the spiral. That is the way of the witch. Nothing ever ends. It simply begins again.

This book is only the beginning of a magical practice. It reflects my thoughts and experience of my journey, and the journey of those I've encountered. Use it to inspire your own path, your own practice. Explore all aspects of paganism. *Gay Witchcraft* is but one view, and you shouldn't deny yourself other material, other views, just because it isn't written from a gay point of view. Educate yourself, but most important, no matter your path, live a magical life.

The Magical Life

Although it can make things easier, magick is not about having an easy life. It's about living a life of integrity and commitment. The commitment is to yourself, your spirituality, the higher good, and the Goddess and God. Witches are ultimately servants and caretakers, though many of us forget that.

My strongest recommendation to you is to do something magical every day. It can be difficult to completely change our lifestyle and outlook. One book does not guarantee it. It takes a daily commitment to the lifestyle, and to me, that starts with small steps. If you can begin a regular meditation and ritual practice, celebrate the Moons and holidays, and work magick into your life, do it. If you feel you can't right now, for whatever reason, try to bring a magical act into you life every day. It doesn't have to be long and involved, but it does have to heartfelt. It does have to ask that you look at the world through magical eyes. If you have a problem or crisis, don't endlessly brood or complain. Meditate on it and ask for guidance. Do a journey with your power animal. Do a ritual to transform it. Call to the universe for help, and expect your call to be heard. Magick has always been meant to be practical as well as spiritual. Through it we do not divorce our bodies and world from spirit, but recognize them all to be part of the larger whole.

Partners and Friends

If you are in a relationship, it is a great thing to share the path with your partner. For me, magical spirituality has been the cornerstone of my marriage. Usually I would tell a date about my life as a witch, either to scare off those with whom I didn't hit it off, or to really test their mettle, because if I liked a man and my path scared him, I wanted to find out quickly. I was very surprised on my first date with my partner. As I announced I studied witchcraft, he looked surprised and then casually mentioned his studies in Hermetic Kabbalah and Norse shamanism and magick. I was blown away. We built upon that mutual interest to create our own family traditions, and now work with a coven of close friends.

If you don't have a partner, sharing the path with friends is another ideal way to practice and develop deep relationships. Magical relationships are some of the most intense ones I've encountered. When they go well and are handled in a mature way, they are rewarding. When they are not, they can be some of the most difficult and dramatic. I hope you already have a partner or friend who will share your interest in this path. If not, I hope your friends will simply be supportive. Don't feel you have to force it on a partner or friend. Witches do not seek to convert others. We live and let others live their own way. Witches are very sensitive to religious intolerance and seek to create a world where everyone is comfortable with expressing their own faith.

Sometimes friends, family, and lovers will be afraid of your practice. Because of popular media stereotypes, the uninformed public equates witchcraft with Satanism, sacrifice, and black magick. It's up to you to be educated on the subject to be able to educate others. Give the basic facts to prevent any fear or misunderstanding. If anyone is interested in more of the practice, discuss it, but remember not to proselytize. Many covens and communities often have open rituals to welcome friends and family members who are not pagan, but seek to explore and understand. I know many couples, where one is pagan and the other will join them for couple's rituals, but the partner doesn't subscribe to the faith. They are there to be supportive, to be involved, and understand, but it's not exactly for them. I have a friend who will do protection magick and healing rituals for his partner, and his partner will join him, and is very interested, but does not seek to be a witch. It's amazing that two people can share something so intimate, and be comfortable with their own boundaries.

If you decide to work with a coven, some practitioners prefer a certain mix of people. Most covens are a mix of ages, genders, and sexualities; that is what I've experienced, and I prefer it that way. Variety provides a good learning opportunity for all of us. However, some witches want a more focused energy. The focus can come from working in a very specific tradition, or having members with a certain energetic focus. Some mysteries can be explored in an all-male or female coven. Other mysteries are explored in an all-queer coven, of both men and women, or separated into covens of gay men and lesbians. The choice is up to you and your covenmates. Each grouping will have its pros and cons. Each will have its own rewards and personal challenges.

Some old texts say that you need the circle to alternate male and female to raise sufficient energy. We know those old stereotypes are not true because we all express a range of gender energy. Find the group that works best for you. If you have a hard time finding an established group, you may want to create your own. New groups can be informal and fun or highly structured and disciplined. See what works best for you.

Embracing Yourself

For me, the biggest part of the craft has been gaining self-esteem. I've learned to embrace the many facets of myself and accept myself unconditionally. I had to embrace my homosexuality, and celebrate it, rather than begrudgingly accept it. I had to embrace my magical self and all my abilities. I developed abilities I didn't know I had and found a fuller expression of my spirit. Through both of these avenues, I had to embrace my magical gay self, and see how the two are intertwined. Both came from the same root, my essence, my soul. I would be less than half the man I am today if I didn't come to acknowledge and love these, and many other parts of myself. As I have, they move beyond a simple descriptive label or title, and simply become a part of me. They always have been, but now I can reveal them, unashamedly, to everyone.

Learn to embrace these things in you. Learn to embrace the Fey, the fairy folk, in all of us. Embrace the fierce Amazon warrior. Embrace the teacher, the parent, the child, and the witch in you. Find your power from it.

Although you may embrace it, not everyone might. As gays, we experience a certain amount of prejudice and stereotyping in the world, particularly if we are very open about our sexuality. The same can be found for those in the pagan community. The world at large still has difficulties with pagans, witches, shamans, and magicians, ranging from accusations of devil worship to simply thinking we're completely crazy. If you claim this path, these are additional considerations to understand. Acceptance of witchcraft is growing, but you may need to be a part of educating the world, so you had better know your history, theory, and practice.

You may even encounter prejudice in the pagan community itself. I would like to say paganism is completely free from homophobia, and in my experience it has been, but others have a different experience. Some pagans are simply stuck on the gender fertility rituals and polarity of Goddess and God in a woman and man. They cannot get beyond their conservative training. Perhaps others have not shed their former, conservative Judeo-Christian backgrounds, even though they claim to be witches. Finally, there are those who haven't been exposed to gay people, don't understand the history, and have no personal basis, so they go along with the dominant opinion, or just fear what they don't know. It is up to us to educate them as well on our sacred history and background, to reclaim our place and purpose in the spiritual traditions.

Magick and Activism

Arthur Evans makes a compelling case for magick and activism when he says, "Magick is one of our most powerful allies in the struggle against patriarchal industrialism" (*Witchcraft and the Gay Counterculture*, p. 149). Although I don't agree with some of Evans's more radical views of violence and activism, I do feel that magick has a powerful place in civil rights, social reform, and the environmental movement. All our thoughts, words, intentions, and actions make up the magick of our lives. Magick and spirituality do not have to be divorced from social consciousness. Everyone must find their place in the changes that are occurring. Everyone must decide what role to play, and what piece of the puzzle they must add. Some witches are very involved in a variety of movements, from civil rights—particularly for pagans, gays, and other unsung minorities—to social, economic, and government reforms. Environmental activities are a common meeting-point among pagans, because of their concern for the divine as expressed through our Mother Earth, plants, animals, and all of creation.

In the process of using your magick to change not only your life, you are changing other lives. You may be modeling a new, magical way of living for others to follow. Simply living an open, honest, and out life, as a gay person or a witch, can do wonders to raise consciousness. You could do specific acts of magick for civil rights legislation, including rights to same-sex marriage or antidiscrimination laws. Some take more confrontational roles, with protests and civil disobedience. Still others have created alternative ways to live through housing, farming, and social cooperatives. Ultimately, the path of the witch is the path of service to the tribe. Ask yourself how you serve the greater good. All ways, big and small, count. Evaluate how you want to contribute to the shift of the ages and the next world.

Age of Aquarius

We find many of our books in the new age section. People talk about the dawning of the new age, the Age of Aquarius. We hear about it in the musical *Hair*, but not many people really understand what it means. I have found it has special significance to the gay community, but no one really mentions us in the myths and prophecies.

The Age of Aquarius refers to the procession of the equinoxes. Roughly every 2,000 years, on the day of the vernal equinox, the constellation that frames the Sun changes. The change is obviously very slow, and it can be very difficult to pinpoint the switch. We live on the cusp of the ages. For the past 2,000 years, we have lived in the Age of Pisces. The age was marked with the rise of Christianity. The highest expression of it has been spirituality, creativity, and unconditional love. We did have a lot of that. The lower expressions are martyrdom, religious zealousness, and institutions. We've had a lot of that, too. We are moving into the Age of Aquarius. What makes it so special is that many tribal and ancient civilizations have had momentous prophecies around this particular change, sometimes signifying mass destruction, but more often an age of enlightenment. Aquarius's lower expressions are violent revolutions, natural disasters, detachment, and unforeseen, sudden change. Its highest expression is equality for all, brotherhood/sisterhood, social and environmental consciousness, new technology, and a chance of utopia.

Aquarius is called the Water Bearer, but it is technically an air sign. The waters Aquarius bears are more like currents of thought and enlightenment than emotion. The Water Bearer is often equated with Ganymede, Zeus's cupbearer. Pouring out his ambrosia, the drink of the gods, he brought power, wisdom, and immortality. In the act of entering this new age, Ganymede is pouring out those potential blessings to us as well. I find it staggering that this divine gay figure is the herald of the new age. In its symbolism I find the potential for all those with our unique blend of male and female energies, those who can be active and receptive, to be the guides into the new age. Not only do I think that gay rights and recognition will change in the new age, I feel it is our sacred duty to get in touch with our spirituality, for we shall be helping to construct the new age. Whatever we are doing at this time in our lives will herald the changes in the new age. What do you want to create for the next 2,000 years? Create it now. Live it now. Make the patterns for future generations to follow, build upon, and grow. You are setting the tone now. Do you want everyone to live a magical life if they so choose? Then live a magical life now!

Bibliography

Adler, Margot. *Drawing Down the Moon: Witches, Druids, Goddess Worshippers, and Other Pagans in America Today*. Boston: Beacon Press, 1979, 1986.

Andrews, Ted. *Animal-Speak: The Spiritual & Magical Powers of Creatures Great and Small*. St. Paul, MN: Lewellyn Publications, 1993.

Beyerl, Paul. *The Master Book of Herbalism*. Custer, WA: Phoenix Publishing, 1984.

Buczynski, Edmund M. *Witchcraft Fact Book*. New York: Magickal Childe Publishing, 1984.

Cabot, Laurie. *A Salem Witch's Herbal Magic*. Salem, MA: Celtic Crow Publishing, 1994.

———— *Witchcraft as a Science I and II*. Class handouts and lecture notes. Salem, MA, 1993.

Cabot, Laurie, with Tom Cowan. *Love Magic: The Way to Love through Rituals, Spells and the Magical Life*. New York: Dell Publishing, 1992.

———— *Power of the Witch: The Earth, the Moon and the Magical Path to Enlightenment*. New York: Dell Publishing, 1989.

Cabot, Laurie, with Jean Mills. *Celebrate the Earth: A Year of Holidays in the Pagan Tradition*. New York: Dell Publishing, 1994.

Casey, Caroline W. *Inner and Outer Space*. Boulder, CO: Sounds True, 1996.

Conner, Randy P. *Blossom of Bone*. San Francisco: HarperSanFrancisco, 1993.

Conner, Randy P., David Hatfield Sparks, and Mariya Sparks. *Cassell's Encyclopedia of Queer Myth, Symbol and Spirit: Gay, Lesbian, Bisexual and Transgender Lore*. London: Cassell, 1997.

Cowan, Tom. *Fire in the Head*. San Francisco: HarperSanFrancisco, 1993.

Conway, D. J. *The Ancient & Shinning Ones*. St. Paul, MN: Llewellyn Publications, 1993.

Crowley, Aleister. *Magick in Theory and Practice*. New York: Dover Publications, 1976.

Crowley, Vivianne. *Wicca, the Old Religion in the New Age*. San Francisco: The Aquarian Press, 1989.

Cunningham, Scott. *The Complete Book of Incense, Oils and Brews*. St. Paul, MN: Llewellyn Publications, 1991.

—— *Cunningham's Encyclopedia of Crystal, Gem & Metal Magic*. St. Paul, MN: Llewellyn Publications, 1992.

—— *Cunningham's Encyclopedia of Magical Herbs*. St. Paul, MN: Llewellyn Publications, 1985.

—— *Wicca: A guide for the Solitary Practitioner*. St. Paul, MN: Llewellyn Publications, 1988.

Danielou, Alain. *The Phallus: Sacred Symbol of Male Creative Power*. Originally published in Puiseaux, France: Editions Pardes, 1993. English Translation, Rochester, VT: Inner Traditions International, 1995.

Evans, Arthur. *Witchcraft and the Gay Counterculture*. Boston: Fag Rag Books, 1978.

Farrar, Janet & Stewart. *Spells and How They Work*. Custer, WA: Phoenix Publishing, 1990.

—— *The Witches' Bible: The Complete Witches Handbook*. Custer, WA: Phoenix Publishing, 1996.

Grahn, Judy. *Another Mother Tongue: Gay Words, Gay Worlds*. Boston: Beacon Press, 1984.

Graves, Robert. *The White Goddess*. New York: Noonday Press, 1997.

Guiley, Rosemary Ellen. *The Encyclopedia of Witches & Witchcraft*. New York: Checkmark Books, 1999.

Harner, Michael. *The Way of the Shaman*. Third Edition. New York: HarperCollins, 1990.

Heflin, Llee. *The Island Dialogues*. San Francisco: Level Press, 1973.

Judith, Anodea. *Wheels of Life*. St. Paul, MN: Llewellyn Publications, 1987.

Kraig, Donald Michael. *Modern Magick: Eleven Lessons in the High Magickal Arts*. St. Paul, MN: Lewellyn Publications, 1988.

—— *Modern Sex Magick: Secrets of Erotic Spirituality*. St. Paul, MN: Llewellyn, 1998.

Three Initiates. *The Kybalion: Hermetic Philosophy*. Chicago: The Yogi Publication Society, 1912.

McKenna, Terrence. *The Search for the Original Tree of Knowledge*. Boulder, CO: Sounds True, 1992.

Monaghan, Patricia. *The Goddess Path*. St. Paul, MN: Llewellyn Publications, 1999.

Myss, Caroline. *Anatomy of the Spirit: The Seven Stages of Power and Healing*. New York: Three Rivers Press, 1996.

Pajeon, Kala & Ketz. *The Candle Magick Workbook*. New York: Citadel Press, 1992.

RavenWolf, Silver. *To Stir A Magick Cauldron*. St. Paul, MN: Llewellyn Publications, 1995.

Richardson, Alen. *Earth God Rising*. St. Paul, MN: Llewellyn Publications, 1990.

Roscoe, Will. *Queer Spirits: a Gay Men's Myth Book*. Boston: Beacon Press, 1995.

Sams, Jamie, and David Carson. *Medicine Cards: The Discovery of Power Through the Ways of the Animals*. Santa Fe: Bear and Company, 1998.

Schindler, William. *Gay Tantra*. Philadelphia: Xlibris Corporation, *www.Xlibris.com*, 2001.

Spence, Lewis. *The Magic Arts in Celtic Britain*. Longwood Pr. Ltd. 1995. New York: Samuel Weiser, Inc., 1970.

Spencer, Colin. *The Gay Kama Sutra*. New York: St. Martin's Press, 1997.

Starhawk. *The Spiral Dance: A Rebirth of the Ancient Religion of the Great Goddess*. San Francisco: HarperSanFrancisco, 1979, 1989.

Stewart, R. J. *Celtic Myths, Celtic Legends*. London: Blandford, 1996.

Stowe, John R. *Gay Spirit Warrior: An Empowerment Workbook for Men Who Love Men*. Findhorn, Scotland: Findhorn Press, 1999.

Talesco, Patricia. *Urban Pagan: Magical Living in a 9 to 5 World*. St. Paul, MN: Lewellyn Publications, 1995.

Thompson, Mark. *Gay Spirit*. New York: St. Martin's Press, 1987.

Thorsson, Edred. *The Book of Ogham*. St. Paul, MN: Llewellyn Publications, 1994.

U. D., Frater. *Secrets of Western Sex Magic*. St. Paul, MN: Llewellyn Publications, 2001.

Walker, Mitch. *Men Loving Men: A Gay Sex Guide & Consciousness Book*. San Francisco: Gay Sunshine Press, 1977.

Weiss, Brian. *Many Lives, Many Masters*. New York: Fireside/Simon & Schuster, 1988.

Wolkstein, Diane, and Samuel Noah Kramer. *Inanna Queen of Heaven and Earth: Her Stories and Hymns from Sumer*. New York: Harper & Row, 1983.

Online Sources

www.bible.crosswalk.com

www.members.home.com/gwydion/page2m.html: Oct 28 2001.

www.faerywolf.com/index2.html: January 24, 2002.

www.fordham.edu/halsall/pwh/copticspell.html: Jan 22. 2002

www.gayguides.com/houstonfaeries/index.html: Feb 20, 2002.

www.geocities.com/SoHo/5756/minbtrad.html: Oct 28, 2001.

www.geocities.com/thegaywiccanvoice/index1.html: January 24, 2002.

www.kinkydragon.com/: Feb 20, 2002

www.phhine.ndirect.co.uk/index.htm.

www.thewellhead.org.uk/GP/gay1.htm Oct 28, 2001.

www.webcastro.com/evans1.htm: Feb 20, 2002.

www.whitecranejournal.com: Feb 20, 2002.

www.wildboysnet.com/: Feb 20, 2002

www.witchvox.com/gay/

www.witchvox.com/gay/gayhistory.html

www.yahoo.com/maletomaletantra